Lyric Poems on Twelve Themes

Lyric Poems on Twelve Themes

Charles H. Kegel

Idaho State University

William J. Shanahan

Idaho State University

Scott, Foresman and Company

E. E. CUMMINGS "next to of course god america i": Copyright, 1926, by Horace
Liveright; renewed, 1954, by E. E. Cummings. Reprinted from his volume, *Poems
1923–1954*, by permission of Harcourt, Brace & World, Inc.   "when any mortal
(even the most odd)": From *95 Poems*, copyright, © 1958, by E. E. Cummings.
Reprinted by permission of Harcourt, Brace & World, Inc.   RICHARD EBER-
HART "The Horse Chestnut Tree" and "The Human Being Is a Lonely Creature":
From *Collected Poems 1930–1960* by Richard Eberhart. © 1960 by Richard Eber-
hart. Reprinted by permission of Oxford University Press, Inc.   T. S. ELIOT
"The Love Song of J. Alfred Prufrock" and "The Hollow Men": From *Collected
Poems 1909–1962* by T. S. Eliot, copyright, 1936, by Harcourt, Brace & World,
Inc.; copyright, © 1963, 1964 by T. S. Eliot. Reprinted by permission of the pub-
lishers.   ROBERT FROST "Bereft," "Birches," "Desert Places," and "Stop-
ping by Woods on a Snowy Evening": From *Complete Poems of Robert Frost*. Copy-
right 1916, 1923, 1928 by Holt, Rinehart and Winston, Inc. Copyright 1936, 1944,
1951, © 1956 by Robert Frost. Copyright © 1964 by Lesley Frost Ballantine. Re-
printed by permission of Holt, Rinehart and Winston, Inc.   THOMAS HARDY
"The Man He Killed," "The Darkling Thrush," "The Impercipient," "In Tenebris
I": Reprinted with permission of the Macmillan Company from *Collected Poems* by
Thomas Hardy. Copyright 1925 by the Macmillan Company.   CECIL HEMLEY
"If He Were Anywhere": Reprinted with the permission of Farrar, Straus & Giroux,
Inc. from *In Midnight Wood* by Cecil Hemley. Copyright © 1951, 1956, 1958 by
Cecil Hemley.   GERARD MANLEY HOPKINS "Pied Beauty," "Carrion
Comfort," "Spring and Fall: To a Young Child": From *Poems*, 4th edition by W. H.
Gardner and N. H. MacKenzie, Oxford University Press, Inc.   A. E. HOUS-
MAN "The Chestnut Casts His Flambeaux": From *The Collected Poems of A. E. Hous-
man*. Copyright 1922 by Holt, Rinehart and Winston, Inc. Copyright 1950 by Bar-
clays Bank Ltd. Reprinted by permission of Holt, Rinehart and Winston, Inc.   "To
an Athlete Dying Young," "1887," and "When I was one-and-twenty": From "A
Shropshire Lad" (Authorised Edition) from *The Collected Poems of A. E. Housman*.

PREFACE

Like other collections of poetry, this one has its particular limits. The editors can claim no mystical significance for the total number of poems included. Only a feeling for symmetry explains why we have collected 144 rather than, let us say, 125 or 150 poems: the even gross allowed us to present twelve poems by twelve different authors on each of twelve major themes.

Within each of the twelve categories we have attempted to present a variety of styles, attitudes, tones, and moods. Thus, the poems on the theme of patriotism range from the blatantly chauvinistic to the openly critical. Similarly, the section on love ranges widely to include the neo-Platonism of Shelley, the *carpe diem* emphasis of Herrick or Marvell, the psychological realism of Meredith, the playful cynicism of Housman. Because we have wished to achieve that variety, we have not included more than one poem by an individual author in any section, though of course some poets are represented several times in the entire collection.

It would be meaningless to suggest that each section contains the twelve best poems on that theme. Although with some misgivings, we have not included any poems in translation. Likewise, the decision to restrict this collection to lyric poetry has necessitated the omission of many excellent narrative or dramatic poems relevant to the various themes. Nevertheless, all of these are good and many of them, great poems.

In deciding upon the nature of the critical apparatus and commentary that should be included, we have kept in mind that this is a book intended primarily for college students in their freshman and sophomore years. Most are not majoring in English, nor do they possess the

long and intimate acquaintance with literary study that would make
extensive commentary necessary – or meaningful. Such students need
first to acquire a lively interest in poetry and to experience the varying
kinds of pleasure that it can convey. And for that purpose there is simply no substitute for a collection of good poems, each communicating
its own thought and emotion. The introductory section, "How to Read a
Poem," sets forth certain basic principles for that experience, and the
study questions at the end of each section attempt to enrich the student's understanding of the poems he has read. Similarly, we have provided in the notes some basic information, biographical and otherwise,
which will further assist the student to understand the works before
him. We have also provided a glossary of literary terms to assist the
student in his understanding of basic technical matters. Other than
that, however, we have tried not to saddle the instructor with our personal critical convictions, preferring instead to allow him maximum
latitude in presenting these poems to his students. He, better than we,
can decide the amount, for example, of biographical or other critical
material needed within the context of his particular course and group
of students.

CONTENTS

POEMS ARRANGED BY THEME

BELIEF AND DOUBT

CHILDHOOD

CONSOLATION

DEATH

DESPAIR

ISOLATION

LOVE

NATURE AND MAN

PATRIOTISM

POETRY AND LITERATURE

SOCIAL CONSCIOUSNESS

WAR

)

POEMS ARRANGED BY AUTHOR

YEATS, WILLIAM BUTLER   (1865 – 1939)

INTRODUCTION:
TO READ A POEM

By the time they arrive in college, most students have had *some* acquaintance with poetry, but that acquaintance is not very sophisticated. In some instances it might be characterized as hostile. This lack of sophistication (perhaps the hostility also) derives in large part from a misunderstanding of the nature and function of poetry. And failing to understand its nature and function, one cannot be an effective reader.

Above all, the effective reader must approach poetry as an art form. Regardless of other effects it might seek to achieve — be they cognitive or emotional — a poem must seek to give pleasure. This, says Samuel Taylor Coleridge, must be "its *immediate* object." Obviously, one does not derive the same sort of pleasure from each poem in this collection. Quite the contrary. Matthew Arnold's "Dover Beach" gives pleasure in a manner almost totally different than Robert Frost's "Birches" or E. E. Cummings' "when any mortal (even the most odd)." In fact, it might be asserted that a good collection should be kaleidoscopic in the kinds of pleasure which its individual poems produce.

But pleasure need not be the ultimate purpose of a poem. It seeks also to communicate some aspects of truth about human experiences. And it does so in ways quite different from those employed, for example, in a scientific treatise. The language of science must be denotative; that is, it must communicate a piece of truth in terms of that which can be empirically determined, of that which can be measured, weighed, and contained. It is highly impersonal and, for the most part, can be written just as well by one scientist as another. The language of poetry, on the other hand, is highly connotative, highly suggestive, highly personal. The poet attempts to translate his own response to emotional and intellectual experience into words that will evoke a similar response in his reader. His concern is not with the factual and quantitative data of life – the number of soldiers killed in Vietnam, the coefficient of elasticity in birch wood – he deals instead with the impact of human experience upon an individual. Thus Whitman's "Vigil Strange I Kept on the Field One Night" deals with the effect of death upon one individual soldier; thus Frost's "Birches" uses the peculiar qualities of birch trees as a point of departure to speculate about man's place in the cosmos.

In communicating his individual response to experience, the poet employs language which, paradoxically, is both exceedingly specific and exceedingly suggestive. He draws clear and accurate pictures of the things he experiences, but he describes them in terms of his own perception. Hence, he is fond of metaphor, simile, symbol, irony, and other forms of figurative language. He associates one thing with another; he allows one thing to symbolize something else; he employs words which by their sound or connotation affect the meaning of other words in the immediate context. In essence the poet attempts through the suggestive impact of figurative language to communicate impressions that literal language would not allow him to convey. Literal language, for example, would only have allowed Hamlet to say of his mother's love for his father, "She loved him very much." Instead, Hamlet uses a simile to communicate the intensity of that love:

> Why, she would hang on him
> As if increase of appetite had grown
> By what it fed on.

The effective reader must, then, approach a poem with a willingness to *participate* in its language. He must involve himself in the nuances of expression, the irony, the paradox, the ambiguity. He must open his mind and sensibility to the intellectual and emotional drama of the individual poem.

This collection contains poems with many moods, many tones, many attitudes. Bitter, resigned, or joyful; hopeful, pessimistic, or cynical; energetic or calm; brutal or gentle; forgiving or vengeful – they all seek to communicate a form of human truth. Carefully and sensitively read, they will provide the student ample opportunity to develop his poetic taste.

TO READ A POEM

Before the student attempts to analyze the poems in this anthology, he should have in mind some system or plan of analysis which he can apply to every poem he reads. Such a formal approach to the study of a poem often seems much more forbidding and difficult than in fact it is. Some students even resent having to analyze a poem, claiming that a disciplined reading of a poem destroys or damages the pleasure in reading it. This is not so. The truth is that any reasonably intelligent student can be taught to analyze a poem with accuracy and perceptivity. The student will discover that knowing how to analyze a poem systematically will increase his appreciation and enjoyment. As he progresses the student will also discover that he will reach at least general agreement with other readers on the meaning or interpretation of specific poems. The value, then, of a systematic, formal approach to reading poetry is twofold: such a method makes the student's interpretation of poetry more accurate and objective, and it heightens and increases his enjoyment and appreciation of poetry.

How do we go about employing a system or method of reading a poem? Basically, there are only three elements to keep in mind in approaching our problem: setting, theme, and language. Our concern in reading a poem should be to analyze each of these elements as it is involved in the specific poem; then we should synthesize or integrate our analysis of each of the three elements so that we can see how they are interrelated and unified into a meaningful comment on human existence. Usually, this process is called explicating a poem.

Let us turn to setting, the first of the three elements to be considered in an explication and ask some necessary questions. Are there any names, dates, references, or other items which require knowledge of things or events outside the poem itself? Are there any autobiographical elements from the poet's own life to be found in the poem? Is the historical context of the poem essential enough to its meaning to require an explanation? Now, these questions will often have no relevance for lyric poetry, and, when they do have relevance, they can usually be disposed of in a sentence or two. In some poetry anthologies, the editors themselves answer these questions (and others like them which vary from poem to poem).

More important questions involving setting include the following. Who is the speaker of the poem? Is there an audience present in the poem as well as a speaker? If so, who is the audience? Does the poem occur at a certain time of the year or in a certain period of history? Does the poem occur in a certain place? In other words, are there any physical, geographical, spatial, or chronological elements which we must discuss before we can understand the poem fully? What we are trying to do, to put the matter in theatrical terms, is to stage the poem in our own minds so that we may appreciate its theme and language completely.

A discussion of theme requires that we answer similar questions. When we turn to theme, we are hoping to take from the poem its central or predominant idea, its comment on human values. We are asking ourselves, "What does the poem say?" Here we are concerned with the "matter" of the poem. In very moralistic poems, the student will usually find the theme put in simple, dogmatic terms. In more sophisticated poems, however, an accurate and sensitive understanding of theme may be much more difficult to achieve.

The beginning student of poetry should understand that there are problems involved in stating a poem's theme accurately. The most common of these is "reading in." A student can easily fool himself into thinking that ideas which are not present in a poem at all are really there, only because he wants to see them there. Such a student's reading of a poem will be distorted by his private beliefs or lack of them.

A second problem concerns the way the student words his statement of a poem's theme. Many lyric poems have no "message" as such at all. There may be observation, comment, and perhaps a plea for thought or action—but there need not be all three. So the student should try to avoid being dogmatic, general, or trite in stating a poem's theme. Theme is always a comment on some aspect of life, though it need not be profound. Again, the student must ask himself, "What does the poem say?" Depending on the complexity of the poem, an answer to this question may be difficult to formulate, but the effort is well worth the trouble, for a poem's theme is ultimately its single most important value.

When we turn from theme to language, the question we ask is not "What does the poem say?" but "How does the poem say it?" Here we must analyze all the elements of language which bear upon the meaning of the poem. These elements include imagery, sound pattern, rhyme scheme, meter, line length, stanzaic form, and punctuation—as well as many others. Just as theme is the "matter" of the poem, so language is the "form" of the poem. At times this part of the analysis will become very detailed, and the student should again recognize that the analysis of language in a poem is a complex and, at times, discouraging process. Still, with some practice the student can expect to become reasonably proficient at understanding poetry's "form."

After the student has discussed a poem's setting, theme, and language, he is ready to attempt a synthesis of these elements. Here the student should ask how the parts of the poem are interrelated to form one unified, coherent whole. Now the student asks the question "Why does the poem say what it does the way it does?" How do the elements of the poem come together (if indeed they do) to make a relevant and enduring comment on human existence in just the particular language which the poem uses? The student might incidentally wish to note that other terms besides setting, theme, and language are sometimes used in the formal analysis of poetry, but, whatever terms are used, the student must concern himself with the problems which have here been labeled by those terms.

A sample explication will help the student understand the process we have been discussing. The editors have chosen Robert Browning's "My Last Duchess" to illustrate for the student the steps he should follow in reading a poem. The text of the poem and the sample explication follow.

MY LAST DUCHESS

Ferrara

That's my last Duchess painted on the wall,
Looking as if she were alive. I call
That piece a wonder, now: Frà Pandolf's hands
Worked busily a day, and there she stands.
5   Will't please you sit and look at her? I said
"Frà Pandolf" by design, for never read
Strangers like you that pictured countenance,
The depth and passion of its earnest glance,
But to myself they turned (since none puts by
10   The curtain I have drawn for you, but I)
And seemed as they would ask me, if they durst,
How such a glance came there; so, not the first
Are you to turn and ask thus. Sir, 'twas not
Her husband's presence only, called that spot
15   Of joy into the Duchess' cheek: perhaps
Frà Pandolf chanced to say "Her mantle laps
Over my Lady's wrist too much," or "Paint
Must never hope to reproduce the faint
Half-flush that dies along her throat:" such stuff
20   Was courtesy, she thought, and cause enough
For calling up that spot of joy. She had
A heart—how shall I say?—too soon made glad,

Too easily impressed; she liked whate'er
She looked on, and her looks went everywhere.
25   Sir, 'twas all one! My favour at her breast,
The dropping of the daylight in the West,
The bough of cherries some officious fool
Broke in the orchard for her, the white mule
She rode with round the terrace—all and each
30   Would draw from her alike the approving speech,
Or blush, at least. She thanked men,—good! but thanked
Somehow—I know not how—as if she ranked
My gift of a nine hundred years old name
With anybody's gift. Who'd stoop to blame
35   This sort of trifling? Even had you skill
In speech—(which I have not)—to make your will
Quite clear to such an one, and say "Just this
Or that in you disgusts me; here you miss,
Or there exceed the mark"—and if she let
40   Herself be lessoned so, nor plainly set
Her wits to yours, forsooth, and made excuse,
—E'en then would be some stooping, and I choose
Never to stoop. Oh, Sir, she smiled, no doubt
Whene'er I passed her; but who passed without
45   Much the same smile? This grew; I gave commands;
Then all smiles stopped together. There she stands
As if alive. Will't please you rise? We'll meet
The company below, then. I repeat,
The Count your Master's known munificence
50   Is ample warrant that no just pretence
Of mine for dowry will be disallowed;
Though his fair daughter's self, as I avowed
At starting, is my object. Nay, we'll go
Together down, Sir! Notice Neptune, tho',
55   Taming a sea-horse, thought a rarity,
Which Claus of Innsbruck cast in bronze for me.

Robert Browning

SETTING

"My Last Duchess" was written by the English poet Robert Browning sometime before 1842. The speaker of the poem is a fictional personage based probably on Alfonso II (1533–1598), the fifth Duke of Ferrara, who was thrice married in his lifetime, the first time to Lucrezia, the daughter of Cosimo de' Medici, Duke of Florence. Only fourteen when she married Ferrara, Lucrezia was dead at seventeen—it is thought by poisoning.

As the poem opens, the Duke has just completed the formalities of negotiating with the emissary of the Count of Tyrol for the hand of the

count's niece. This emissary, then, serves as the immediate audience
for the speaker of the poem. The two men have evidently been discussing the financial terms of the forthcoming marriage. They have passed
in front of a portrait of the Duke's first wife, a portrait which hangs
near the top of a splendid staircase within the Duke's palace. In front of
the picture there is evidently a bench on which the two men sit before
they finally, at the poem's end, descend to meet the company below.
Throughout the poem an atmosphere of sumptuous elegance and artistic
taste, mingled with cold formality, forms an essential part of the setting.

THEME

"My Last Duchess" is a character study, and the theme of the poem is
closely involved with the way the Duke reveals his true self and that of
his first wife to the emissary. To make the discussion of theme conven-
ient, we can think of the poem's structure as being roughly divided into
three parts.

In the first part (ll. 1–13), the Duke uncovers his late wife's portrait to his visitor, explaining as he does so that the artist was Friar
Pandolf. In response to a question, the Duke rather calmly and objec-
tively comments on the "depth and passion" of his wife's "earnest
glance."

There is a dramatic difference in the picture the Duke gives us of
himself in the second section (ll. 13–46). Whether he realizes it or
not—there is scholarly dispute on this point—the Duke in this section
bares his resentment that others besides himself could bring "that
spot / Of joy into the Duchess' cheek." At this point the poem becomes a
study of the Duke's pride, and we watch with fascinated horror as his
jealousy finally drives him to bring about her death:

> . . . who passed without
> Much the same smile? This grew; I gave commands;
> Then all smiles stopped together.

In the third section (ll. 46–56), the Duke easily shifts from confes-
sional comments to summarize the business that had been discussed
before the opening of the poem. Note especially the Duke's facility in
using diplomatic language as he talks of his intended bride and her
dowry. The last three and a half lines provide a revealing final glimpse
of the Duke's character. The emissary, out of respect for the Duke's
superior rank, has evidently made some gesture inviting the Duke to
descend the staircase before him. The Duke's refusal to stand upon this
matter of protocol amounts to a clever flattery of his guest, and this in
itself can be a form of condescension. He also takes this opportunity to
change the subject abruptly, indicating to the emissary that he wishes
to carry the discussion of marriage arrangements no further. Hence his
invitation that the emissary notice the bronze statue of Neptune taming a sea horse (perhaps the portrait of his former wife and the bronze

statue are of equal value to the Duke as works of art). The last line may contain a final bit of subtle flattery, for Innsbruck was not only the capital of Tyrol, but also the home of the historical personage who was the actual envoy.

What does the poem say? It tells us of an enormously proud man, capable of great self-deception – capable, in fact, of murder. Yet he has considerable diplomatic skill and a highly developed appreciation of art. The Duke is a consummate hypocrite and courtly liar; although the poem is built around the portrait of his wife, it is really a superbly and realistically drawn character sketch of the Duke himself. If we wish to express the theme simply, we could say that "My Last Duchess" is a study of heartless murder, passionless pride, and hypocritical self-deception.

LANGUAGE

The poem is a dramatic monologue. Its verse form is the rhymed couplet, and the line length is pentameter. The poetic foot basically employed is the iamb. The poem makes such extensive use of enjambment that persons who hear the poem read aloud are often unaware that rhymed couplets are employed in it. These elements together impart a casual, conversational tone to a poem that is written in a very rigid, artificial form. Since we are supposed to believe that the Duke is talking, this conversational effect makes the poem seem all the more realistic and believable.

Images of all kinds abound, most of which are associated with the late Duchess and most of which depend on color. The effect of these visual images is to make us contrast the aristocratic coldness of the Duke with the warmth, sweetness, and vitality of the girl whose death he brought about.

There are also shifts in the pace and flavor of the language, corresponding to the poem's structural shifts. In the first section, for example, the Duke speaks rather indifferently and even dispassionately of the portrait. In the second section, as the Duke's pride draws him into a moment of self-revelation, his language moves faster and he interrupts himself; even now, he becomes excited and angry when he thinks of his late wife's imagined insults to his "nine-hundred-years-old name." Finally, the Duke is all diplomacy and grace in the third section, mouthing the conventional protestations of love connected with a state marriage.

Any discussion of prosody can become as detailed as one would like to make it. This is especially true in the case of a poet like Browning, who was one of the most skillful and conscious artists in the history of English poetry. In most analyses, however, it is enough for the student to mention the specific elements of language which the poet employs in his poem, being certain to relate those elements to the poem's meaning. Again, the student should be careful to comment on the effectiveness of a poem's language. For example, rhymed couplets would not normally be effective when used in a "conversation" poem like "My Last Duchess." Yet, because of the devices Browning uses to vary the pace, pitch, and tone of his couplets, they work with almost unequaled success.

SYNTHESIS

Browning was particularly fascinated by the Italian Renaissance; the paradoxical mingling of religion and worldliness captivated him, and the complex personality of a character like the Duke of Ferrara gave him material for one of the great psychological studies in English poetry. What Browning says in a poem of fifty-six lines about our endless capacity for self-deception, our hypocrisy, our greed, our pride, and our ability to murder stands as a permanent and persuasive comment on the evil we do, made all the more effective because Browning does not moralize directly.

And it is hard to imagine his comments on human nature being put any better than they are in this dramatic monologue. The visual imagery associated with the first duchess suggests just how lovely a creature the Duke had killed. The Duke's self-exposure provides another dimension to an already satanic personality. The very way the lines are constructed—so conversational and flowing—makes us relax as we read them; again, Browning is deliberately failing to prepare us fully for the Duke's horrifying disclosure so that we will be even more repelled when we learn of it. Nor should we forget the presence of the silent audience, acting both as a stimulus for the Duke's comments and as an intermediary for the reader. The sumptuous palace, the objects of art, the company waiting to be entertained, the velvet and marble, and the details concerning the kindnesses done the late Duchess are further selected elements which underline realistically the perfidious character of the Duke. Lastly, there is the Duke's easy swing from thoughts of murder to preparations for marriage. In few poems has the character of the true Machiavellian been so fully sketched, so realistically and chillingly rendered.

BELIEF AND DOUBT

Throughout recorded time man has affirmed, speculated about, or openly doubted the existence of a divine being. Indeed, some of the great poems of the world, lyric or otherwise, have treated the general subject of belief and doubt. The twelve lyric poems in this section—all written during the last three and a half centuries of the Christian era—provide a representative selection of various attitudes toward God, and they record in poignant language man's eternal and essentially personal struggle to find the meaning of life and death.

The earliest poem anthologized here is "Holy Sonnet XIV" by John Donne, a famous seventeenth-century clergyman of the Church of England. The imagery in this remarkable sonnet has been justly praised for its unusual strength and freshness. The key to appreciating the sonnet lies in the bizarre manner in which Donne addresses God: God becomes a looter of towns; he even becomes a rapist. Were it not for Donne's evident sincerity, we would find the poem repulsive and even blasphemous. However, because of the poem's sincerity, we can accept the central paradox on which it depends. What is this paradox? Simply, it is that we as humans are such sinful creatures that God must force Himself upon us, and this is what Donne urges God to do in this devotional poem.

George Herbert's poem "The Collar" also expresses piety and devotion, again in an unusual manner. Throughout the poem Herbert, who was also a clergyman, resents Christian restrictions on behavior and the rigid system of morality by which he, as a Christian, must live. Yet at the end of the poem, after the speaker has raved and shouted his rebellious feelings, he gives in completely. He acknowledges that he is, finally, in spite of his resentment about the fact, a simple child of God.

John Keble's "Morning" first appeared in a volume of devotional verse called *The Christian Year,* which was one of the best sellers of nineteenth-century England. A leading clergyman in the Oxford Movement, Keble wrote his poems to express simple, honest piety. "Morning" speaks of the miracle we should find with the dawn of each new day; the most common, ordinary event—like the beauty of morning—can direct our attention to God and remind us of our heavenly destiny. In fact, the chief excellence in the poem lies in the ability of Keble to see transcendent greatness even in the commonplace.

In its totality "In Memoriam A. H. H." is a deeply complex and moving poem prompted by the unexpected death of Tennyson's best friend and brother-in-law to-be, Arthur Henry Hallam. Tennyson's faith in God had already been tested by his reading, particularly of recent scientific discoveries. The death of Hallam, a young man of great promise, caused him to ponder life even more deeply to determine its possible meaning. In a very real sense the entire poem, written over a period of seventeen years, expresses with piercing accuracy the religious doubts of the mid-nineteenth century. This background explains why these introductory stanzas (actually written after the rest of the poem was completed) so persistently ask God's forgiveness for having doubted him.

The next poem, Matthew Arnold's "Stanzas from the Grande Chartreuse," was written shortly after he had visited the ascetic Carthusian monastery high in the Alps. Unlike some other poems in this section, Arnold's does not make a strong, affirmative statement of faith. Indeed the key to the poem lies in the two lines:

> Wandering between two worlds, one dead,
> The other powerless to be born.

In other words, Arnold recognizes that recent intellectual developments have made the faith of the monks unacceptable; yet he remains unwilling to settle for a life of "action and pleasure"—a life without faith or a sense of human dignity. Hence the "children" in the poem remain in the shade of the monastery, wishing only for peace and tranquility. Put literally, Arnold's generation cannot accept the old, comfortable assumptions of religion; neither can it find a new foundation on which life becomes meaningful.

"Pied Beauty," by the Jesuit priest Gerard Manley Hopkins, provides a significant contrast to the tortured uncertainty of Arnold's poem. Hopkins rests comfortable in the assurance that a benevolent God directs the universe. *Pied,* a word meaning *speckled,* symbolizes the central idea of the poem. Hopkins, because of his faith in God, is able to perceive beauty in plain, ordinary, "speckled" things—in things not often considered beautiful. This is Hopkins in one mood—ecstatic and jubilant over God's creation. He also, however, experienced moods of profound despair, one of which is described in his "Carrion Comfort" on page 146.

The tone of Robert Frost's poem "Bereft" indicates still another aspect of the relationship between God and man. Drained of all other resources, Frost finally turns to God. The lines in this poem, which is written in an interlocking rhyme scheme, show a man totally deprived of any other source of comfort, affection, or companionship save God's. Of particular interest is Frost's ability to suggest a lonely mood through a series of selected symbols.

In "The World's Wonders" Robinson Jeffers speaks, not directly to or about God, but of the nature of man (which may come close to the same thing). Writing in his old age and disillusioned by man's capacity to destroy himself, Jeffers looks back over a lifetime of war and violence. When Jeffers writes that "you are doomed as Oedipus," he is telling us that our limitless abilities to destroy ourselves will in the end win out. The poem properly belongs in this section because Jeffers profoundly doubts man's capability of surviving; the implication follows that no Divine Being providentially guards the universe.

The brief poem "when any mortal (even the most odd)" by E. E. Cummings twists an old cliché about evil in the world so that it becomes an attack on man, not God. The substance of the poem comes from John Milton's *Paradise Lost*, in which Milton states specifically that his intention in writing is to justify the ways of God to man — to explain the evil and suffering in the universe. Clearly, Cummings feels that God's part in the sorrows of man is not nearly so hard to explain as man's abuse of God.

W. H. Auden's poem "Sext" is another work, like "The World's Wonders," which says more about man than God, although indirectly the poem sings of God also. The poem is reminiscent of the Puritan ethic, in that Auden suggests that man reaches his best when he works at something which interests and absorbs him. Auden also strongly implies that the brotherhood of man sustains us when all else fails. The poem ends with a reference to Christ's death, a death which by implication unites us and makes us better human beings.

"Meditations of an Old Woman" by Theodore Roethke resembles the Auden poem in that Roethke concerns himself primarily not with God, but with man. In a series of splendid, provocative images, Roethke speaks mostly of the loneliness, unhappiness, and desolation of an elderly woman. The central image — that of the bus ride — evokes these feelings poignantly. Then, at the very end of the poem, we learn from the woman that

> In such times, lacking a god,
> I am still happy.

The late and rather unexpected introduction of God into the poem lends an effectively startling shock value to the old woman's musings. When we come to this point in the poem, we no longer are dealing simply with the ravings of an old person; we are confronted with the naked horror of an old person who has little left in life and nothing to look forward to. Then the fact that the woman can become happy — if only on rare occasions — seems heroic.

Philip Larkin's poem "Church Going" presents still a different point of view. Here, a man, evidently a tourist in Ireland, tells of his stopping to visit a deserted church. The poem suggests that belief in God now is outworn and dead. Churches become in the poet's vision curiosities — museums of questionable value and interest. Yet because of our humanity, because a church remains "A serious house on serious earth," churches will endure and the human need for them likewise will last, even though the doctrines of a specific religion may die.

We discover that poems on belief and doubt range from stark pessimism to strong testimony of faith. In general, it can be said with fairness that older poems on this subject tend to emphasize belief, while more recent ones tend to emphasize doubt. The reasons for the shift are indeed complex, but it remains true that every thinking man must decide how he feels about belief in God; these twelve poems give tongue to that voiceless moment of truth we all must face.

HOLY SONNET XIV (Batter my heart)

Batter my heart, three-personed God; for you
As yet but knock, breathe, shine, and seek to mend;
That I may rise and stand, o'erthrow me and bend
Your force to break, blow, burn and make me new.
5   I, like an usurped town, to another due,
Labour to admit.you, but Oh, to no end;
Reason, your viceroy in me, me should defend,
But is captived and proves weak or untrue.
Yet dearly I love you and would be loved fain,
10   But am betrothed unto your enemy:
Divorce me, untie or break that knot again,
Take me to you, imprison me, for I
Except you enthrall me, never shall be free,
Nor ever chaste, except you ravish me.

John Donne   (1571?–1631)

THE COLLAR

I struck the board, and cried, "No more!
I will abroad!
What? Shall I ever sigh and pine?
My lines and life are free, free as the road,
5   Loose as the wind, as large as store.
Shall I be still in suit?
Have I no harvest but a thorn
To let me blood, and not restore
What I have lost with cordial fruit?
10   Sure there was wine
Before my sighs did dry it. There was corn
Before my tears did drown it.
Is the year only lost to me?
Have I no bays to crown it?
15   No flowers, no garlands gay? All blasted?
All wasted?
Not so, my heart! But there is fruit,
And thou hast hands.
Recover all thy sigh-blown age
20   On double pleasures. Leave thy cold dispute
Of what is fit and not. Forsake thy cage,
Thy rope of sands,

Which petty thoughts have made, and made to thee
Good cable, to enforce and draw,
25   And be thy law,
While thou didst wink and wouldst not see.
Away! Take heed!
I will abroad!
Call in thy death's head there! Tie up thy fears!
30   He that forbears
To suit and serve his need
Deserves his load."
But as I raved, and grew more fierce and wild
At every word,
35   Methoughts I heard one calling, "Child!"
And I replied, "My Lord!"

George Herbert   (1593 – 1633)

MORNING

Hues of the rich unfolding morn,
That, ere the glorious sun be born,
By some soft touch invisible
Around his path are taught to dwell; —

5   Thou rustling breeze so fresh and gay,
That dancest forth at opening day,
And brushing by with joyous wing,
Wakenest each little leaf to sing; —

Ye fragrant clouds of dewy steam,
10   By which deep grove and tangled stream
Pay, for soft rains in season given,
Their tribute to the genial heaven; —

Why waste your treasures of delight
Upon our thankless, joyless sight;
15   Who day by day to sin awake,
Seldom of heaven and you partake?

Oh! timely happy, timely wise,
Hearts that with rising morn arise!
Eyes that the beam celestial view,
20   Which evermore makes all things new!

New every morning is the love
Our wakening and uprising prove;
Through sleep and darkness safely brought,
Restor'd to life, and power, and thought.

25 New mercies, each returning day,
Hover around us while we pray;
New perils past, new sins forgiven,
New thoughts of God, new hopes of Heaven.

If on our daily course our mind
30 Be set to hallow all we find,
New treasures still, of countless price,
God will provide for sacrifice.

Old friends, old scenes, will lovelier be,
As more of Heaven in each we see:
35 Some softening gleam of love and prayer
Shall dawn on every cross and care.

As for some dear familiar strain
Untir'd we ask, and ask again,
Ever, in its melodious store,
40 Finding a spell unheard before;

Such is the bliss of souls serene,
When they have sworn, and steadfast mean,
Counting the cost, in all to' espy
Their God, in all themselves deny.

45 O could we learn that sacrifice,
What lights would all around us rise!
How would our hearts with wisdom talk
Along Life's dullest, dreariest walk!

We need not bid, for cloister'd cell,
50 Our neighbor and our work farewell,
Nor strive to wind ourselves too high
For sinful man beneath the sky:

The trivial round, the common task,
Would furnish all we ought to ask;
55 Room to deny ourselves; a road
To bring us, daily, nearer God.

Seek we no more; content with these,
Let present Rapture, Comfort, Ease,
As Heaven shall bid them, come and go: —
60 The secret this of Rest below.

Only, O Lord, in thy dear love
Fit us for perfect Rest above;
And help us, this and every day,
To live more nearly as we pray.

John Keble   (1792 – 1866)

from IN MEMORIAM A. H. H.

Prologue

Strong Son of God, immortal Love,
   Whom we, that have not seen thy face,
   By faith, and faith alone, embrace,
Believing where we cannot prove;

5   Thine are these orbs of light and shade;
   Thou madest Life in man and brute;
   Thou madest Death; and lo, thy foot
Is on the skull which thou hast made.

Thou wilt not leave us in the dust:
10   Thou madest man, he knows not why,
   He thinks he was not made to die;
And thou hast made him; thou art just.

Thou seemest human and divine,
   The highest, holiest manhood, thou.
15   Our wills are ours, we know not how;
Our wills are ours, to make them thine.

Our little systems have their day;
   They have their day and cease to be;
   They are but broken lights of thee,
20   And thou, O Lord, art more than they.

We have but faith; we cannot know,
   For knowledge is of things we see;
   And yet we trust it comes from thee,
A beam in darkness; let it grow.

25   Let knowledge grow from more to more,
   But more of reverence in us dwell;
   That mind and soul, according well,
May make one music as before,

30 But vaster. We are fools and slight;
    We mock thee when we do not fear.
    But help thy foolish ones to bear;
Help thy vain worlds to bear thy light.

Forgive what seemed my sin in me,
    What seemed my worth since I began;
35   For merit lives from man to man,
And not from man, O Lord, to thee.

Forgive my grief for one removed,
    Thy creature, whom I found so fair.
    I trust he lives in thee, and there
40 I find him worthier to be loved.

Forgive these wild and wandering cries,
    Confusions of a wasted youth;
    Forgive them where they fail in truth,
And in thy wisdom make me wise.

Alfred, Lord Tennyson   (1809 – 1892)

STANZAS FROM THE GRANDE CHARTREUSE

Through Alpine meadows soft-suffused
With rain, where thick the crocus blows,
Past the dark forges long disused,
The mule-track from Saint Laurent goes.
5 The bridge is cross'd, and slow we ride,
Through forest, up the mountain-side.

The autumnal evening darkens round,
The wind is up, and drives the rain;
While, hark! far down, with strangled sound
10 Doth the Dead Guier's stream complain,
Where that wet smoke, among the woods,
Over his boiling cauldron broods.

Swift rush the spectral vapours white
Past limestone scars with ragged pines,
15 Showing — then blotting from our sight! —
Halt — through the cloud-drift something shines!
High in the valley, wet and drear,
The huts of Courrerie appear.

        Strike leftward! cries our guide; and higher
20   Mounts up the stony forest-way.
        At last the encircling trees retire;
        Look! through the showery twilight grey
        What pointed roofs are these advance?—
        A palace of the Kings of France?

25   Approach, for what we seek is here!
        Alight, and sparely sup, and wait
        For rest in this outbuilding near;
        Then cross the sward and reach that gate.
        Knock; pass the wicket! Thou art come
30   To the Carthusians' world-famed home.

        The silent courts, where night and day
        Into their stone-carved basins cold
        The splashing icy fountains play—
        The humid corridors behold!
35   Where, ghostlike in the deepening night,
        Cowl'd forms brush by in gleaming white.

        The chapel, where no organ's peal
        Invests the stern and naked prayer—
        With penitential cries they kneel
40   And wrestle; rising then, with bare
        And white uplifted faces stand,
        Passing the Host from hand to hand;

        Each takes, and then his visage wan
        Is buried in his cowl once more.
45   The cells!—the suffering Son of Man
        Upon the wall—the knee-worn floor—
        And where they sleep, that wooden bed,
        Which shall their coffin be, when dead!

        The library, where tract and tome
50   Not to feed priestly pride are there,
        To hymn the conquering march of Rome,
        Nor yet to amuse, as ours are!
        They paint of souls the inner strife,
        Their drops of blood, their death in life.

55   The garden, overgrown—yet mild,
        See, fragrant herbs are flowering there!
        Strong children of the Alpine wild
        Whose culture is the brethren's care;
        Of human tasks their only one,
60   And cheerful works beneath the sun.

Those halls, too, destined to contain
Each its own pilgrim-host of old,
From England, Germany, or Spain—
All are before me! I behold
65   The House, the Brotherhood austere!
—And what am I, that I am here?

For rigorous teachers seized my youth,
And purged its faith, and trimm'd its fire,
Show'd me the high white star of Truth,
70   There bade me gaze, and there aspire;
Even now their whispers pierce the gloom:
What dost thou in this living tomb?

Forgive me, masters of the mind!
At whose behest I long ago
75   So much unlearnt, so much resign'd—
I come not here to be your foe!
I seek these anchorites, not in ruth,
To curse and to deny your truth;

Not as their friend, or child, I speak!
80   But as, on some far northern strand,
Thinking of his own Gods, a Greek
In pity and mournful awe might stand
Before some fallen Runic stone—
For both were faiths, and both are gone.

85   Wandering between two worlds, one dead,
The other powerless to be born,
With nowhere yet to rest my head,
Like these, on earth I wait forlorn.
Their faith, my tears, the world deride—
90   I come to shed them at their side.

Oh, hide me in your gloom profound,
Ye solemn seats of holy pain!
Take me, cowl'd forms, and fence me round,
Till I possess my soul again;
95   Till free my thoughts before me roll;
Not chafed by hourly false control!

For the world cries your faith is now
But a dead time's exploded dream;
My melancholy, sciolists say,
100   Is a pass'd mode, an outworn theme—
As if the world had ever had
A faith, or sciolists been sad!

Ah, if it *be* pass'd, take away,
At least, the restlessness, the pain;
105   Be man henceforth no more a prey
To these out-dated stings again!
The nobleness of grief is gone —
Ah, leave us not the fret alone!

But — if you cannot give us ease
110   Last of the race of them who grieve
Here leave us to die out with these
Last of the people who believe!
Silent, while years engrave the brow;
Silent — the best are silent now.

115   Achilles ponders in his tent,
The kings of modern thought are dumb;
Silent they are, though not content,
And wait to see the future come.
They have the grief men had of yore,
120   But they contend and cry no more.

Our fathers water'd with their tears
This sea of time whereon we sail,
Their voices were in all men's ears
Who pass'd within their puissant hail.
125   Still the same ocean round us raves,
But we stand mute, and watch the waves.

For what avail'd it, all the noise
And out cry of the former men? —
Say, have their sons achieved more joys,
130   Say, is life lighter now than then?
The sufferers died, they left their pain —
The pangs which tortured them remain.

What helps it now, that Byron bore,
With haughty scorn which mock'd the smart,
135   Through Europe to the Aetolian shore
The pageant of his bleeding heart?
That thousands counted every groan,
And Europe made his woe her own?

What boots it, Shelley! that the breeze
140   Carried thy lovely wail away,
Musical through Italian trees
Which fringe thy soft blue Spezzian bay?
Inheritors of thy distress
Have restless hearts one throb the less?

145   Or are we easier, to have read,
      O Obermann! the sad, stern page,
      Which tells us how thou hidd'st thy head
      From the fierce tempest of thine age
      In the lone brakes of Fontainebleau,
150   Or chalets near the Alpine snow?

      Ye slumber in your silent grave! —
      The world, which for an idled day
      Grace to your mood of sadness gave,
      Long since hath flung her weeds away.
155   The eternal trifler breaks your spell;
      But we — we learnt your lore too well!

      Years hence, perhaps, may dawn an age,
      More fortunate, alas! than we,
      Which without hardness will be sage,
160   And gay without frivolity,
      Sons of the world, ho, speed those years;
      But, while we wait, allow our tears!

      Allow them! We admire with awe
      The exulting thunder of your race;
165   You give the universe your law,
      You triumph over time and space!
      Your pride of life, your tireless powers,
      We laud them, but they are not ours.

      We are like children rear'd in shade
170   Beneath some old-world abbey wall,
      Forgotten in a forest-glade,
      And secret from the eyes of all.
      Deep, deep the greenwood round them waves,
      Their abbey, and its close of graves!

175   But, where the road runs near the stream,
      Oft through the trees they catch a glance
      Of passing troops in the sun's beam —
      Pennon, and plume, and flashing lance!
      Forth to the world those soldiers fare,
180   To life, to cities, and to war!

      And through the wood, another way,
      Faint bugle-notes from far are borne,
      Where hunters gather, staghounds bay,
      Round some fair forest-lodge at morn.
185   Gay dames are there, in sylvan green;
      Laughter and cries — those notes between!

The banners flashing through the trees
Make their blood dance and chain their eyes;
That bugle-music on the breeze
190   Arrests them with a charm'd surprise.
Banner by turns and bugle woo:
Ye shy recluses, follow too!

O children, what do ye reply?—
'Action and pleasure, will ye roam
195   Through these secluded dells to cry
And call us?—but too late ye come!
Too late for us your call ye blow,
Whose bent was taken long ago.

'Long since we pace this shadow'd nave,
200   We watch those yellow tapers shine,
Emblems of hope over the grave,
In the high altar's depth divine;
The organ carries to our ear
Its accents of another sphere.

205   'Fenced early in this cloistral round
Of reverie, of shade, of prayer,
How should we grow in other ground?
How can we flower in foreign air?
Pass, banners, pass, and bugles, cease,
210   And leave our desert to its peace!'

Matthew Arnold   (1822 – 1888)

PIED BEAUTY

Glory be to God for dappled things—
    For skies of couple-colour as a brinded cow;
        For rose-moles all in stipple upon trout that swim;
Fresh-firecoal chestnut-falls; finches' wings;
5   Landscape plotted and pieced—fold, fallow, and plough;
        And all trades, their gear and tackle and trim.

All things counter, original, spare, strange;
    Whatever is fickle, freckled (who knows how?)
        With swift, slow; sweet, sour; adazzle, dim;
10   He fathers-forth whose beauty is past change:
            Praise him.

Gerard Manley Hopkins   (1844 – 1889)

BEREFT

Where had I heard this wind before
Change like this to a deeper roar?
What would it take my standing there for,
Holding open a restive door,
5   Looking down hill to a frothy shore?
Summer was past and day was past.
Somber clouds in the west were massed.
Out in the porch's sagging floor,
Leaves got up in a coil and hissed,
10   Blindly struck at my knee and missed.
Something sinister in the tone
Told me my secret must be known:
Word I was in the house alone
Somehow must have gotten abroad,
15   Word I was in my life alone,
Word I had no one left but God.

Robert Frost (1874–1963)

THE WORLD'S WONDERS

Being now three or four years more than sixty,
I have seen strange things in my time. I have seen a merman standing
    waist-deep in the ocean off my rock shore,

Unmistakably human and unmistakably a sea-beast: he submerged
    and never came up again,
While we stood watching. I do not know what he was, and I have no
    theory: but this was the least of wonders.

I have seen the United States grow up the strongest and wealthiest of
5   nations, and swim in the wind over bankruptcy.
I have seen Europe, for twenty-five hundred years the crown of the
    world, become its beggar and cripple.

I have seen my people, fooled by ambitious men and a froth of senti-
    ment, waste themselves on three wars.
None was required, all futile, all grandly victorious. A fourth is forming.

I have seen the invention of human flight; a chief desire of man's
    dreaming heart for ten thousand years;
10   And men have made it the chief of the means of massacre.

I have seen the far stars weighed and their distance measured, and the
   powers that make the atom put into service —
For what? — To kill. To kill half a million flies — men I should say — at
   one slap.

I have also seen doom. You can stand up and struggle or lie down and
   sleep — you are doomed as Oedipus.
A man and a civilization grow old, grow fatally — as we say — ill: courage and the will are bystanders.

15
It is easy to know the beauty of inhuman things, sea, storm and mountain; it is their soul and their meaning.
Humanity has its lesser beauty, impure and painful; we have to harden
   our hearts to bear it.

I have hardened my heart only a little: I have learned that happiness is
   important, but pain *gives* importance.
The use of tragedy: Lear becomes as tall as the storm he crawls in; and
   a tortured Jew became God.

Robinson Jeffers   (1887 – 1962)

WHEN ANY MORTAL (EVEN THE MOST ODD)

when any mortal (even the most odd)

can justify the ways of man to God
i'll think it strange that normal mortals can

not justify the ways of God to man

E. E. Cummings   (1894 – 1962)

from HORAE CANONICAE SEXT

1

You need not see what someone is doing
to know if it is his vocation,

you have only to watch his eyes:
a cook mixing a sauce, a surgeon

5   making a primary incision,
        a clerk completing a bill of lading,

        wear the same rapt expression,
        forgetting themselves in a function.

        How beautiful it is,
10   that eye-on-the-object look.

        To ignore the appetitive goddesses,
        to desert the formidable shrines

        of Rhea, Aphrodite, Demeter, Diana,
        to pray instead to St. Phocas,

15   St. Barbara, San Saturnino,
        or whoever one's patron is,

        that one may be worthy of their mystery,
        what a prodigious step to have taken.

        There should be monuments, there should be odes,
20   to the nameless heroes who took it first,

        to the first flaker of flints
        who forgot his dinner,

        the first collector of sea-shells
        to remain celibate.

25   Where should we be but for them?
        Feral still, un-housetrained, still

        wandering through forests without
        a consonant to our names,

        slaves of Dame Kind, lacking
30   all notion of a city

        and, at this noon, for this death,
        there would be no agents.

        2

        You need not hear what orders he is giving
        to know if someone has authority,

35   you have only to watch his mouth:
        when a besieging general sees

a city wall breached by his troops,
when a bacteriologist

40   realizes in a flash what was wrong
with his hypothesis, when,

from a glance at the jury, the prosecutor
knows the defendant will hang,

their lips and the lines around them
relax, assuming an expression,

45   not of simple pleasure at getting
their own sweet way but of satisfaction

of being right, an incarnation
of *Fortitudo, Justicia, Nous.*

You may not like them much
50   (Who does?) but we owe them

basilicas, divas,
dictionaries, pastoral verse,

the courtesies of the city:
without these judicial mouths

55   (which belong for the most part
to very great scoundrels)

how squalid existence would be,
tethered for life to some hut village,

afraid of the local snake
60   or the local ford demon,

speaking the local patois
of some three hundred words

(think of the family squabbles and the
poison-pens, think of the inbreeding)

65   and, at this noon, there would be no authority
to command this death.

3

Anywhere you like, somewhere
on broad-chested life-giving Earth,

anywhere between her thirstlands
70   and undrinkable Ocean,

the crowd stands perfectly still,
its eyes (which seem one) and its mouths

(which seem infinitely many)
expressionless, perfectly blank.

75   The crowd does not see (what everyone sees)
a boxing match, a train wreck,

a battleship being launched,
does not wonder (as everyone wonders)

who will win, what flag she will fly,
80   how many will be burned alive,

is never distracted
(as everyone is always distracted)

by a barking dog, a smell of fish,
a mosquito on a bald head:

85   the crowd sees only one thing
(which only the crowd can see),

an epiphany of that
which does whatever is done.

Whatever god a person believes in,
90   in whatever way he believes

(no two are exactly alike),
as one of the crowd he believes

and only believes in that
in which there is only one way of believing.

95   Few people accept each other and most
will never do anything properly,

but the crowd rejects no one, joining the crowd
is the only thing all men can do.

Only because of that can we say
100   all men are our brothers,

superior, because of that,
to the social exoskeletons: When

have they ever ignored their queens,
for one second stopped work

105   on their provincial cities, to worship
The Prince of this world like us,

at this noon, on this hill,
in the occasion of this dying.

W. H. Auden   (1907 –   )

MEDITATIONS OF AN OLD WOMAN

First Meditation

1

On love's worst ugly day,
The weeds hiss at the edge of the field,
The small winds make their chilly indictments.
Elsewhere, in houses, even pails can be sad;
5   While stones loosen on the obscure hillside,
And a tree tilts from its roots,
Toppling down an embankment.

The spirit moves, but not always upward,
While animals eat to the north,
10   And the shale slides an inch in the talus,
The bleak wind eats at the weak plateau,
And the sun brings joy to some.
But the rind, often, hates the life within.

How can I rest in the days of my slowness?
15   I've become a strange piece of flesh,
Nervous and cold, bird-furtive, whiskery,
With a cheek soft as a hound's ear.
What's left is light as a seed;
I need an old crone's knowing.

2

20   Often I think of myself as riding —
Alone, on a bus through western country.
I sit above the back wheels, where the jolts are hardest,
And we bounce and sway along toward the midnight,
The lights tilting up, skyward, as we come over a little rise,
25   Then down, as we roll like a boat from a wave-crest.

All journeys, I think, are the same:
The movement is forward, after a few wavers,
And for a while we are all alone,
Busy, obvious with ourselves,
30   The drunken soldier, the old lady with her peppermints;
And we ride, we ride, taking the curves
Somewhat closer, the trucks coming
Down from behind the last ranges,
Their black shapes breaking past;
35   And the air claps between us,
Blasting the frosted windows,
And I seem to go backward,
Backward in time:

      Two song sparrows, one within a greenhouse,
40   Shuttling its throat while perched on a wind-vent,
      And another, outside, in the bright day,
      With a wind from the west and the trees all in motion.
      One sang, then the other,
      The songs tumbling over and under the glass,
45   And the men beneath them wheeling in dirt to the cement
          benches,
      The laden wheelbarrows creaking and swaying,
      And the up-spring of the plank when a foot left the runway.

Journey within a journey:
The ticket mislaid or lost, the gate
50   Inaccessible, the boat always pulling out
From the rickety wooden dock,
The children waving;
Or two horses plunging in snow, their lines tangled,
A great wooden sleigh careening behind them,
55   Swerving up a steep embankment.
For a moment they stand above me,
Their black skins shuddering:
Then they lurch forward,
Lunging down a hillside.

3

60   As when silt drifts and sifts down through muddy pond-water,
Settling in small beads around weeds and sunken branches,
And one crab, tentative, hunches himself before moving along the bot-
      tom,
Grotesque, awkward, his extended eyes looking at nothing in particular,
Only a few bubbles loosening from the ill-matched tentacles,
65   The tail and smaller legs slipping and sliding slowly backward—
So the spirit tries for another life,
Another way and place in which to continue;

70

75

80

85

90

95

Or a salmon, tired, moving up a shallow stream,
Nudges into a back-eddy, a sandy inlet,
Bumping against sticks and bottom-stones, then swinging
Around, back into the tiny maincurrent, the rush of brownish-white
    water,
Still swimming forward —
So, I suppose, the spirit journeys.

4

I have gone into the waste lonely places
Behind the eye; the lost acres at the edge of smoky cities.
What's beyond never crumbles like an embankment,
Explodes like a rose, or thrusts wings over the Caribbean.
There are no pursuing forms, faces on walls:
Only the motes of dust in the immaculate hallways,
The darkness of falling hair, the warnings from lint and spiders,
The vines graying to a fine powder.
There is no riven tree, or lamb dropped by an eagle.

There are still times, morning and evening:
The cerulean, high in the elm,
Thin and insistent as a cicada,
And the far phoebe, singing,
The long plaintive notes floating down,
Drifting through leaves, oak and maple,
Or the whippoorwill, along the smoky ridges,
A single bird calling and calling;
A fume reminds me, drifting across wet gravel;
A cold wind comes over stones;
A flame, intense, visible,
Plays over the dry pods,
Runs fitfully along the stubble,
Moves over the field,
Without burning.
        In such times, lacking a god,
        I am still happy.

Theodore Roethke   (1908 – 1963)

CHURCH GOING

Once I am sure there's nothing going on
I step inside, letting the door thud shut.
Another church: matting, seats, and stone,
And little books; sprawlings of flowers, cut

5   For Sunday, brownish now; some brass and stuff
     Up at the holy end; the small neat organ;
     And a tense, musty, unignorable silence,
     Brewed God knows how long. Hatless, I take off
     My cycle-clips in awkward reverence,

10   Move forward, run my hand around the font.
     From where I stand, the roof looks almost new —
     Cleaned, or restored? Someone would know: I don't.
     Mounting the lectern, I peruse a few
     Hectoring large-scale verses, and pronounce
15   'Here endeth' much more loudly than I'd meant.
     The echoes snigger briefly. Back at the door
     I sign the book, donate an Irish sixpence,
     Reflect the place was not worth stopping for.

     Yet stop I did: in fact I often do,
20   And always end much at a loss like this,
     Wondering what to look for; wondering, too,
     When churches fall completely out of use
     What we shall turn them into, if we shall keep
     A few cathedrals chronically on show,
25   Their parchment, plate and pyx in locked cases,
     And let the rest rent-free to rain and sheep.
     Shall we avoid them as unlucky places?

     Or, after dark, will dubious women come
     To make their children touch a particular stone;
30   Pick simples for a cancer; or in some
     Advised night see walking a dead one?
     Power of some sort or other will go on
     In games, in riddles, seemingly at random;
     But superstition, like belief, must die,
35   And what remains when disbelief has gone?
     Grass, weedy pavement, brambles, buttress, sky,

     A shape less recognisable each week,
     A purpose more obscure. I wonder who
     Will be the last, the very last, to seek
40   This place for what it was; one of the crew
     That tap and jot and know what rood-lofts were?
     Some ruin-bibber, randy for antique,
     Or Christmas-addict, counting on a whiff
     Of gown-and-bands and organ-pipes and myrrh?
45   Or will he be my representative,

     Bored, uninformed, knowing the ghostly silt
     Dispersed, yet tending to this cross of ground
     Through suburb scrub because it held unspilt

So long and equably what since is found
50 Only in separation—marriage, and birth,
And deaths, and thoughts of these—for whom was built
This special shell? For, though I've no idea
What this accoutred frowsty barn is worth,
It pleases me to stand in silence here;

55 A serious house on serious earth it is,
In whose blent air all our compulsions meet,
Are recognised, and robed as destinies.
And that much never can be obsolete,
Since someone will forever be surprising
60 A hunger in himself to be more serious,
And gravitating with it to this ground,
Which, he once heard, was proper to grow wise in,
If only that so many dead lie round.

Philip Larkin   (1922 –   )

QUESTIONS FOR DISCUSSION AND FURTHER STUDY

HOLY SONNET XIV (BATTER MY HEART)

1. In terms of grammar, what mood predominates in this poem — indicative, subjunctive, or imperative? Why is Donne's choice of mood particularly important?
2. There is an image which predominates in each quatrain of this sonnet. Identify the images and discuss their appropriateness.
3. At one point in the poem Donne compares God to a rapist. Were it not for Donne's evident sincerity, this image would be inappropriate, even blasphemous. Why does the image succeed, making the poem even more effective?

THE COLLAR

1. One of the more difficult but important questions to be asked about this poem is: What is the significance of the title? Of what does the "collar" consist? Is it related to the phrase "rope of sands"?
2. How does Herbert use images of food and wine to present one pole toward which he is attracted? How does he use images from law and philosophy ("be still in suit," "cold dispute") to represent the other pole?
3. In the poem the speaker moves from rebellion to piety. Is his motivation for this change given by Herbert? If not, does this constitute a weakness in the poem? Why or why not?

MORNING

1. Wordsworth has written of his own poetry that he wished it to make the ordinary and commonplace fresh and new. In what sense could "Morning" be called a Wordsworthian poem?
2. Discuss the imagery based on light in this poem. References to the sense of sight occur several times. Given his theme, why does Keble use images of this sort?
3. Much of Keble's poem is a hymn of praise to God. One difficulty for a poet in writing about God is that God is an abstraction; He cannot be described concretely. Do you think Keble overcomes this problem? Why or why not?

FROM IN MEMORIAM A. H. H.

1.   The first stanza suggests that we should accept God's existence as a matter of faith; we cannot prove it. Do you feel that Tennyson's idea is anti-intellectual? Why or why not? Do you feel that faith without knowledge is sufficient basis for belief in God?
2.   In light of the recent assassinations of public figures in this country, do you feel that we are facing the same spiritual dilemma Tennyson faced when Hallam died?
3.   Discuss the rather unusual rhyme scheme Tennyson uses in his four-line stanza. What effects are gained by the separation of the first rhyme (ll. 1–4)?

STANZAS FROM THE GRANDE CHARTREUSE

1.   In this poem Arnold suggests that we are "between two worlds, one dead, one powerless to be born." There were a number of scientific discoveries in the nineteenth century which seemed to conflict with traditional religious belief. The theory of evolution is an example. In terms of the foregoing, what is the poem really about? What is Arnold's attitude toward older religious beliefs? Is he glad to see them weakened, or does he regret their passing?
2.   What is Arnold's attitude toward the monks in the poem? Does he approve of the way they have solved or at least sublimated the conflict between faith and doubt? Or does he feel that their pattern of life holds some weakness?
3.   Images of light and dark predominate in this poem. Discuss the meaning of these images, and indicate their effectiveness in terms of the poem's overall meaning.

PIED BEAUTY

1.   For what does Hopkins praise God in this poem? Remember that the word *pied* means *speckled*. How is the notion that we should give glory to God, "whose beauty is past change," related to the first question?
2.   Discuss Hopkins' use of alliteration. Where does he use pairs or sets of alliterative words in the poem?
3.   Discuss the descriptive qualities of the poem's third line. What about this line makes it so powerfully suggestive?

BEREFT

1. What state, according to the poem, must a human being reach before he is ready to come to God? Do you agree with Frost's judgment?
2. The time of year, the time of day, the weather, and the condition of the house mentioned in the poem help to suggest what emotional state being experienced by the poem's speaker? What is the speaker's "secret"?
3. Note that the door is "restive," the clouds are "massed," and the leaves have "hissed." What effect does Frost gain by attributing animate qualities to inanimate objects?

THE WORLD'S WONDERS

1. What is the speaker's attitude toward the United States? Would you say it is patriotic or unpatriotic? Why?
2. Why does Jeffers refer to Lear? What relevance has a tragic hero to a poem about "The World's Wonders"? For that matter, why does Jeffers mention Christ, by implication, in the poem's last line? Can you draw a comparison between the poet's attitude toward his country and his attitude toward religion?
3. How does the poet compare himself to his country? Be specific in terms of age, health, wisdom, and virtue.

WHEN ANY MORTAL (EVEN THE MOST ODD)

1. What contrast is made in this poem between a "normal" mortal and an "odd" one? What is the thematic significance of this contrast?
2. Is it possible for man to abuse God? How? What religious assumptions would underlie such a possibility?
3. Attempt to write a paraphrase of this poem, employing fewer words than Cummings does.

FROM HORAE CANONICAE SEXT

1. What attitude toward work is taken by Auden in this poem? Is all work of basically the same value and importance to Auden? Why?
2. What attitude toward belief is taken by Auden? How is his attitude toward belief related to his attitude toward work? What is your opinion of the relationship?

3.   What is the poem really about? At first it seems to be a hymn to work, later, a hymn to belief, finally, a hymn to brotherhood. How are the first two elements related to the third? What role does Christ play in the union of these three?

MEDITATIONS OF AN OLD WOMAN (FIRST MEDITATION)

1.   Describe the setting used to stage the woman's meditations. What concrete details does Roethke use to symbolize externally the old woman's internal state?
2.   What dreams or meditations does the woman experience? What thematic significance does the bus journey have? When the woman speaks of the bus journey, is she symbolizing another journey also? If so, what is that other journey? Why is the ticket mislaid or lost?
3.   What is the old woman's attitude toward God and religion? In connection with this, what compensations does she find in life? Where do these compensations spring from? Are the compensations symbolized by specific details? If so, what are they?

CHURCH GOING

1.   Does the poet feel that religion is outworn, or does he think it is still of some value? Would you characterize his attitude toward religion as a simple or complex one? If religion still has value, wherein does that value lie?
2.   Note the use of detail: the speaker's removal of his cycle clip, for example. What effect does such detail have on involving the reader more immediately in the setting of the poem?
3.   Discuss the points of similarity and difference between this poem and Arnold's "Stanzas from the Grande Chartreuse." Which poem do you consider more effective? Why?

CHILDHOOD

Many poems about childhood are really studies of recollection in which the poet looks back upon some aspect of his early youth. The attitude of poets toward their childhood varies widely, as the poems in this section clearly show.

There is a special problem involved in reading poems about childhood. A poet who writes about the distant past in his own life must rely on memory, and memory plays tricks. As a result, the way childhood appears to a poet when he writes about it as an adult may be far different from the way it really was. The poet may idealize his childhood, for example. The student should be aware that often there are problems of point of view in studying poems on this theme; in fact, the student should pay special attention to the tone of each poem, asking himself if he can really rely on the accuracy of the observations the poet makes, or if he must allow for the poet's sentimentality or cynicism (or any other emotion which might color his ideas).

The two oldest poems of recollection in this group, both written in the seventeenth century, are "The Retreat" and "Innocence." Henry Vaughan's poem "The Retreat" pleads the innocence of childhood and even suggests the doctrine of preexistence. According to this doctrine, a person's soul waits in union with God in heaven until it is time to be born. Then the soul is imprisoned, as it were, in the body. Children are therefore holier than adults because they are closer to their heavenly home. When Plato taught this doctrine, he believed that the soul forgot its divine origins at birth, but many poets suggest that we remember them at least dimly. In any event, Vaughan is interested in seeing the spiritual symbols and meanings which lie just beneath the veil of the material world. He yearns for the innocence and sanctity of childhood, both of which he sees as being inevitably interwoven with God and heaven.

Thomas Traherne's "Innocence," also written in the seventeenth century, resembles Vaughan's poem in that it too pleads for a return to the purity and goodness of childhood. Again, the innocence of youth is contrasted with the corruption of adulthood; again, the doctrine of pre-existence is suggested, however dimly; again, the urge to become a child again, so strong in Vaughan's poem, suggests a union among childhood, salvation, and perfect happiness.

Probably the most famous poem suggesting preexistence is Words-worth's "Intimations" ode. It is helpful to think of this poem in three parts. In the first four stanzas Wordsworth asks what has happened to the "visionary gleam" he once experienced as a child. (This gleam is the child's awareness of his heavenly beginnings, which he gradually loses as he gets older. We are born "trailing clouds of glory," but as we become adults we lose our instinctive awareness of God and heaven.) In stanzas 5–8 Wordsworth answers his question; we lose our sensitiv-ity to nature (and God) as we grow older and travel further from heaven, our home. Stanzas 9–11 are often called "compensatory" stanzas in that they describe with lyric rejoicing the compensations that adult-hood brings.

Thomas Hood's simple but sincere poem "I Remember, I Remem-ber" does not share with the "Intimations" ode its philosophical com-plexity, nor does the doctrine of preexistence appear with anything but the slightest hint. Neither does it use Wordsworth's argument that adulthood has its compensations. Yet Hood does effectively suggest in the ending the theme shared by so many poets of childhood:

> But now 'tis little joy
> To know I'm farther off from heav'n
> Than when I was a boy.

Longfellow's poem "My Lost Youth" possesses something in com-mon with the Wordsworth ode. In a number of stanzas, each ending the same way, Longfellow remembers many of the scenes of his childhood; as in the Wordsworth poem, "There are thoughts that make the strong heart weak," and there is a "joy that is almost pain." The contrast be-tween a boy's emotional state and the emotional state of an adult look-ing back on it is touching and effective; sadly, the difference between the two is vast, even cosmic.

In Walt Whitman's "There Was a Child Went Forth" the emphasis is not so much on what occurs before birth. He provides instead a barrage of images, appealing to all the five senses, which serve in effect to cata-log the natural influences upon the child. Basically, Whitman is inter-ested in the unity of mankind and the cyclical way all life repeats itself. All life is one; all generations are one; all time is repetitious; existence moves in a cycle, everywhere repeating its themes and variations in all times and places.

The tone of resignation in "Birches" is stronger than in the other poems discussed so far. In this quietly moving poem Robert Frost shows us how temporarily desirable it would be for us to be more than we are — more than human. He does this by picturing a boy who swings on slender birch trees, going for a time toward heaven but always ending back on earth. Reaching for heaven is a good thing in a temporary sense, Frost says, but "Earth's the right place for love." The poem then ends on a chord of contentment and tranquillity.

Some poems about childhood stress not the innocence and beauty so much as the brevity and fleetingness not only of youth but of life itself. Both "Spring and Fall: To a Young Child" and "The Horse Chestnut Tree" do this. In the first poem Hopkins points out to Margaret that she is really mourning for herself when she thinks she is grieving because spring is turning to fall. Unknown to herself, the little girl is subconsciously identifying with nature and sensing her own passing ("It is the blight man was born for") as she mourns the transitoriness of the beautiful things about her.

The ideas of the quick passage of time and the permanence of nature are also expressed by the narrator of "The Horse Chestnut Tree." As a boy, he too stole horse chestnuts with his friends, hurrying "the work of nature for their pleasure." Now, as a man, he chases other boys away who wish to do the same thing. This leads the speaker to the metaphorical consideration that we are all outlaws, stealing a moment's "tangible good" from "God's property," and we too will be driven from the scene — by death. The brevity and restlessness of our lives are contrasted with the enduring permanence of nature, "the great flowing world unbroken yet."

A different kind of alienation appears in "My Parents Kept Me from Children Who Were Rough." Here the narrator sees himself as a sensitive, delicate child, unable to win fights or to make friends with rougher children, and "they never smiled." This understatement, in other words, suggests that companionship or acceptance between the "children who were rough" and the lonely narrator never did exist.

The two remaining poems in this section both deal with the innocence of childhood. In "The Lamb" William Blake, as it were, teaches catechism to a child. The poem suggests that the innocence of children makes them like Christ, here symbolized by the lamb. Because of their mutual goodness, the child and God are one. The language of the poem is very simple, but it escapes being ludicrous because of the obvious sincerity of its tone.

"Frost at Midnight" is also about innocence, but in this poem Coleridge sustains an important contrast. As his infant son Hartley sleeps by his side, Coleridge meditates on the difference between his childhood and the one he hopes his son will have. Coleridge was raised in the city; his son will be raised in the country, where the tonic, beneficial, healing powers of nature will keep the young child innocent and good. Although Coleridge is known widely for narrative poems dealing with the supernatural, this poem's quiet, conversational, and human tone makes it most powerful.

From this discussion the student can see that poets have traditionally been interested in the subject of childhood. They have written about it in a variety of ways, but one constant factor which seems to appear in most poems on childhood is the notion that this is the most innocent, virtuous period of human life.

THE RETREAT

Happy those early days, when I
Shined in my angel-infancy!
Before I understood this place
Appointed for my second race,
5   Or taught my soul to fancy ought
But a white, celestial thought;
When yet I had not walked above
A mile or two from my first love;
And looking back, at that short space,
10   Could see a glimpse of his bright face;
When on some gilded cloud or flower
My gazing soul would dwell an hour,
And in those weaker glories spy
Some shadows of eternity;
15   Before I taught my tongue to wound
My conscience with a sinful sound,
Or had the black art to dispense
A several sin to every sense,
But felt through all this fleshy dress
20   Bright shoots of everlastingness.
    O how I long to travel back,
And tread again that ancient track!
That I might once more reach that plain,
Where first I left my glorious train;
25   From whence the enlightened spirit sees
That shady City of Palm trees.
But ah! my soul with too much stay
Is drunk, and staggers in the way!
Some men a forward motion love,
30   But I by backward steps would move;
And, when this dust falls to the urn,
In that state I came, return.

        Henry Vaughan   (1622 – 1695)

INNOCENCE

1

But that which most I wonder at, which most
I did esteem my bliss, which most I boast,
And ever shall enjoy, is that within
    I felt no stain nor spot of sin.

5   No darkness then did overshade,
But all within was pure and bright;
No guilt did crush nor fear invade,
But all my soul was full of light.

A joyful sense and purity
10   Is all I can remember;
The very night to me was bright,
'Twas summer in December.

2

A serious meditation did employ
My soul within, which, taken up with joy
15   Did seem no outward thing to note, but fly
All objects that do feed the eye.

While it those very objects did
Admire and prize and praise and love,
Which in their glory most are hid,
20   Which presence only doth remove.

Their constant daily presence I
Rejoicing at, did see,
And that which takes them from the eye
Of others offered them to me.

3

25   No inward inclination did I feel
To avarice or pride; my soul did kneel
In admiration all the day. No lust, nor strife,
Polluted then my infant life.

No fraud nor anger in me moved,
30   No malice, jealousy, or spite;
All that I saw I truly loved:
Contentment only and delight

Were in my soul. O Heaven! what bliss
Did I enjoy and feel!
35   What powerful delight did this
Inspire! for this I daily kneel.

4

Whether it be that nature is so pure,
And custom only vicious; or that sure
God did by miracle the guilt remove,
40   And made my soul to feel His love

So early; or that 'twas one day
Wherein this happiness I found,
Whose strength and brightness so do ray,
That still it seems me to surround —

45   Whate'er it is, it is a light
               So endless unto me
          That I a world of true delight
          Did then, and to this day do see.

               5

          That prospect was the gate of Heaven, that day
50   The ancient light of Eden did convey
          Into my soul: I was an Adam there,
               A little Adam in a sphere

          Of joys! Oh, there my ravished sense
          Was entertained in Paradise,
55   And had a sight of innocence,
          Which was beyond all bound and price.

          An antepast of Heaven sure!
               I on the earth did reign;
          Within, without me, all was pure:
60   I must become a child again.

                              Thomas Traherne   (1638? – 1674)

THE LAMB

          Little Lamb, who made thee?
               Dost thou know who made thee?
          Gave thee life, and bid thee feed,
          By the stream and o'er the mead;
5   Gave thee clothing of delight,
          Softest clothing, woolly, bright;
          Gave thee such a tender voice,
          Making all the vales rejoice?
               Little Lamb, who made thee?
10   Dost thou know who made thee?

               Little Lamb, I'll tell thee,
               Little Lamb, I'll tell thee:
          He is called by thy name,
          For he calls himself a Lamb,

15   He is meek, and he is mild;
He became a little child.
I a child, and thou a lamb,
We are called by his name.
    Little Lamb, God bless thee!
20   Little Lamb, God bless thee!

               William Blake   (1757 – 1827)

ODE: INTIMATIONS OF IMMORTALITY
FROM RECOLLECTIONS OF EARLY CHILDHOOD

The Child is father of the Man;
And I could wish my days to be
Bound each to each by natural piety.

1

There was a time when meadow, grove, and stream,
The earth, and every common sight,
      To me did seem
    Apparelled in celestial light,
5   The glory and the freshness of a dream.
It is not now as it hath been of yore; —
      Turn wheresoe'er I may,
        By night or day,
The things which I have seen I now can see no more.

2

10   The Rainbow comes and goes,
      And lovely is the Rose,
      The Moon doth with delight
    Look round her when the heavens are bare,
      Waters on a starry night
15   Are beautiful and fair;
    The sunshine is a glorious birth;
    But yet I know, where'er I go,
That there hath past away a glory from the earth.

3

Now, while the birds thus sing a joyous song,
20   And while the young lambs bound
      As to the tabor's sound,

To me alone there came a thought of grief:
A timely utterance gave that thought relief,
    And I again am strong:
25 The cataracts blow their trumpets from the steep;
Nor more shall grief of mine the season wrong;
I hear the Echoes through the mountains throng,
The Winds come to me from the fields of sleep,
    And all the earth is gay:
30   Land and sea
    Give themselves up to jollity,
        And with the heart of May
    Doth every Beast keep holiday; —
        Thou Child of Joy,
35 Shout round me, let me hear thy shouts, thou happy
        Shepherd-boy!

    4

Ye blessèd Creatures, I have heard the call
    Ye to each other make; I see
The heavens laugh with you in your jubilee:
40   My heart is at your festival,
        My head hath its coronal,
The fulness of your bliss, I feel — I feel it all.
    Oh evil day! if I were sullen
    While Earth herself is adorning,
45   This sweet May-morning,
    And the Children are culling
        On every side,
    In a thousand valleys far and wide,
    Fresh flowers; while the sun shines warm,
50 And the Babe leaps up on his Mother's arm: —
    I hear, I hear, with joy I hear!
    — But there's a Tree, of many, one,
A single Field which I have looked upon,
Both of them speak of something that is gone:
55   The Pansy at my feet
        Doth the same tale repeat:
Whither is fled the visionary gleam?
Where is it now, the glory and the dream?

    5

Our birth is but a sleep and a forgetting:
60 The Soul that rises with us, our life's Star,
        Hath had elsewhere its setting,
            And cometh from afar:
        Not in entire forgetfulness,
        And not in utter nakedness,

65   But trailing clouds of glory do we come
        From God, who is our home:
     Heaven lies about us in our infancy!
     Shades of the prison-house begin to close
        Upon the growing Boy,
70   But He beholds the light, and whence it flows,
        He sees it in his joy;
     The Youth, who daily farther from the east
        Must travel, still is Nature's Priest,
        And by the vision splendid
75   Is on his way attended;
     At length the Man perceives it die away,
     And fade into the light of common day.

     6

     Earth fills her lap with pleasures of her own;
     Yearnings she hath in her own natural kind,
80   And, even with something of a Mother's mind,
        And no unworthy aim,
        The homely Nurse doth all she can
     To make her Foster-child, her Inmate Man,
        Forget the glories he hath known,
85   And that imperial palace whence he came.

     7

     Behold the Child among his new-born blisses,
     A six years' Darling of a pigmy size!
     See, where 'mid work of his own hand he lies,
     Fretted by sallies of his mother's kisses,
90   With light upon him from his father's eyes!
     See, at his feet, some little plan or chart,
     Some fragment from his dream of human life,
     Shaped by himself with newly-learned art;
        A wedding or a festival,
95   A mourning or a funeral;
           And this hath now his heart,
        And unto this he frames his song:
           Then will he fit his tongue
     To dialogues of business, love, or strife;
100   But it will not be long
        Ere this be thrown aside,
        And with new joy and pride
     The little Actor cons another part;
     Filling from time to time his "humorous stage"
105 With all the Persons, down to palsied Age,
     That Life brings with her in her equipage;
        As if his whole vocation
        Were endless imitation.

8

Thou, whose exterior semblance doth belie
110   Thy Soul's immensity;
Thou best Philosopher, who yet dost keep
Thy heritage, thou Eye among the blind,
That, deaf and silent, read'st the eternal deep,
Haunted for ever by the eternal mind, —
115   Mighty Prophet! Seer blest!
                On whom those truths do rest,
Which we are toiling all our lives to find,
In darkness lost, the darkness of the grave;
Thou, over whom thy Immortality
120   Broods like the Day, a Master o'er a Slave,
A Presence which is not to be put by;
Thou little Child yet glorious in the might
Of heaven-born freedom on thy being's height,
Why with such earnest pains dost thou provoke
125   The years to bring the inevitable yoke,
Thus blindly with thy blessedness at strife?
Full soon thy Soul shall have her earthly freight,
And custom lie upon thee with a weight,
Heavy as frost, and deep almost as life!

9

130   Oh joy! that in our embers
                Is something that doth live,
                That nature yet remembers
                What was so fugitive!
The thought of our past years in me doth breed
135   Perpetual benediction: not indeed
For that which is most worthy to be blest;
Delight and liberty, the simple creed
Of Childhood, whether busy or at rest,
With new-fledged hope still fluttering in his breast: —
140   Not for these I raise
                The song of thanks and praise;
            But for those obstinate questionings
                Of sense and outward things,
                Fallings from us, vanishings;
145   Blank misgivings of a Creature
Moving about in worlds not realised,
High instincts before which our mortal Nature
Did tremble like a guilty Thing surprised:
                But for those first affections,
150   Those shadowy recollections,
            Which, be they what they may,
Are yet the fountain-light of all our day,
Are yet a master-light of all our seeing;

Uphold us, cherish, and have power to make
155 Our noisy years seem moments in the being
Of the eternal Silence: truths that wake,
   To perish never:
Which neither listlessness, nor mad endeavour,
   Nor Man nor Boy,
160 Nor all that is at enmity with joy,
Can utterly abolish or destroy!
   Hence in a season of calm weather
   Though inland far we be,
Our Souls have sight of that immortal sea
165   Which brought us hither,
   Can in a moment travel thither,
And see the Children sport upon the shore,
And hear the mighty waters rolling evermore.

10

Then sing, ye Birds, sing, sing, a joyous song!
170   And let the young Lambs bound
   As to the tabor's sound!
We in thought will join your throng,
   Ye that pipe and ye that play,
   Ye that through your hearts today
175   Feel the gladness of the May!
What though the radiance which was once so bright
Be now for ever taken from my sight,
   Though nothing can bring back the hour
Of splendour in the grass, of glory in the flower,
180   We will grieve not, rather find
   Strength in what remains behind;
   In the primal sympathy
   Which having been must ever be;
   In the soothing thoughts that spring
185   Out of human suffering;
   In the faith that looks through death,
In years that bring the philosophic mind.

11

And O, ye Fountains, Meadows, Hills, and Groves,
Forebode not any severing of our loves!
190 Yet in my heart of hearts I feel your might;
I only have relinquished one delight
To live beneath your more habitual sway.
I love the Brooks which down their channels fret,
Even more than when I tripped lightly as they;
195 The innocent brightness of a new-born Day
   Is lovely yet;

The Clouds that gather round the setting sun
Do take a sober colouring from an eye
That hath kept watch o'er man's mortality;
200   Another race hath been, and other palms are won.
Thanks to the human heart by which we live,
Thanks to its tenderness, its joys, and fears,
To me the meanest flower that blows can give
Thoughts that do often lie too deep for tears.

                 William Wordsworth   *(1770 – 1850)*

FROST AT MIDNIGHT

The frost performs its secret ministry,
Unhelped by any wind. The owlet's cry
Came loud — and hark, again! loud as before.
The inmates of my cottage, all at rest,
5   Have left me to that solitude, which suits
Abstruser musings: save that at my side
My cradled infant slumbers peacefully.
'Tis calm indeed! so calm, that it disturbs
And vexes meditation with its strange
10   And extreme silentness. Sea, hill, and wood,
This populous village! Sea, and hill, and wood,
With all the numberless goings-on of life,
Inaudible as dreams! the thin blue flame
Lies on my low-burnt fire, and quivers not;
15   Only that film, which fluttered on the grate,
Still flutters there, the sole unquiet thing.
Methinks, its motion in this hush of nature
Gives it dim sympathies with me who live,
Making it a companionable form,
20   Whose puny flaps and freaks the idling Spirit
By its own moods interprets, everywhere
Echo or mirror seeking of itself,
And makes a toy of Thought.

                     But O! how oft,
How oft, at school, with most believing mind,
25   Presageful, have I gazed upon the bars,
To watch that fluttering stranger! and as oft
With unclosed lids, already had I dreamt
Of my sweet birth-place, and the old church-tower,
Whose bells, the poor man's only music, rang
30   From morn to evening, all the hot Fair-day,

So sweetly, that they stirred and haunted me
With a wild pleasure, falling on mine ear
Most like articulate sounds of things to come!
So gazed I, till the soothing things, I dreamt,
35 Lulled me to sleep, and sleep prolonged my dreams!
And so I brooded all the following morn,
Awed by the stern preceptor's face, mine eye
Fixed with mock study on my swimming book:
Save if the door half opened, and I snatched
40 A hasty glance, and still my heart leaped up,
For still I hoped to see the *stranger's* face,
Townsman, or aunt, or sister more beloved,
My playmate when we both were clothed alike!

Dear Babe, that sleepest cradled by my side,
45 Whose gentle breathings, heard in this deep calm,
Fill up the interspersèd vacancies
And momentary pauses of the thought!
My babe so beautiful! it thrills my heart
With tender gladness, thus to look at thee,
50 And think that thou shalt learn far other lore,
And in far other scenes! For I was reared
In the great city, pent 'mid cloisters dim,
And saw nought lovely but the sky and stars.
But *thou*, my babe! shalt wander like a breeze
55 By lakes and sandy shores, beneath the crags
Of ancient mountain, and beneath the clouds,
Which image in their bulk both lakes and shores
And mountain crags: so shalt thou see and hear
The lovely shapes and sounds intelligible
60 Of that eternal language, which thy God
Utters, who from eternity doth teach
Himself in all, and all things in himself.
Great universal Teacher! he shall mold
Thy spirit, and by giving make it ask.

65 Therefore all seasons shall be sweet to thee,
Whether the summer clothe the general earth
With greenness, or the redbreast sit and sing
Betwixt the tufts of snow on the bare branch
Of mossy apple-tree, while the nigh thatch
70 Smokes in the sun-thaw; whether the evedrops fall
Heard only in the trances of the blast,
Of if the secret ministry of frost
Shall hang them up in silent icicles,
Quietly shining to the quiet Moon.

Samuel Taylor Coleridge   (1772 – 1834)

I REMEMBER, I REMEMBER

I remember, I remember,
The house where I was born,
The little window where the sun
Came peeping in at morn;
5   He never came a wink too soon,
Nor brought too long a day,
But now, I often wish the night
Had borne my breath away!

I remember, I remember,
10   The roses, red and white,
The vi'lets, and the lily-cups,
Those flowers made of light!
The lilacs where the robin built,
And where my brother set
15   The laburnum on his birthday, —
The tree is living yet!

I remember, I remember,
Where I was used to swing,
And thought the air must rush as fresh
20   To swallows on the wing;
My spirit flew in feathers then,
That is so heavy now,
And summer pools could hardly cool
The fever on my brow!

25   I remember, I remember,
The fir trees dark and high;
I used to think their slender tops
Were close against the sky:
It was a childish ignorance,
30   But now 'tis little joy
To know I'm farther off from heav'n
Than when I was a boy.

       Thomas Hood   (1799 – 1845)

MY LOST YOUTH

Often I think of the beautiful town
   That is seated by the sea;
Often in thought go up and down
The pleasant streets of that dear old town,
5   And my youth comes back to me.

And a verse of a Lapland song
Is haunting my memory still:
"A boy's will is the wind's will,
And the thoughts of youth are long, long thoughts."

10   I can see the shadowy lines of its trees,
    And catch, in sudden gleams,
The sheen of the far-surrounding seas,
And islands that were the Hesperides
    Of all my boyish dreams.
15   And the burden of that old song,
       It murmurs and whispers still:
       "A boy's will is the wind's will,
And the thoughts of youth are long, long thoughts."

I remember the black wharves and the slips,
20   And the sea-tides tossing free;
And Spanish sailors with bearded lips,
And the beauty and mystery of the ships,
       And the magic of the sea.
       And the voice of that wayward song
25   Is singing and saying still:
       "A boy's will is the wind's will,
And the thoughts of youth are long, long thoughts."

I remember the bulwarks by the shore,
    And the fort upon the hill;
30   The sunrise gun, with its hollow roar,
The drum-beat repeated o'er and o'er,
    And the bugle wild and shrill.
       And the music of that old song
       Throbs in my memory still:
35   "A boy's will is the wind's will,
And the thoughts of youth are long, long thoughts."

I remember the sea-fight far away,
    How it thundered o'er the tide!
And the dead sea-captains, as they lay
40   In their graves, o'erlooking the tranquil bay
    Where they in battle died.
       And the sound of that mournful song
       Goes through me with a thrill:
       "A boy's will is the wind's will,
45   And the thoughts of youth are long, long thoughts."

I can see the breezy dome of groves,
    The shadows of Deering's Woods;
And the friendships old and the early loves
Come back with a Sabbath sound, as of doves
50   In quiet neighborhoods.

And the verse of that sweet old song,
It flutters and murmurs still:
"A boy's will is the wind's will,
And the thoughts of youth are long, long thoughts."

55   I remember the gleams and glooms that dart
            Across the school-boy's brain;
        The song and the silence in the heart,
        That in part are prophecies, and in part
            Are longings wild and vain.
60   And the voice of that fitful song
                Sings on, and is never still:
                "A boy's will is the wind's will,
        And the thoughts of youth are long, long thoughts."

        There are things of which I may not speak;
65   There are dreams that cannot die;
        There are thoughts that make the strong heart weak,
        And bring a pallor into the cheek,
            And a mist before the eye.
                And the words of that fatal song
70   Come over me like a chill:
                "A boy's will is the wind's will,
        And the thoughts of youth are long, long thoughts."

        Strange to me now are the forms I meet
            When I visit the dear old town;
75   But the native air is pure and sweet,
        And the trees that o'ershadow each well-known street,
            As they balance up and down,
                Are singing the beautiful song,
                Are sighing and whispering still:
80   "A boy's will is the wind's will,
        And the thoughts of youth are long, long thoughts."

        And Deering's Woods are fresh and fair,
            And with joy that is almost pain
        My heart goes back to wander there,
85   And among the dreams of the days that were,
            I find my lost youth again.
                And the strange and beautiful song,
                The groves are repeating it still:
                "A boy's will is the wind's will,
90   And the thoughts of youth are long, long thoughts."

                Henry Wadsworth Longfellow   (1807 – 1882)

THERE WAS A CHILD WENT FORTH

There was a child went forth every day,
And the first object he look'd upon, that object he became,
And that object became part of him for the day or a certain part of the day,
Or for many years or stretching cycles of years.
5   The early lilacs became part of this child.
And grass and white and red morning-glories, and white and red clo-
    ver, and the song of the phoebe-bird,
And the Third-month lambs and the sow's pink-faint litter, and the
    mare's foal and cow's calf,
And the noisy brood of the barnyard or by the mire of the pond-side,
And the fish suspending themselves so curiously below there, and the
    beautiful curious liquid,
10   And the water-plants with their graceful flat heads, all became part of him.
The field-sprouts of the Fourth-month and Fifth-month became part of
    him,
Winter-grain sprouts and those of the light-yellow corn and the escu-
    lent roots of the garden,
And the apple-trees cover'd with blossoms and the fruit afterward and
    wood-berries, and the commonest weeds by the road,
And the old drunkard staggering home from the outhouse of the tavern
    when he had lately risen,
15   And the schoolmistress that pass'd on her way to the school,
And the friendly boys that pass'd, and the quarrelsome boys,
And the tidy and fresh-cheek'd girls, and the barefoot negro boy and
    girl,
And all the changes of city and country wherever he went.

His own parents, he that had father'd him and she that had conceiv'd
    him in her womb and birth'd him,
20   They gave this child more of themselves than that,
They gave him afterward every day, they became part of him.

The mother at home quietly placing the dishes on the supper-table.
The mother with mild words, clean her cap and gown, a wholesome
    odor falling off her person and clothes as she walks by,
The father, strong, self-sufficient, manly, mean, anger'd, unjust,
25   The blow, the quick loud word, the tight bargain, the crafty lure
The family usages, the language, the company, the furniture, the yearn-
    ing and swelling heart,
Affection that will not be gainsay'd, the sense of what is real, the
    thought if after all it should prove unreal,
The doubts of day-time and the doubts of night-time, the curious
    whether and how,
Whether that which appears so is so, or is it all flashes and specks?

30 Men and women crowding fast in the streets, if they are not flashes and
   specks what are they?
  The streets themselves and the façades of houses, and goods in the
   windows,
  Vehicles, teams, the heavy-plank'd wharves, the huge crossing at the
   ferries,
  The village on the highland seen from afar at sunset, the river between,
  Shadows, aureola and mist, the light falling on roofs and gables of
   white or brown two miles off,
35 The schooner near by sleepily dropping down the tide, the little boat
   slack-tow'd astern,
  The hurrying tumbling waves, quick-broken crests, slapping,
  The strata of color'd clouds, the long bar of maroon-tint away solitary
   by itself, the spread of purity it lies motionless in,
  The horizon's edge, the flying sea-crow, the fragrance of salt marsh
   and shore mud,
  These became part of that child who went forth every day, and who
   now goes, and will always go forth every day.

Walt Whitman (1819 – 1892)

SPRING AND FALL: TO A YOUNG CHILD

  Márgarét, are you gríeving
  Over Goldengrove unleaving?
  Leáves, líke the things of man, you
  With your fresh thoughts care for, can you?
5 Áh! ás the heart grows older
  It will come to such sights colder
  By and by, nor spare a sigh
  Though worlds of wanwood leafmeal lie;
  And yet you wíll weep and know why.
10 Now no matter, child, the name:
  Sórrow's springs áre the same,
  Nor mouth had, no nor mind, expressed
  What heart heard of, ghost guessed:
  It ís the blight man was born for,
15 It is Margaret you mourn for.

Gerard Manley Hopkins (1844 – 1889)

BIRCHES

When I see the birches bend to left and right
Across the lines of straighter darker trees,
I like to think some boy's been swinging them.
But swinging doesn't bend them down to stay.
5   Ice-storms do that. Often you must have seen them
Loaded with ice a sunny winter morning
After a rain. They click upon themselves
As the breeze rises, and turn many-coloured
As the stir cracks and crazes their enamel.
10   Soon the sun's warmth makes them shed crystal shells
Shattering and avalanching on the snowcrust —
Such heaps of broken glass to sweep away
You'd think the inner dome of heaven had fallen.
They are dragged to the withered bracken by the load,
15   And they seem not to break; though once they are bowed
So low for long, they never right themselves:
You may see their trunks arching in the woods
Years afterwards, trailing their leaves on the ground
Like girls on hands and knees that throw their hair
20   Before them over their heads to dry in the sun.
But I was going to say when Truth broke in
With all her matter-of-fact about the ice-storm
(Now am I free to be poetical?)
I should prefer to have some boy bend them
25   As he went out and in to fetch the cows —
Some boy too far from town to learn baseball,
Whose only play was what he found himself,
Summer or winter, and could play alone.
One by one he subdued his father's trees
30   By riding them down over and over again
Until he took the stiffness out of them,
And not one but hung limp, not one was left
For him to conquer. He learned all there was
To learn about not launching out too soon
35   And so not carrying the tree away
Clear to the ground. He always kept his poise
To the top branches, climbing carefully
With the same pains you use to fill a cup
Up to the brim, and even above the brim.
40   Then he flung outward, feet first, with a swish,
Kicking his way down through the air to the ground.

So was I once myself a swinger of birches;
And so I dream of going back to be.
It's when I'm weary of considerations,

45   And life is too much like a pathless wood
      Where your face burns and tickles with the cobwebs
      Broken across it, and one eye is weeping
      From a twig's having lashed it open,
      I'd like to get away from earth a while
50   And then come back to it and begin over.
      May no fate wilfully misunderstand me
      And half grant what I wish and snatch me away
      Not to return. Earth's the right place for love:
      I don't know where it's likely to go better.
55   I'd like to go by climbing a high birch tree,
      And climb black branches up a snow-white trunk
      Toward heaven, till the tree could bear no more,
      But dipped its top and set me down again.
      That would be good both going and coming back.
60   One could do worse than be a swinger of birches.

                              Robert Frost   *(1874 – 1963)*

THE HORSE CHESTNUT TREE

      Boys in sporadic but tenacious droves
      Come with sticks, as certainly as Autumn,
      To assault the great horse chestnut tree.

      There is a law governs their lawlessness.
5   Desire is in them for a shining amulet
      And the best are those that are highest up.

      They will not pick them easily from the ground.
      With shrill arms they fling to the higher branches,
      To hurry the work of nature for their pleasure.

10   I have seen them trooping down the street
      Their pockets stuffed with chestnuts shucked, unshucked.
      It is only evening keeps them from their wish.

      Sometimes I run out in a kind of rage
      To chase the boys away; I catch an arm,
15   Maybe, and laugh to think of being the lawgiver.

      I was once such a young sprout myself
      And fingered in my pocket the prize and trophy.
      But still I moralize upon the day

20 And see that we, outlaws on God's property,
Fling out imagination beyond the skies
Wishing a tangible good from the unknown.

And likewise death will drive us from the scene
With the great flowering world unbroken yet,
Which we held in idea, a little handful.

Richard Eberhart   (1904 –   )

MY PARENTS KEPT ME FROM CHILDREN WHO WERE ROUGH

My parents kept me from children who were rough
Who threw words like stones and who wore torn clothes.
Their thighs showed through rags. They ran in the street
And climbed cliffs and stripped by the country streams.

5 I feared more than tigers their muscles like iron
Their jerking hands and their knees tight on my arms.
I feared the salt coarse pointing of those boys
Who copied my lisp behind me on the road.

They were lithe, they sprang out behind hedges
10 Like dogs to bark at my world. They threw mud
While I looked the other way, pretending to smile.
I longed to forgive them, but they never smiled.

Stephen Spender   (1909 –   )

QUESTIONS FOR DISCUSSION AND FURTHER STUDY

THE RETREAT

1. Describe the poem's meter, line length, and rhyme scheme.
2. What is literally meant by the statement "But ah! my soul with too much stay / Is drunk, and staggers in the way!"?
3. Compare this poem with Wordsworth's "Intimations" ode. What is similar about the attitudes expressed toward childhood? How do the two attitudes differ?

INNOCENCE

1. This poem compares well with "The Retreat." Both poems, for example, praise the goodness and innocence of childhood. Do you feel that either or both Vaughan and Traherne idealize childhood subjectively? What part does memory play in poems like these two?
2. Discuss the light imagery to be found in this poem. Given Traherne's attitude toward childhood, what makes this kind of imagery help to sustain his theme?
3. The last line of the poem reads "I must become a child again." In terms of the entire poem, what is the meaning of this line? Is the line related to Traherne's statement that once he was a "little Adam"? What are the biblical overtones of the line?

THE LAMB

1. Name the speaker and audience in this poem. How are the speaker, the audience, and the third person mentioned in the poem related?
2. The first of the two stanzas asks a series of rhetorical questions. How effective are they? The second stanza provides answers to the questions asked earlier. What religious point of view is implied by the answers given?
3. A poem such as this one could easily become unintentionally funny. Why? How does Blake avoid letting his poem become ludicrous?

ODE: INTIMATIONS OF IMMORTALITY FROM RECOLLECTIONS OF EARLY CHILDHOOD

1. Define an ode. Why did Wordsworth choose this poetic form to express his change in personality and outlook rather than any other? Is there some special effect he gains by the use of this particular form?

2. Discuss the doctrine of preexistence indicated in this poem. Do we lose our sense of heavenly beginnings completely at birth or gradually as we grow older?

3. Wordsworth once stated, in defense of his Christian beliefs, that this poem was not meant to express a philosophic truth, but only a poetic one. By such a statement Wordsworth hoped to defend both his orthodoxy and his poetry. What is your opinion of such a defense?

4. Compare Wordsworth's attitude toward childhood in this poem and in "Tintern Abbey." What are the differences in the way he views childhood in the two poems?

FROST AT MIDNIGHT

1. The "stranger" mentioned in the poem refers to a burning piece of coal or wood which falls on an open-fire grate, still fluttering. According to popular custom of the day, this was supposed to foreshadow a visitor. Hence the child Coleridge longs for company after seeing a "stranger." How are Coleridge's plans for Hartley's education going to help the son avoid the melancholia from which the father suffered?

2. Discuss the techniques by which Coleridge achieves the calm, tranquil, meditative tone of the poem. How does the setting itself add to that tone?

3. Is only tranquil nature to be an educative force on young Hartley? Or is nature in her harsher aspects also to play a part in his development?

I REMEMBER, I REMEMBER

1. A single image dominates each of the four stanzas in this lyric. Identify each image and explain why it exemplifies an aspect of childhood.

2. Why does Hood "often wish the night/Had borne my breath away"? In answering this question, consider the last three lines of the poem.

3. Like other poems in this group, "I Remember, I Remember" identifies childhood with goodness and innocence. How does Hood's poem compare with similar poems, and why is it that an adult is "farther off from heav'n" than is a child? Is there something necessarily evil about adulthood?

MY LOST YOUTH

1. Compare and contrast the imagery of Longfellow's poem with that of Whitman's "There Was a Child Went Forth." What basic differences do you find? Which is more concrete?

2.   The last two lines of every stanza end in a refrain. What is the meaning of the first line of the refrain, and how is the second line related to the theme?
3.   In this poem, as in many about childhood, the influence and possible distortion of adult memory on childhood experience must be considered. What evidence is there in the poem to suggest that Longfellow may, at least in part, be idealizing childhood?

THERE WAS A CHILD WENT FORTH

1.   Is this poem about one child, or is it really about every child? The last two lines of the poem can help you decide.
2.   How effective is the repetition of "and" and "the" with which Whitman begins many of his lines? Does his use of this repetition have something to do with the nature of free verse?
3.   In the poem Whitman presents a sweeping canvas on which is painted much that is in nature and man. What imagery helps him do this?
4.   We never get "inside" the boy's mind or personality. Whitman rather uses the boy to symbolize his own cyclical theory of life. Does this lack of identification between the boy's mind and the reader's weaken the poem? Why or why not?

SPRING AND FALL: TO A YOUNG CHILD

1.   What does Hopkins mean when he says to Margaret that it is herself she grieves for? What does this grief have to do with the title and with the passing of the seasons?
2.   Note the rhyme in lines three and four: "man, you" / " can you?" Why is this rhyme unusual, and how effective do you feel it is?
3.   The accents over certain syllables indicate that Hopkins wished those syllables to be stressed when the poem was read. By stressing those syllables when you read the poem, how is its sound changed?

BIRCHES

1.   Discuss the setting in the poem. What techniques does Frost use to achieve such a remarkably realistic and poignant setting? Does he concentrate on visual imagery, for example?
2.   Discuss the conversational tone of the poem. The language Frost uses seems quite natural and relaxed, even "chatty." Why does the ease of diction enhance the theme and effect of a nature poem like this one?
3.   Discuss focus in this poem. Who is the more important character, the boy swinging on birch trees or the narrator? What is the reason for your answer?

THE HORSE CHESTNUT TREE

1. The boys stealing chestnuts are compared to all men being outlaws on God's property. In what sense can we be considered "outlaws"? The narrator sees himself as driving the boys away; who
   or what drives the "outlaws" away?
2. The poem's structure is interesting. All but the last seven lines
   are narrative; what function is performed by those lines? Are
   there other poems in this section which use the last few lines for
   a similar purpose?
3. Discuss the various references to law made in this poem. How
   does the poem's meaning depend on these references?

MY PARENTS KEPT ME FROM CHILDREN WHO WERE ROUGH

1. What is the narrator's attitude toward the rough children? What
   makes it complex? Given their treatment of him, why does he feel
   as he does about them in the last line? In answering this question,
   are you stating the poem's theme?
2. Spender relies primarily upon specific detail to describe the rough
   children. He uses the simile very sparingly. Can you suggest a
   reason for his doing so?
3. What inferences can you make about the personality, family life,
   and economic status of the narrator from what he tells us of
   himself?

CONSOLATION

In modern times the term *elegy* refers to a poem commemorating a death. It may commemorate the death of a particular person or group, or it may commemorate the general fact of death as it applies to all mankind, and most elegies go beyond a statement of grief to some general comment about mankind. Often this comment is not necessarily about death itself; indeed, poets have used the elegaic form to criticize a social, political, or religious institution while ostensibly mourning the dead. Rising above mere grief for a specific death, seeking instead the meaning and purpose of death, elegies provide a source of consolation. However, any tribute to a dead person is a form of consolation, both to the writer and to the audience or reader. For similar reasons, at the conclusion of an elegy the poet will generally find in the face of death some reason for resignation, acceptance, or joy. The poems in this collection clearly and eloquently exemplify the characteristics discussed above.

"To the Memory of My Beloved the Author, Mr. William Shakespeare," the oldest elegy in the collection, was written by the seventeenth-century poet and dramatist Ben Jonson. Published with the first (1623) folio edition of Shakespeare's plays, the poem uses heroic couplets to praise Shakespeare's qualities as a man and a dramatist. Of particular interest is the high place Jonson awards Shakespeare in the history of great playwrights.

Like Jonson, Thomas Carew praises primarily the literary qualities of his subject, John Donne. "An Elegy upon the Death of Doctor Donne, Dean of Paul's" also shares with the Jonson poem the fact that it too prefaced the first (1633) full edition of its subject's works. Like the Jonson poem, Carew's is written in heroic couplets. Carew takes special pains to praise Donne's "wit"; by this is meant that Donne, a metaphysical poet, possessed great skill in creating unusual images and in using the English language in a particularly fresh and original way.

The pastoral elegy is represented in this collection by three poems, the earliest of which is John Milton's "Lycidas." The pastoral elegy is a specific type of personal elegy in which the dead person is presented as a shepherd being mourned by his fellows. Here the person mourned by Milton is Edward King, a young classmate and friend who was tragically drowned in the Irish Sea. In lines of varying length and rhyme scheme, Milton not only eulogizes King, he also uses the poem to express his own fears of an early death, to comment upon the nature of worldly fame, and to attack the corrupt clergy of the Church of England.

John Dryden's "To the Memory of Mr. Oldham," like several other elegies in this section, pays tribute to a fellow writer. John Oldham (1653–1683) died at an early age, before his poetic talents had matured. Jonson's elegy to Shakespeare and Carew's to Donne could praise the considerable literary contribution of a full lifetime; Dryden's elegy to Oldham cannot do so. Instead, Dryden laments the tragedy of one cut off by death from the fulfillment of his poetic potential. The emphasis is upon an untimely death as it was in Milton's "Lycidas."

Pope's "Elegy: To the Memory of an Unfortunate Lady," also in heroic couplets, tells the story of an anonymous young woman who, presumably because of a guardian's cruelty, stabs herself. Since she committed suicide, normal Christian burial rites are denied to her. By way of compensation, Pope indicates that nature and the angels will adorn her grave. Since Pope seems to be so distant from the subject of his elegy, most readers of the poem find it very formal and perhaps even artificial.

In contrast, Gray's "Elegy Written in a Country Churchyard" speaks with a quiet sincerity. Each quatrain has a measured, meditative pace; the lines, written in iambic pentameter, read slowly; and even the alternating rhyme pattern keeps the somber, stately tone. This elegy, by the way, is one of those which does not mourn a particular person. Rather, it tells of the lives of unknown, lowly villagers, and it instructs us to remember that these lives, lived in anonymous seclusion, nonetheless had purpose and meaning.

"Adonais" mourns the youthful and tragic death of John Keats (1795–1821), who died of tuberculosis. Shelley grieves genuinely for Keats, but he also is concerned with his own troubles. In stanzas 31–34, he describes himself as one who "in another's fate now wept his own." In the tradition of the greatest elegies, Shelley's abject grief for the death of Keats gives way to acceptance of the fact of death and ultimately to rejoicing. Keats has become "a portion of the Eternal," "one with Nature," bright with the "white radiance of Eternity." Death even becomes desirable, and the last stanza of the poem is a strange presentiment of Shelley's own death in a sailing accident the following year.

Whitman's "When Lilacs Last in the Dooryard Bloom'd" is perhaps the greatest elegy that America has yet produced. The best-known of the four elegies Whitman wrote to celebrate the death of Abraham Lincoln, this free verse poem makes superb use of soft, liquid sounds to create a tone of quiet, profound meditation; indeed, a kind of tranquillity emerges as Whitman praises the mysterious cycle of life and death. The symbolism of the lilac, the western star (Lincoln himself), and the thrush—all introduced early in the poem—are pursued throughout and fused together significantly in the final lines.

Matthew Arnold's "Thyrsis," another pastoral elegy, commemorates the death of his close friend and fellow poet Arthur Hugh Clough. The poem employs some of the same symbols as does "The Scholar Gipsy," a work which Clough admired and which appears elsewhere in this anthology. Unlike some other elegies, "Thyrsis" does not progress from a hymn of grief to a praise of death and immortality; rather, Arnold speaks here of the difficulty with which the search for truth (symbolized by Clough and the Scholar Gipsy) survives in modern life. Set in the Oxford surroundings that he and Clough had so often visited in their undergraduate days, the poem achieves a sort of stoic resolution for Arnold—that he, the survivor, should persist in the quest they had started together.

A group is eulogized in Allen Tate's "Ode to the Confederate Dead." Like Whitman, Tate writes in free verse, although Tate's free verse is less expansive. The poem moves from speaking about the graves of the dead soldiers to the graves of all humanity, and there is scant comfort in Tate's statement that life is just a series of distractions between two nights, one a beginning, one an end. Tate offers no hope of an afterlife nor even of a meaningful participation in the totality of nature. Even the names on the headstones yield to the elements, and the grave is seen as a place of "verdurous anonymity."

Nor is there any suggestion of personal immortality in W. H. Auden's poem "In Memory of W. B. Yeats." The first two parts of the poem, written in free verse, praise Yeats's skill as a poet, contrasting the indifference of the world with the death of a great man. The third part of the poem, written in tetrameter to suggest an incantation, testifies to the instructive value of poetry and suggests that the poetry of a man like Yeats can teach the human heart how to love and how to understand.

The last poem in this section, Karl Shapiro's "Elegy for a Dead Soldier," is set in the South Pacific during World War II. A young soldier has died, and his companions at arms attend a makeshift funeral service before burying the man. Although the soldiers are concerned with the possibility of their own deaths, they grieve for their comrade, and suggestions of brotherhood and compassion echo throughout the poem. The poem stresses the particularity and individuality of death, and that emphasis persists through the brief epitaph which ends the poem.

We have seen elegies which mourn for the death of one person, the death of a group, and even the ultimate death of all mankind. While sobering, elegies unite us and comfort us by giving us a sense of ourselves as fellow human beings. Like the poems in the section on death, elegies treat of our most binding, universal experience.

TO THE MEMORY OF MY BELOVED THE AUTHOR, MR. WILLIAM SHAKESPEARE, AND WHAT HE HATH LEFT US

To draw no envy, Shakespeare, on thy name,
Am I thus ample to thy book and fame;
While I confess thy writings to be such
As neither man nor Muse can praise too much.
'Tis true, and all men's suffrage. But these ways
Were not the paths I meant unto thy praise;
For silliest ignorance on these may light,
Which, when it sounds at best, but echoes right;
Or blind affection, which doth ne'er advance
The truth, but gropes, and urgeth all by chance;
Or crafty malice might pretend this praise,
And think to ruin, where it seemed to raise.
These are, as some infamous bawd or whore
Should praise a matron. What could hurt her more?
But thou art proof against them, and indeed,
Above the ill fortune of them, or the need.
I therefore will begin. Soul of the age!
The applause, delight, the wonder of our stage!
My Shakespeare, rise! I will not lodge thee by
Chaucer, or Spenser, or bid Beaumont lie
A little further, to make thee a room;
Thou art a monument without a tomb,
And art alive still while thy book doth live
And we have wits to read and praise to give
That I not mix thee so, my brain excuses,
I mean with great, but disproportioned Muses;
For if I thought my judgment were of years,
I should commit thee surely with thy peers,
And tell how far thou didst our Lyly outshine,
Or sporting Kyd, or Marlowe's mighty line.
And though thou hadst small Latin and less Greek,
From thence to honor thee I would not seek
For names; but call forth thundering Aeschylus,
Euripides, and Sophocles to us;
Pacuvius, Accius, him of Cordova dead,
To life again, to hear thy buskin tread,
And shake a stage; or, when thy socks were on,
Leave thee alone for the comparison
Of all that insolent Greece or haughty Rome
Sent forth, or since did from their ashes come.
Triumph, my Britain, thou hast one to show
To whom all scenes of Europe homage owe.
He was not of an age, but for all time!
And all the Muses still were in their prime,
When, like Apollo, he came forth to warm

Our ears, or like a Mercury to charm!
Nature herself was proud of his designs
And joyed to wear the dressing of his lines,
Which were so richly spun, and woven so fit,
50   As, since, she will vouchsafe no other wit.
The merry Greek, tart Aristophanes,
Neat Terence, witty Plautus, now not please,
But antiquated and deserted lie,
As they were not of Nature's family.
55   Yet must I not give Nature all; thy art,
My gentle Shakespeare, must enjoy a part.
For though the poet's matter Nature be,
His art doth give the fashion; and, that he
Who casts to write a living line, must sweat
60   (Such as thine are) and strike the second heat
Upon the Muses' anvil; turn the same
(And himself with it) that he thinks to frame,
Or, for the laurel, he may gain a scorn;
For a good poet's made, as well as born.
65   And such wert thou! Look how the father's face
Lives in his issue; even so the race
Of Shakespeare's mind and manners brightly shines
In his well-turnèd, and true-filèd lines;
In each of which he seems to shake a lance,
70   As brandished at the eyes of ignorance.
Sweet Swan of Avon! what a sight it were
To see thee in our waters yet appear,
And make those flights upon the banks of Thames,
That so did take Eliza, and our James!
75   But stay, I see thee in the hemisphere
Advanced, and made a constellation there!
Shine forth, thou star of poets, and with rage
Or influence, chide or cheer the drooping stage,
Which, since thy flight from hence, hath mourned like night,
80   And despairs day, but for thy volume's light.

Ben Jonson   (1573–1637)

AN ELEGY UPON THE DEATH OF DOCTOR DONNE, DEAN OF PAUL'S

Can we not force from widowed poetry,
Now thou art dead, great Donne, one elegy
To crown thy hearse? Why yet did we not trust,
Though with unkneaded dough-baked prose, thy dust,

5   Such as the unscissored lect'rer from the flower
       Of fading rhet'ric, short-lived as his hour,
       Dry as the sand that measures it, might lay
       Upon the ashes, on the funeral day?
       Have we nor tune nor voice? Didst thou dispense
10   Through all our language both the words and sense?
       'Tis a sad truth. The pulpit may her plain
       And sober Christian precepts still retain;
       Doctrines it may, and wholesome uses, frame;
       Grave homilies and lectures, but the flame
15   Of thy brave soul, that shot such heat and light
       As burnt our earth and made our darkness bright,
       Committed holy rapes upon the will,
       Did through the eye the melting heart distil,
       And the deep knowledge of dark truths so teach
20   As sense might judge where fancy could not reach,
       Must be desired for ever. So the fire
       That fills with spirit and heat the Delphic choir,
       Which, kindled first by thy Promethean breath,
       Glowed here a while, lies quenched now in thy death.
25   The Muses' garden, with pedantic weeds
       O'erspread, was purged by thee; the lazy seeds
       Of servile imitation thrown away,
       And fresh invention planted; thou didst pay
       The debts of our penurious bankrupt age;
30   Licentious thefts, that make poetic rage
       A mimic fury, when our souls must be
       Possessed, or with Anacreon's ecstasy
       Or Pindar's, not their own; the subtle cheat
       Of sly exchanges, and the juggling feat
35   Of two-edged words, or whatsoever wrong
       By ours was done the Greek or Latin tongue,
       Thou hast redeemed, and opened us a mine
       Of rich and pregnant fancy; drawn a line
       Of masculine expression, which had good
40   Old Orpheus seen, or all the ancient brood
       Our superstitious fools admire and hold
       Their lead more precious than thy burnished gold,
       Thou hadst been their exchequer, and no more
       They each in other's dung had searched for ore.
45   Thou shalt yield no precedence, but of time
       And the blind fate of language, whose tuned chime
       More charms the outward sense; yet thou mayst claim
       From so great disadvantage greater fame,
       Since to the awe of thy imperious wit
50   Our troublesome language bends, made only fit
       With her tough thick-ribbed hoops to gird about

Thy giant fancy, which had proved too stout
For their soft melting phrases. As in time
They had the start, so did they cull the prime
55 Buds of invention many a hundred year,
And left the rifled fields, besides the fear
To touch their harvest; yet from those bare lands
Of what was only thine, thy only hands,
And that their smallest work, have gleanèd more
60 Than all those times and tongues could reap before.
    But thou art gone, and thy strict laws will be
Too hard for libertines in poetry;
They will recall the goodly exiled train
Of gods and goddesses, which in thy just reign
65 Were banished nobler poems; now with these,
The silenced tales i' th' *Metamorphoses*,
Shall stuff their lines, and swell the windy page,
Till verse, refined by thee in this last age,
Turn ballad-rhyme, or those old idols be
70 Adored again with new apostasy.
    O, pardon me, that break with untuned verse
The reverend silence that attends thy hearse,
Whose solemn awful murmurs were to thee,
More than these rude lines, a loud elegy,
75 That did proclaim in a dumb eloquence
The death of all the arts; whose influence,
Grown feeble, in these panting numbers lies,
Gasping short-winded accents, and so dies.
So doth the swiftly turning wheel not stand
80 In the instant we withdraw the moving hand,
But some short time retain a faint weak course,
By virtue of the first impulsive force;
And so, whilst I cast on thy funeral pile
The crown of bays, oh, let it crack awhile,
85 And spit disdain, till the devouring flashes
Suck all the moisture up, then turn to ashes.
    I will not draw thee envy to engross
All thy perfections, or weep all the loss;
Those are too numerous for one elegy,
90 And this too great to be expressed by me.
Let others carve the rest; it shall suffice
I on thy grave this epitaph incise:
    Here lies a king that ruled as he thought fit
    The universal monarchy of wit;
95   Here lie two flamens, and both those the best,
    Apollo's first, at last the true God's priest.

Thomas Carew   (1595? – 1639?)

LYCIDAS

In this monody the author bewails a learned friend, unfortunately drowned in his passage from Chester on the Irish Seas, 1637; and by occasion foretells the ruin of our corrupted clergy, then in their height.

Yet once more, O ye laurels, and once more
Ye myrtles brown, with ivy never sere,
I come to pluck your berries harsh and crude,
And with forced fingers rude,
5 Shatter your leaves before the mellowing year.
Bitter constraint, and sad occasion dear,
Compels me to disturb your season due:
For Lycidas is dead, dead ere his prime,
Young Lycidas, and hath not left his peer.
10 Who would not sing for Lycidas? He knew
Himself to sing, and build the lofty rhyme.
He must not float upon his watery bier
Unwept, and welter to the parching wind,
Without the meed of some melodious tear.
15   Begin then, sisters of the sacred well,
That from beneath the seat of Jove doth spring,
Begin, and somewhat loudly sweep the string.
Hence with denial vain and coy excuse;
So may some gentle muse
20 With lucky words favor my destined urn,
And as he passes turn,
And bid fair peace be to my sable shroud.
For we were nursed upon the self-same hill,
Fed the same flock, by fountain, shade, and rill.
25   Together both, ere the high lawns appeared
Under the opening eyelids of the morn,
We drove afield, and both together heard
What time the gray-fly winds her sultry horn,
Battening our flocks with the fresh dews of night,
30 Oft till the star that rose, at evening, bright,
Toward heaven's descent had sloped his westering wheel.
Meanwhile the rural ditties were not mute,
Tempered to the oaten flute,
Rough satyrs danced, and fauns with cloven heel,
35 From the glad sound would not be absent long,
And old Damaetas loved to hear our song.
    But O the heavy change, now thou art gone,
Now thou art gone, and never must return!
Thee, shepherd, thee the woods and desert caves,
40 With wild thyme and the gadding vine o'ergrown,
And all their echoes mourn.

The willows and the hazel copses green
Shall now no more be seen,
Fanning their joyous leaves to thy soft lays.
45   As killing as the canker to the rose,
Or taint-worm to the weanling herds that graze,
Or frost to flowers, that their gay wardrobe wear,
When first the white-thorn blows:
Such, Lycidas, thy loss to shepherd's ear.
50   Where were ye, nymphs, when the remorseless deep
Closed o'er the head of your loved Lycidas?
For neither were ye playing on the steep,
Where your old bards, the famous druids, lie,
Nor on the shaggy top of Mona high,
55   Nor yet where Deva spreads her wizard stream:
Ay me, I fondly dream!
"Had ye been there" — for what could that have done?
What could the Muse herself that Orpheus bore,
The Muse herself for her enchanting son
60   Whom universal nature did lament,
When by the rout that made the hideous roar,
His gory visage down the stream was sent,
Down the swift Hebrus to the Lesbian shore?
    Alas! What boots it with uncessant care
65   To tend the homely slighted shepherd's trade,
And strictly meditate the thankless Muse?
Were it not better done, as others use,
To sport with Amaryllis in the shade,
Or with the tangles of Neaera's hair?
70   Fame is the spur that the clear spirit doth raise
(That last infirmity of noble mind)
To scorn delights, and live laborious days;
But the fair guerdon when we hope to find,
And think to burst out into sudden blaze,
75   Comes the blind Fury with the abhorrèd shears,
And slits the thin-spun life. "But not the praise,"
Phoebus replied, and touched my trembling ears:
"Fame is no plant that grows on mortal soil,
Nor in the glistering foil
80   Set off to the world, nor in broad rumor lies,
But lives and spreads aloft by those pure eyes
And perfect witness of all-judging Jove;
As he pronounces lastly on each deed,
Of so much fame in heaven expect thy meed."
85   O fountain Arethuse, and thou honored flood,
Smooth-sliding Mincius, crowned with vocal reeds,
That strain I heard was of a higher mood.
But now my oat proceeds,
And listens to the herald of the sea,
90   That came in Neptune's plea.

He asked the waves and asked the felon-winds,
What hard mishap hath doomed this gentle swain,
And questioned every gust of rugged wings
That blows from off each beakèd promontory.
95   They knew not of his story,
And sage Hippotades their answer brings:
That not a blast was from his dungeon strayed;
The air was calm, and on the level brine,
Sleek Panopë with all her sisters played.
100   It was that fatal and perfidious bark
Built in the eclipse, and rigged with curses dark,
That sunk so low that sacred head of thine.
      Next Camus, reverend sire, went footing slow,
His mantle hairy, and his bonnet sedge,
105   Inwrought with figures dim, and on the edge
Like to that sanguine flower inscribed with woe.
"Ah, who hath reft," quoth he, "my dearest pledge?"
Last came, and last did go,
The pilot of the Galilean Lake;
110   Two massy keys he bore of metals twain
(The golden opes, the iron shuts amain).
He shook his mitered locks, and stern bespake:
"How well could I have spared for thee, young swain,
Enow of such as for their bellies' sake
115   Creep, and intrude, and climb into the fold!
Of other care they little reckoning make,
Than how to scramble at the shearers' feast,
And shove away the worthy bidden guest.
Blind mouths, that scarce themselves know how to hold
120   A sheep hook, or have learned aught else the least
That to the faithful herdman's art belongs!
What recks it them? What need they? They are sped,
And when they list, their lean and flashy songs
Grate on their scrannel pipes of wretched straw.
125   The hungry sheep look up and are not fed,
But swollen with wind, and the rank mist they draw,
Rot inwardly, and foul contagion spread;
Besides what the grim wolf with privy paw
Daily devours apace, and nothing said;
130   But that two-handed engine at the door
Stands ready to smite once, and smite no more."
      Return, Alpheus, the dread voice is past,
That shrunk thy streams; return, Sicilian Muse,
And call the vales, and bid them hither cast
135   Their bells and flowerets of a thousand hues.
Ye valleys low, where the mild whispers use
Of shades and wanton winds and gushing brooks,
On whose fresh lap the swart star sparely looks,
Throw hither all your quaint enameled eyes,

140 That on the green turf suck the honeyed showers,
 And purple all the ground with vernal flowers.
 Bring the rathe primrose that forsaken dies,
 The tufted crow-toe, and pale jessamine,
 The white pink, and the pansy freaked with jet,
145 The glowing violet,
 The musk-rose, and the well-attired woodbine,
 With cowslips wan that hang the pensive head,
 And every flower that sad embroidery wears.
 Bid amaranthus all his beauty shed,
150 And daffodillies fill their cups with tears,
 To strew the laureate hearse where Lycid lies.
 For so to interpose a little ease,
 Let our frail thoughts dally with false surmise.
 Ay me! Whilst thee the shores and sounding seas
155 Wash far away, where'er thy bones are hurled,
 Whether beyond the stormy Hebrides,
 Where thou perhaps under the whelming tide
 Visitest the bottom of the monstrous world;
 Or whether thou to our moist vows denied,
160 Sleepest by the fable of Bellerus old,
 Where the great vision of the guarded mount
 Looks toward Namancos and Bayona's hold;
 Look homeward, Angel, now, and melt with ruth.
 And, O ye dolphins, waft the hapless youth.
165 Weep no more, woeful shepherds, weep no more,
 For Lycidas your sorrow is not dead,
 Sunk though he be beneath the watery floor,
 So sinks the day-star in the ocean bed,
 And yet anon repairs his drooping head,
170 And tricks his beams, and with new-spangled ore
 Flames in the forehead of the morning sky:
 So Lycidas sunk low, but mounted high,
 Through the dear might of him that walked the waves
 Where, other groves and other streams along,
175 With nectar pure his oozy locks he laves,
 And hears the unexpressive nuptial song,
 In the blest kingdoms meek of joy and love.
 There entertain him all the saints above
 In solemn troops and sweet societies
180 That sing, and singing in their glory move,
 And wipe the tears forever from his eyes.
 Now, Lycidas, the shepherds weep no more;
 Henceforth thou art the genius of the shore,
 In thy large recompense, and shalt be good
185 To all that wander in that perilous flood.
  Thus sang the uncouth swain to the oaks and rills,
 While the still morn went out with sandals gray;
 He touched the tender stops of various quills,

190

> With eager thought warbling his Doric lay.
> And now the sun had stretched out all the hills,
> And now was dropped into the western bay.
> At last he rose, and twitched his mantle blue:
> Tomorrow to fresh woods, and pastures new.

John Milton   (1608 – 1674)

TO THE MEMORY OF MR. OLDHAM

> Farewell, too little and too lately known,
> Whom I began to think and call my own:
> For sure our souls were near allied, and thine
> Cast in the same poetic mold with mine.

5

> One common note on either lyre did strike,
> And knaves and fools we both abhorred alike.
> To the same goal did both our studies drive:
> The last set out the soonest did arrive.
> Thus Nisus fell upon the slippery place,

10

> Whilst his young friend performed and won the race.
> O early ripe! to thy abundant store
> What could advancing age have added more?
> It might (what nature never gives the young)
> Have taught the numbers of thy native tongue.

15

> But satire needs not those, and wit will shine
> Through the harsh cadence of a rugged line.
> A noble error, and but seldom made,
> When poets are by too much force betray'd.
> Thy generous fruits, though gathered ere their prime,

20

> Still showed a quickness; and maturing time
> But mellows what we write to the dull sweets of rhyme.
> Once more, hail, and farewell! farewell, thou young,
> But ah! too short, Marcellus of our tongue!
> Thy brows with ivy and with laurels bound;

25

> But Fate and gloomy night encompass thee around.

John Dryden   (1631 – 1700)

ELEGY TO THE MEMORY OF AN UNFORTUNATE LADY

> What beck'ning ghost, along the moonlight shade
> Invites my steps, and points to yonder glade?
> 'Tis she!—but why that bleeding bosom gor'd,
> Why dimly gleams the visionary sword?

5 Oh ever beauteous, ever friendly! tell,
Is it, in heav'n, a crime to love too well?
To bear too tender, or too firm a heart,
To act a Lover's, or a Roman's part?
Is there no bright reversion in the sky,
10 For those who greatly think, or bravely die?
    Why bade ye else, ye Pow'rs! her soul aspire
Above the vulgar flight of low desire?
Ambition first sprung from your blest abodes;
The glorious fault of Angels and of Gods;
15 Thence to their Images on earth it flows,
And in the breasts of Kings and Heroes glows!
Most souls, 'tis true, but peep out once an age,
Dull sullen pris'ners in the body's cage:
Dim lights of life, that burn a length of years,
20 Useless, unseen, as lamps in sepulchres;
Like Eastern Kings, a lazy state they keep,
And close confin'd to their own palace, sleep.
    From these perhaps (ere nature bade her die)
Fate snatch'd her early to the pitying sky.
25 As into air the purer spirits flow,
And sep'rate from their kindred dregs below;
So flew the soul to its congenial place,
Nor left one virtue to redeem her Race.
    But thou, false guardian of a charge too good,
30 Thou, mean deserter of thy brother's blood!
See on these ruby lips the trembling breath,
These cheeks now fading at the blast of death:
Cold is that breast which warm'd the world before,
And those love-darting eyes must roll no more.
35 Thus, if Eternal justice rules the ball,
Thus shall your wives, and thus your children fall;
On all the line a sudden vengeance waits,
And frequent herses shall besiege your gates.
There passengers shall stand, and pointing say,
40 (While the long fun'rals blacken all the way)
"Lo these were they, whose souls the Furies steel'd,
And curs'd with hearts unknowing how to yield."
Thus unlamented pass the proud away,
The gaze of fools, and pageant of a day!
45 So perish all, whose breast ne'er learn'd to glow
For others' good, or melt at others' woe.
    What can atone (oh ever-injur'd shade!)
Thy fate unpity'd, and thy rites unpaid?
No friend's complaint, no kind domestic tear
50 Pleas'd thy pale ghost, or grac'd thy mournful bier.
By foreign hands thy dying eyes were clos'd,
By foreign hands thy decent limbs compos'd,
By foreign hands thy humble grave adorn'd,

By strangers honour'd, and by strangers mourn'd!
55   What tho' no friends in sable weeds appear,
Grieve for an hour, perhaps, then mourn a year,
And bear about the mockery of woe
To midnight dances, and the public show?
What tho' no weeping Loves thy ashes grace,
60   Nor polish'd marble emulate thy face?
What tho' no sacred earth allow thee room,
Nor hallow'd dirge be mutter'd o'er thy tomb?
Yet shall thy grave with rising flow'rs be drest,
And the green turf lie lightly on thy breast:
65   There shall the morn her earliest tears bestow,
There the first roses of the year shall blow;
While Angels with their silver wings o'ershade
The ground, now sacred by thy reliques made.
    So peaceful rests, without a stone, a name,
70   What once had beauty, titles, wealth, and fame.
How lov'd, how honour'd once, avails thee not,
To whom related, or by whom begot;
A heap of dust alone remains of thee,
'Tis all thou art, and all the proud shall be!
75   Poets themselves must fall, like those they sung,
Deaf the prais'd ear, and mute the tuneful tongue.
Ev'n he, whose soul now melts in mournful lays,
Shall shortly want the gen'rous tear he pays;
Then from his closing eyes thy form shall part,
80   And the last pang shall tear thee from his heart,
Life's idle business at one gasp be o'er,
The Muse forgot, and thou be lov'd no more!

Alexander Pope   (1688 – 1744)

ELEGY WRITTEN IN A COUNTRY CHURCHYARD

The Curfew tolls the knell of parting day,
The lowing herd wind slowly o'er the lea,
The plowman homeward plods his weary way,
And leaves the world to darkness and to me.

5   Now fades the glimmering landscape on the sight,
And all the air a solemn stillness holds,
Save where the beetle wheels his droning flight,
And drowsy tinklings lull the distant folds;

Save that from yonder ivy-mantled tow'r
10   The mopeing owl does to the moon complain
Of such, as wand'ring near her secret bow'r,
Molest her ancient solitary reign.

Beneath those rugged elms, that yew-tree's shade,
Where heaves the turf in many a mould'ring heap,
15   Each in his narrow cell for ever laid,
The rude Forefathers of the hamlet sleep.

The breezy call of incense-breathing Morn,
The shallow twitt'ring from the straw-built shed,
The cock's shrill clarion, or the echoing horn,
20   No more shall rouse them from their lowly bed.

For them no more the blazing hearth shall burn,
Or busy housewife ply her evening care:
No children run to lisp their sire's return,
Or climb his knees the envied kiss to share.

25   Oft did the harvest to their sickle yield,
Their furrow oft the stubborn glebe has broke;
How jocund did they drive their team afield!
How bow'd the woods beneath their sturdy stroke!

Let not Ambition mock their useful toil,
30   Their homely joys, and destiny obscure;
Nor Grandeur hear with a disdainful smile,
The short and simple annals of the poor.

The boast of heraldry, the pomp of pow'r,
And all that beauty, all that wealth e'er gave,
35   Awaits alike th' inevitable hour.
The paths of glory lead but to the grave.

Nor you, ye Proud, impute to These the fault,
If Mem'ry o'er their Tomb no Trophies raise,
Where thro' the long-drawn isle and fretted vault
40   The pealing anthem swells the note of praise.

Can storied urn or animated bust
Back to its mansion call the fleeting breath?
Can Honour's voice provoke the silent dust,
Or Flatt'ry sooth the dull cold ear of Death?

45   Perhaps in this neglected spot is laid
Some heart once pregnant with celestial fire;
Hands, that the rod of empire might have sway'd,
Or wak'd to extasy the living lyre.

But Knowledge to their eyes her ample page
50   Rich with the spoils of time did ne'er unroll;
Chill Penury repress'd their noble rage,
And froze the genial current of the soul.

Full many a gem of purest ray serene,
The dark unfathom'd caves of ocean bear:
55   Full many a flower is born to blush unseen,
And waste its sweetness on the desert air.

Some village-Hampden, that with dauntless breast
The little Tyrant of his fields withstood;
Some mute inglorious Milton here may rest,
60   Some Cromwell guiltless of his country's blood.

Th' applause of list'ning senates to command,
The threats of pain and ruin to despise,
To scatter plenty o'er a smiling land,
And read their hist'ry in a nation's eyes,

65   Their lot forbad: nor circumscrib'd alone
Their growing virtues, but their crimes confin'd;
Forbad to wade through slaughter to a throne,
And shut the gates of mercy on mankind,

The struggling pangs of conscious truth to hide,
70   To quench the blushes of ingenuous shame,
Or heap the shrine of Luxury and Pride
With incense kindled at the Muse's flame.

Far from the madding crowd's ignoble strife,
Their sober wishes never learn'd to stray;
75   Along the cool sequester'd vale of life
They kept the noiseless tenor of their way.

Yet ev'n these bones from insult to protect
Some frail memorial still erected nigh,
With uncouth rhimes and shapeless sculpture deck'd,
80   Implores the passing tribute of a sigh.

Their name, their years, spelt by th' unletter'd muse,
The place of fame and elegy supply:
And many a holy text around she strews,
That teach the rustic moralist to die.

85   For who to dumb Forgetfulness a prey,
This pleasing anxious being e'er resign'd,
Left the warm precincts of the chearful day,
Nor cast one longing ling'ring look behind?

On some fond breast the parting soul relies,
90   Some pious drops the closing eye requires;
Ev'n from the tomb the voice of Nature cries,
Ev'n in our Ashes live their wonted Fires.

For thee, who mindful of th' unhonour'd Dead
Dost in these lines their artless tale relate;
95   If chance, by lonely contemplation led,
Some kindred Spirit shall inquire thy fate,

Haply some hoary-headed Swain may say,
"Oft have we seen him at the peep of dawn
Brushing with hasty steps the dews away
100   To meet the sun upon the upland lawn.

There at the foot of yonder nodding beech
That wreathes its old fantastic roots so high,
His listless length at noontide would he stretch,
And pore upon the brook that babbles by.

105   Hard by yon wood, now smiling as in scorn,
Mutt'ring his wayward fancies he would rove,
Now drooping, woeful wan, like one forlorn,
Or craz'd with care, or cross'd in hopeless love.

One morn I miss'd him on the custom'd hill,
110   Along the heath and near his fav'rite tree;
Another came; nor yet beside the rill,
Nor up the lawn, nor at the wood was he;

The next with dirges due in sad array
Slow thro' the church-way path we saw him born.
115   Approach and read (for thou can'st read) the lay,
Grav'd on the stone beneath yon aged thorn."

The Epitaph.

Here rests his head upon the lap of Earth
A Youth to Fortune and to Fame unknown.
Fair Science frown'd not on his humble birth,
120   And Melancholy mark'd him for her own.

Large was his bounty, and his soul sincere,
Heav'n did a recompence as largely send:
He gave to Mis'ry all he had, a tear,
He gain'd from Heav'n ('twas all he wish'd) a friend.

125   No farther seek his merits to disclose,
         Or draw his frailties from their dread abode,
         (There they alike in trembling hope repose,)
         The bosom of his Father and his God.

                              Thomas Gray   (1716–1771)

ADONAIS

I

         I weep for Adonais—he is dead!
         O, weep for Adonais! though our tears
         Thaw not the frost which binds so dear a head!
         And thou, sad Hour, selected from all years
5   To mourn our loss, rouse thy obscure compeers,
         And teach them thine own sorrow, say: 'With me
         Died Adonais; till the Future dares
         Forget the Past, his fate and fame shall be
An echo and a light unto eternity!'

II

10   Where wert thou, mighty Mother, when he lay,
         When thy Son lay, pierced by the shaft which flies
         In darkness? where was lorn Urania
         When Adonais died? With veilèd eyes,
         'Mid listening Echoes, in her Paradise
15   She sate, while one, with soft enamoured breath,
         Rekindled all the fading melodies,
         With which, like flowers that mock the corse beneath,
He had adorned and hid the coming bulk of Death.

III

         Oh, weep for Adonais—he is dead!
20   Wake, melancholy Mother, wake and weep!
         Yet wherefore? Quench within their burning bed
         Thy fiery tears, and let thy loud heart keep
         Like his, a mute and uncomplaining sleep;
         For he is gone, where all things wise and fair
25   Descend;—oh, dream not that the amorous Deep
         Will yet restore him to the vital air;
Death feeds on his mute voice, and laughs at our despair.

IV

Most musical of mourners, weep again!
Lament anew, Urania! — He died,
30   Who was the Sire of an immortal strain,
Blind, old, and lonely, when his country's pride,
The priest, the slave, and the liberticide,
Trampled and mocked with many a loathèd rite
Of lust and blood; he went, unterrified,
35   Into the gulf of death; but his clear Sprite
Yet reigns o'er earth; the third among the sons of light.

V

Most musical of mourners, weep anew!
Not all to that bright station dared to climb;
And happier they their happiness who knew,
40   Whose tapers yet burn through that night of time
In which suns perished; others more sublime,
Struck by the envious wrath of man or god,
Have sunk, extinct in their refulgent prime;
And some yet live, treading the thorny road,
45   Which leads, through toil and hate, to Fame's serene abode.

VI

But now, thy youngest, dearest one, has perished —
The nursling of thy widowhood, who grew,
Like a pale flower by some sad maiden cherished,
And fed with true-love tears, instead of dew;
50   Most musical of mourners, weep anew!
Thy extreme hope, the loveliest and the last,
The bloom, whose petals nipped before they blew
Died on the promise of the fruit, is waste;
The broken lily lies — the storm is overpast.

VII

55   To that high Capital, where kingly Death
Keeps his pale court in beauty and decay,
He came; and bought, with price of purest breath,
A grave among the eternal. — Come away!
Haste, while the vault of blue Italian day
60   Is yet his fitting charnel-roof! while still
He lies, as if in dewy sleep he lay;
Awake him not! surely he takes his fill
Of deep and liquid rest, forgetful of all ill.

VIII

He will awake no more, oh, never more!—
65   Within the twilight chamber spreads apace
The shadow of white Death, and at the door
Invisible Corruption waits to trace
His extreme way to her dim dwelling-place;
The eternal Hunger sits, but pity and awe
70   Soothe her pale rage, nor dares she to deface
So fair a prey, till darkness, and the law
Of change, shall o'er his sleep the mortal curtain draw.

IX

Oh, weep for Adonais!—The quick Dreams,
The passion-wingèd Ministers of thought,
75   Who were his flocks, whom near the living streams
Of his young spirit he fed, and whom he taught
The love which was its music, wander not,—
Wander no more, from kindling brain to brain,
But droop there, whence they sprung; and mourn their lot
80   Round the cold heart, where, after their sweet pain,
They ne'er will gather strength, or find a home again.

X

And one with trembling hands clasps his cold head,
And fans him with her moonlight wings, and cries;
'Our love, our hope, our sorrow, is not dead;
85   See, on the silken fringe of his faint eyes,
Like dew upon a sleeping flower, there lies
A tear some Dream has loosened from his brain.'
Lost Angel of a ruined Paradise!
She knew not 'twas her own; as with no stain
90   She faded, like a cloud which had outwept its rain.

XI

One from a lucid urn of starry dew
Washed his light limbs as if embalming them;
Another clipped her profuse locks, and threw
The wreath upon him, like an anadem,
95   Which frozen tears instead of pearls begem;
Another in her wilful grief would break
Her bow and wingèd reeds, as if to stem
A greater loss with one whjch was more weak;
And dull the barbèd fire against his frozen cheek.

XII

100   Another Splendour on his mouth alit,
          That mouth, whence it was wont to draw the breath
          Which gave it strength to pierce the guarded wit,
          And pass into the panting heart beneath
          With lightning and with music: the damp death
105   Quenched its caress upon his icy lips;
          And, as a dying meteor stains a wreath
          Of moonlight vapour, which the cold night clips,
     It flushed through his pale limbs, and passed to its eclipse.

XIII

          And others came . . . Desires and Adorations,
110   Wingèd Persuasions and veiled Destinies,
          Splendours, and Glooms, and glimmering Incarnations
          Of hopes and fears, and twilight Phantasies;
          And Sorrow, with her family of Sighs,
          And Pleasure, blind with tears, led by the gleam
115   Of her own dying smile instead of eyes,
          Came in slow pomp; — the moving pomp might seem
     Like pageantry of mist on an autumnal stream.

XIV

          All he had loved, and moulded into thought,
          From shape, and hue, and odour, and sweet sound,
120   Lamented Adonais. Morning sought
          Her eastern watch-tower, and her hair unbound,
          Wet with the tears which should adorn the ground,
          Dimmed the aëreal eyes that kindle day;
          Afar the melancholy thunder moaned,
125   Pale Ocean in unquiet slumber lay,
     And the wild Winds flew round, sobbing in their dismay.

XV

          Lost Echo sits amid the voiceless mountains,
          And feeds her grief with his remembered lay,
          And will no more reply to winds or fountains,
130   Or amorous birds perched on the young green spray,
          Or herdsman's horn, or bell at closing day;
          Since she can mimic not his lips, more dear
          Than those for whose disdain she pined away
          Into a shadow of all sounds: — a drear
135 Murmur, between their songs, is all the woodmen hear.

XVI

Grief made the young Spring wild, and she threw down
Her kindling buds, as if she Autumn were,
Or they dead leaves; since her delight is flown,
For whom should she have waked the sullen year?
140   To Phoebus was not Hyacinth so dear
Nor to himself Narcissus, as to both
Thou, Adonais: wan they stand and sere
Amid the faint companions of their youth,
With dew all turned to tears; odour, to sighing ruth.

XVII

145   Thy spirit's sister, the lorn nightingale
Mourns not her mate with such melodious pain;
Not so the eagle, who like thee could scale
Heaven, and could nourish in the sun's domain
Her mighty youth with morning, doth complain,
150   Soaring and screaming round her empty nest,
As Albion wails for thee: the curse of Cain
Light on his head who pierced thy innocent breast,
And scared the angel soul that was its earthly guest!

XVIII

Ah, woe is me! Winter is come and gone,
155   But grief returns with the revolving year;
The airs and streams renew their joyous tone;
The ants, the bees, the swallows reappear;
Fresh leaves and flowers deck the dead Seasons' bier;
The amorous birds now pair in every brake,
160   And build their mossy homes in field and brere;
And the green lizard, and the golden snake,
Like unimprisoned flames, out of their trance awake.

XIX

Through wood and stream and field and hill and Ocean
A quickening life from the Earth's heart has burst
165   As it has ever done, with change and motion,
From the great morning of the world when first
God dawned on Chaos; in its stream immersed,
The lamps of Heaven flash with a softer light;
All baser things pant with life's sacred thirst;
170   Diffuse themselves; and spend in love's delight,
The beauty and the joy of their renewèd might.

XX

The leprous corpse, touched by this spirit tender,
Exhales itself in flowers of gentle breath;
Like incarnations of the stars, when splendour
175 Is changed to fragrance, they illumine death
And mock the merry worm that wakes beneath;
Nought we know, dies. Shall that alone which knows
Be as a sword consumed before the sheath
By sightless lightning? — the intense atom glows
180 A moment, then is quenched in a most cold repose.

XXI

Alas! that all we loved of him should be,
But for our grief, as if it had not been,
And grief itself be mortal! Woe is me!
Whence are we, and why are we? of what scene
185 The actors or spectators? Great and mean
Meet massed in death, who lends what life must borrow.
As long as skies are blue, and fields are green,
Evening must usher night, night urge the morrow,
Month follow month with woe, and year wake year to sorrow.

XXII

190 *He* will awake no more, oh, never more!
'Wake thou,' cried Misery, 'childless Mother, rise
Out of thy sleep, and slake, in thy heart's core,
A wound more fierce than his, with tears and sighs.'
And all the Dreams that watched Urania's eyes,
195 And all the Echoes whom their sister's song
Had held in holy silence, cried: 'Arise!'
Swift as a Thought by the snake Memory stung,
From her ambrosial rest the fading Splendour sprung.

XXIII

She rose like an autumnal Night, that springs
200 Out of the East, and follows wild and drear
The golden Day, which, on eternal wings,
Even as a ghost abandoning a bier,
Had left the Earth a corpse. Sorrow and fear
So struck, so roused, so rapt Urania;
205 So saddened round her like an atmosphere
Of stormy mist; so swept her on her way
Even to the mournful place where Adonais lay.

XXIV

Out of her secret Paradise she sped,
Through camps and cities rough with stone, and steel,
210 And human hearts, which to her aery tread
Yielding not, wounded the invisible
Palms of her tender feet where'er they fell:
And barbèd tongues, and thoughts more sharp than they,
Rent the soft Form they never could repel,
215 Whose sacred blood, like the young tears of May,
Paved with eternal flowers that undeserving way.

XXV

In the death-chamber for a moment Death,
Shamed by the presence of that living Might,
Blushed to annihilation, and the breath
220 Revisited those lips, and Life's pale light
Flashed through those limbs, so late her dear delight.
'Leave me not wild and drear and comfortless,
As silent lightning leaves the starless night!
Leave me not!' cried Urania: her distress
225 Roused Death: Death rose and smiled, and met her vain caress.

XXVI

'Stay yet awhile! speak to me once again;
Kiss me, so long but as a kiss may live;
And in my heartless breast and burning brain
That word, that kiss, shall all thoughts else survive,
230 With food of saddest memory kept alive,
Now thou art dead, as if it were a part
Of thee, my Adonais! I would give
All that I am to be as thou now art!
But I am chained to Time, and cannot thence depart!

XXVII

235 'O gentle child, beautiful as thou wert,
Why didst thou leave the trodden paths of men
Too soon, and with weak hands though mighty heart
Dare the unpastured dragon in his den?
Defenceless as thou wert, oh, where was then
240 Wisdom the mirrored shield, or scorn the spear?
Or hadst thou waited the full cycle, when
Thy spirit should have filled its crescent sphere,
The monsters of life's waste had fled from thee like deer.

XXVIII

'The herded wolves, bold only to pursue;
245   The obscene ravens, clamorous o'er the dead;
        The vultures to the conqueror's banner true
        Who feed where Desolation first has fed,
        And whose wings rain contagion; — how they fled,
        When, like Apollo, from his golden bow
250   The Pythian of the age one arrow sped
        And smiled! — The spoilers tempt no second blow,
They fawn on the proud feet that spurn them lying low.

XXIX

'The sun comes forth, and many reptiles spawn;
        He sets, and each ephemeral insect then
255   Is gathered into death without a dawn,
        And the immortal stars awake again;
        So is it in the world of living men:
        A godlike mind soars forth, in its delight
        Making earth bare and veiling heaven, and when
260   It sinks, the swarms that dimmed or shared its light
Leave to its kindred lamps the spirit's awful night.'

XXX

        Thus ceased she: and the mountain shepherds came,
        Their garlands sere, their magic mantles rent;
        The Pilgrim of Eternity, whose fame
265   Over his living head like Heaven is bent,
        An early but enduring monument,
        Came, veiling all the lightnings of his song
        In sorrow; from her wilds Ierne sent
        The sweetest lyrist of her saddest wrong,
270   And Love taught Grief to fall like music from his tongue.

XXXI

        Midst others of less note, came one frail Form,
        A phantom among men; companionless
        As the last cloud of an expiring storm
        Whose thunder is its knell; he, as I guess,
275   Had gazed on Nature's naked loveliness,
        Actaeon-like, and now he fled astray
        With feeble steps o'er the world's wilderness,
        And his own thoughts, along that rugged way,
Pursued, like raging hounds, their father and their prey.

XXXII

280
A pardlike Spirit beautiful and swift—
A Love in desolation masked;—a Power
Girt round with weakness;—it can scarce uplift
The weight of the superincumbent hour;
It is a dying lamp, a falling shower,
285
A breaking billow;—even whilst we speak
Is it not broken? On the withering flower
The killing sun smiles brightly: on a cheek
The life can burn in blood, even while the heart may break.

XXXIII

His head was bound with pansies overblown,
290
And faded violets, white, and pied, and blue;
And a light spear topped with a cypress cone,
Round whose rude shaft dark ivy-tresses grew
Yet dripping with the forest's noonday dew,
Vibrated, as the ever-beating heart
295
Shook the weak hand that grasped it; of that crew
He came the last, neglected and apart;
A herd-abandoned deer struck by the hunter's dart.

XXXIV

All stood aloof, and at his partial moan
Smiled through their tears; well knew that gentle band
300
Who in another's fate now wept his own,
As in the accents of an unknown land
He sung new sorrow; sad Urania scanned
The Stranger's mien, and murmured: 'Who art thou?'
He answered not, but with a sudden hand
305
Made bare his branded and ensanguined brow,
Which was like Cain's or Christ's—oh! that it should be so!

XXXV

What softer voice is hushed over the dead?
Athwart what brow is that dark mantle thrown?
What form leans sadly o'er the white death-bed,
310
In mockery of monumental stone,
The heavy heart heaving without a moan?
If it be He, who, gentlest of the wise,
Taught, soothed, loved, honoured the departed one,
Let me not vex, with inharmonious sighs,
315
The silence of that heart's accepted sacrifice.

XXXVI

    Our Adonais has drunk poison—oh!
    What deaf and viperous murderer could crown
    Life's early cup with such a draught of woe?
    The nameless worm would now itself disown:
320   It felt, yet could escape, the magic tone
    Whose prelude held all envy, hate, and wrong,
    But what was howling in one breast alone,
    Silent with expectation of the song,
Whose master's hand is cold, whose silver lyre unstrung.

XXXVII

325   Live thou, whose infamy is not thy fame!
    Live! fear no heavier chastisement from me,
    Thou noteless blot on a remembered name!
    But be thyself, and know thyself to be!
    And ever at thy season be thou free
330   To spill the venom when thy fangs o'erflow;
    Remorse and Self-contempt shall cling to thee;
    Hot Shame shall burn upon thy secret brow,
And like a beaten hound tremble thou shalt—as now.

XXXVIII

    Nor let us weep that our delight is fled
335   Far from these carrion kites that scream below;
    He wakes or sleeps with the enduring dead;
    Thou canst not soar where he is sitting now.—
    Dust to the dust! but the pure spirit shall flow
    Back to the burning fountain whence it came,
340   A portion of the Eternal, which must glow
    Through time and change, unquenchably the same,
Whilst thy cold embers choke the sordid hearth of shame.

XXXIX

    Peace, peace! he is not dead, he doth not sleep—
    He hath awakened from the dream of life—
345   'Tis we, who lost in stormy visions, keep
    With phantoms an unprofitable strife,
    And in mad trance, strike with our spirit's knife
    Invulnerable nothings.—We decay
    Like corpses in a charnel; fear and grief
350   Convulse us and consume us day by day,
And cold hopes swarm like worms within our living clay.

XL

He has outsoared the shadow of our night;
Envy and calumny and hate and pain,
And that unrest which men miscall delight,
355 Can touch him not and torture not again;
From the contagion of the world's slow stain
He is secure, and now can never mourn
A heart grown cold, a head grown gray in vain;
Nor, when the Spirit's self has ceased to burn,
360 With sparkless ashes load an unlamented urn.

XLI

He lives, he wakes — 'tis Death is dead, not he;
Mourn not for Adonais. — Thou young Dawn,
Turn all thy dew to splendour, for from thee
The spirit thou lamentest is not gone;
365 Ye caverns and ye forests, cease to moan!
Cease, ye faint flowers and fountains, and thou Air,
Which like a mourning veil thy scarf hadst thrown
O'er the abandoned Earth, now leave it bare
Even to the joyous stars which smile on its despair!

XLII

370 He is made one with Nature: there is heard
His voice in all her music, from the moan
Of thunder, to the song of night's sweet bird;
He is a presence to be felt and known
In darkness and in light, from herb and stone,
375 Spreading itself where'er that Power may move
Which has withdrawn his being to its own;
Which wields the world with never-wearied love,
Sustains it from beneath, and kindles it above.

XLIII

He is a portion of the loveliness
380 Which once he made more lovely: he doth bear
His part, while the one Spirit's plastic stress
Sweeps through the dull dense world, compelling there,
All new successions to the forms they wear;
Torturing th' unwilling dross that checks its flight
385 To its own likeness, as each mass may bear;
And bursting in its beauty and its might
From trees and beasts and men into the Heaven's light.

XLIV

The splendours of the firmament of time
May be eclipsed, but are extinguished not;
390   Like stars to their appointed height they climb,
And death is a low mist which cannot blot
The brightness it may veil. When lofty thought
Lifts a young heart above its mortal lair,
And love and life contend in it, for what
395   Shall be its earthly doom, the dead live there
And move like winds of light on dark and stormy air.

XLV

The inheritors of unfulfilled renown
Rose from their thrones, built beyond mortal thought,
Far in the Unapparent. Chatterton
400   Rose pale,—his solemn agony had not
Yet faded from him; Sidney, as he fought
And as he fell and as he lived and loved
Sublimely mild, a Spirit without spot,
Arose; and Lucan, by his death approved:
405   Oblivion as they rose shrank like a thing reproved.

XLVI

And many more, whose names on Earth are dark,
But whose transmitted effluence cannot die
So long as fire outlives the parent spark,
Rose, robed in dazzling immortality.
410   'Thou art become as one of us,' they cry,
'It was for thee yon kingless sphere has long
Swung blind in unascended majesty,
Silent alone amid an Heaven of Song.
Assume thy wingèd throne, thou Vesper of our throng!'

XLVII

415   Who mourns for Adonais? Oh, come forth,
Fond wretch! and know thyself and him aright.
Clasp with thy panting soul the pendulous Earth;
As from a centre, dart thy spirit's light
Beyond all worlds, until its spacious might
420   Satiate the void circumference: then shrink
Even to a point within our day and night;
And keep thy heart light lest it make thee sink
When hope has kindled hope, and lured thee to the brink.

XLVIII

425   Or go to Rome, which is the sepulchre,
      Oh, not of him, but of our joy: 'tis nought
      That ages, empires, and religions there
      Lie buried in the ravage they have wrought;
      For such as he can lend,—they borrow not
      Glory from those who made the world their prey;
430   And he is gathered to the kings of thought
      Who waged contention with their time's decay,
And of the past are all that cannot pass away.

XLIX

      Go thou to Rome,—at once the Paradise,
      The grave, the city, and the wilderness;
435   And where its wrecks like shattered mountains rise,
      And flowering weeds, and fragrant copses dress
      The bones of Desolation's nakedness
      Pass, till the spirit of the spot shall lead
      Thy footsteps to a slope of green access
440   Where, like an infant's smile, over the dead
A light of laughing flowers along the grass is spread;

L

      And gray walls moulder round, on which dull Time
      Feeds, like slow fire upon a hoary brand;
      And one keen pyramid with wedge sublime,
445   Pavilioning the dust of him who planned
      This refuge for his memory, doth stand
      Like flame transformed to marble; and beneath,
      A field is spread, on which a newer band
      Have pitched in Heaven's smile their camp of death,
450   Welcoming him we lose with scarce extinguished breath.

LI

      Here pause: these graves are all too young as yet
      To have outgrown the sorrow which consigned
      Its charge to each; and if the seal is set,
      Here, on one fountain of a mourning mind,
455   Break it not thou! too surely shalt thou find
      Thine own well full, if thou returnest home,
      Of tears and gall. From the world's bitter wind
      Seek shelter in the shadow of the tomb.
What Adonais is, why fear we to become?

LII

460 The One remains, the many change and pass;
 Heaven's light forever shines, Earth's shadows fly;
 Life, like a dome of many-coloured glass,
 Stains the white radiance of Eternity,
 Until Death tramples it to fragments. — Die,
465 If thou wouldst be with that which thou dost seek!
 Follow where all is fled! — Rome's azure sky,
 Flowers, ruins, statues, music, words, are weak
The glory they transfuse with fitting truth to speak.

LIII

 Why linger, why turn back, why shrink, my Heart?
470 Thy hopes are gone before: from all things here
 They have departed; thou shouldst now depart!
 A light is passed from the revolving year,
 And man, and woman; and what still is dear
 Attracts to crush, repels to make thee wither.
475 The soft sky smiles, — the low wind whispers near:
 'Tis Adonais calls! oh, hasten thither,
No more let Life divide what Death can join together.

LIV

 That Light whose smile kindles the Universe,
 That Beauty in which all things work and move,
480 That Benediction which the eclipsing Curse
 Of birth can quench not, that sustaining Love
 Which through the web of being blindly wove
 By man and beast and earth and air and sea,
 Burns bright or dim, as each are mirrors of
485 The fire for which all thirst; now beams on me,
Consuming the last clouds of cold mortality.

LV

 The breath whose might I have invoked in song
 Descends on me; my spirit's bark is driven,
 Far from the shore, far from the trembling throng
490 Whose sails were never to the tempest given;
 The massy earth and spherèd skies are riven!
 I am borne darkly, fearfully, afar;
 Whilst, burning through the inmost veil of Heaven,
 The soul of Adonais, like a star,
495 Beacons from the abode where the Eternal are.

Percy Bysshe Shelley (1792 – 1822)

WHEN LILACS LAST IN THE DOORYARD BLOOM'D

1

When lilacs last in the dooryard bloom'd,
And the great star early droop'd in the western sky in the night,
I mourn'd, and yet shall mourn with ever-returning spring.

Ever-returning spring, trinity sure to me you bring,
5   Lilac blooming perennial and drooping star in the west,
And I thought of him I love.

2

O powerful western fallen star!
O shades of night—O moody, tearful night!
O great star disappear'd—O the black murk that hides the star!
10   O cruel hands that hold me powerless—O helpless soul of me!
O harsh surrounding cloud that will not free my soul.

3

In the dooryard fronting an old farm-house near the whitewash'd
    palings,
Stands the lilac-bush tall-growing with heart-shaped leaves of rich
    green,
With many a pointed blossom rising delicate, with the perfume strong I
    love,
15   With every leaf a miracle—and from this bush in the dooryard,
With delicate-color'd blossoms and heart-shaped leaves of rich green,
A sprig with its flower I break.

4

In the swamp in secluded recesses,
A shy and hidden bird is warbling a song.
20   Solitary the thrush,
The hermit withdrawn to himself, avoiding the settlements,
Sings by himself a song.

Song of the bleeding throat,
Death's outlet song of life, (for well, dear brother, I know,
25   If thou wast not granted to sing thou would'st surely die.)

5

Over the breast of the spring, the land, amid cities,
Amid lanes and through old woods, where lately the violets peep'd from
        the ground, spotting the grey debris,
Amid the grass in the fields each side of the lanes, passing the endless
        grass,
Passing the yellow-spear'd wheat, every grain from its shroud in the
        dark-brown fields uprisen,
30   Passing the apple-tree blows of white and pink in the orchards,
Carrying a corpse to where it shall rest in the grave,
Night and day journeys a coffin.

6

Coffin that passes through lanes and streets,
Through day and night with the great cloud darkening the land,
35   With the pomp of the inloop'd flags with the cities draped in black,
With the show of the States themselves as of crepe-veil'd women
        standing,
With processions long and winding and the flambeaus of the night,
With the countless torches lit, with the silent sea of faces and the un-
        bared heads,
With the waiting depot, the arriving coffin, and the somber faces,
40   With dirges through the night, with the thousand voices rising strong
        and solemn,
With all the mournful voices of the dirges pour'd around the coffin,
The dim-lit churches and the shuddering organs—where amid these
        you journey,
With the tolling tolling bells' perpetual clang,
Here, coffin that slowly passes,
45   I give you my sprig of lilac.

7

(Nor for you, for one alone,
Blossoms and branches green to coffins all I bring,
For fresh as the morning, thus would I chant a song for you
        O sane and sacred death.

50   All over bouquets of roses,
O death, I cover you over with roses and early lilies,
But mostly and now the lilac that blooms the first,
Copious I break, I break the sprigs from the bushes,
With loaded arms I come, pouring for you,
55   For you and the coffins all of you O death.)

8

O western orb sailing the heaven,
Now I know what you must have meant as a month since I walked,
As I walked in silence the transparent shadowy night,
As I saw you had something to tell as you bent to me night after night,
60   As you droop'd from the sky low down as if to my side, (while the other
      stars all look'd on,)
As we wandered together the solemn night, (for something I know not
      what kept me from sleep,)
As the night advanced, and I saw on the rim of the west how full you
      were of woe,
As I stood on the rising ground in the breeze in the cool transparent
      night,
As I watch'd where you pass'd and was lost in the netherward black
      of the night,
65   As my soul in its trouble dissatisfied sank, as where you sad orb,
Concluded, dropt in the night, and was gone.

9

Sing on there in the swamp,
O singer bashful and tender, I hear your notes, I hear your call,
I hear, I come presently, I understand you,
70   But a moment I linger, for the lustrous star has detain'd me,
The star my departing comrade holds and detains me.

10

O how shall I warble myself for the dead one there I loved?
And how shall I deck my song for the large sweet soul that has gone?
And what shall my fortune be for the grave of him I love?

75   Sea-winds blown from east and west,
Blown from the Eastern sea and blown from the Western sea, till there
      on the prairies meeting,
These and with these and the breath of my chant,
I'll perfume the grave of him I love.

11

O what shall I hang on the chamber walls?
80   And what shall the pictures be that I hang on the walls,
To adorn the burial-house of him I love?

Pictures of growing spring and farms and homes,
With the Fourth-month eve at sundown, and the gray smoke lucid and
      bright,

With floods of the yellow gold of the gorgeous, indolent, sinking sun, burning, expanding the air,
85 With the fresh sweet herbage under foot, and the pale green leaves of the trees prolific,
In the distance the flowing glaze, the breast of the river, with a wind-dapple here and there,
With ranging hills on the banks, with many a line against the sky, and shadows,
And the city at hand with dwellings so dense, and stacks of chimneys,
And all the scenes of life and the workshops, and the workmen homeward returning.

12

90 Lo, body and soul — this land,
My own Manhattan with spires, and the sparkling and hurrying tides, and the ships,
The varied and ample land, the South and the North in the light, Ohio's shores and flashing Missouri,
And ever the far-spreading prairies cover'd with grass and corn.
Lo, the most excellent sun so calm and haughty,
95 The violet and purple morn with just-felt breezes,
The gentle soft-born measureless light,
The miracle spreading bathing all, the fulfill'd noon,
The coming eve delicious, the welcoming night and the stars,
Over my cities shining all, enveloping man and land.

13

100 Sing on, sing on you gray-brown bird,
Sing from the swamps, the recesses, pour your chant from the bushes,
Limitless out of the dusk, out of the cedars and pines.
Sing on dearest brother, warble your reedy song,
Loud human song, with voice of uttermost woe.
105 O liquid and free and tender!
O wild and loose to my soul — O wondrous singer!
You only I hear — yet the star holds me, (but will soon depart,)
Yet the lilac with mastering odor holds me.

14

Now while I sat in the day and look'd forth,
110 In the close of the day with its light and the fields of spring, and the farmers preparing their crops,
In the large unconscious scenery of my land with its lakes and forests,
In the heavenly aerial beauty, (after the perturb'd winds and the storms,)
Under the arching heavens of the afternoon swift passing, and the voices of children and women,

The many-moving sea-tides, and I saw the ships how they sail'd,
115   And the summer approaching with richness, and the fields all busy
      with labor,
      And the infinite separate houses, how they all went on, each with its
      meals and minutia of daily usages,
      And the streets how their throbbings throbb'd, and the cities pent—lo,
      then and there,
      Falling upon them all and among them all, enveloping me with the
      rest,
      Appear'd the cloud, appear'd the long black trail,
120   And I knew death, its thought, and the sacred knowledge of death.

      Then with the knowledge of death as walking one side of me,
      And the thought of death close-walking the other side of me,
      And I in the middle as with companions, and as holding the hands of
      companions,
      I fled forth to the hiding receiving night that talks not,
125   Down to the shores of the water, the path by the swamp in the dimness,
      To the solemn shadowy cedars and ghostly pines so still.

      And the singer so shy to the rest receiv'd me,
      The gray-brown bird I know receiv'd us comrades three,
      And he sang the carol of death, and a verse for him I love.
130   From deep secluded recesses,
      From the fragrant cedars and the ghostly pines so still,
      Came the carol of the bird.

      And the charm of the carol rapt me,
      As I held as if by their hands my comrades in the night,
135   And the voice of my spirit tallied the song of the bird.

      Come lovely and soothing death,
      Undulate round the world, serenely arriving, arriving,
      In the day, in the night, to all, to each,
      Sooner or later delicate death.

140   *Prais'd be the fathomless universe,*
      For life and joy, and for objects and knowledge curious,
      And for love, sweet love—but praise! praise! praise!
      For the sure-enwinding arms of cool-enfolding death.

      Dark mother always gliding near with soft feet,
145   *Have none chanted for thee a chant of fullest welcome?*
      Then I chant it for thee, I glorify thee above all,
      I bring thee a song that when thou must indeed come, come
      unfalteringly.

      Approach strong deliveress,
      When it is so, when thou hast taken them I joyously sing the dead,

150   Lost in the loving floating ocean of thee,
      Laved in the flood of thy bliss, O death.

      From me to thee glad serenades,
      Dances for thee I propose saluting thee, adornments and feastings for
            thee,
      And the sights of the open landscape and the high-spread sky are
            fitting,
155   And life and the fields, and the huge and thoughtful night.

      The night in silence under many a star,
      The ocean shore and the husky whispering wave whose voice I know,
      And the soul turning to thee, O vast and well-veil'd death,
      And the body gratefully nestling close to thee.

160   Over the tree-tops I float thee a song,
      Over the rising and sinking waves, over the myriad fields and the
            prairies wide,
      Over the dense-pack'd cities all and the teeming wharves and ways,
      I float this carol with joy, with joy to thee, O death.

      15

      To the tally of my soul,
165   Loud and strong kept up the gray-brown bird,
      With pure deliberate notes spreading filling the night.

      Loud in the pines and cedars dim,
      Clear in the freshness moist and the swamp-perfume,
      And I with my comrades there in the night.

170   While my sight that was bound in my eyes unclosed,
      As to long panoramas of visions.

      And I saw askant the armies,
      I saw as in noiseless dreams hundreds of battle-flags,
      Borne through the smoke of the battles and pierc'd with missiles I saw
            them,
175   And carried hither and yon through the smoke, and torn and bloody,
      And at last but a few shreds left on the staffs, (and all in silence,)
      And the staffs all splinter'd and broken.

      I saw battle-corpses, myriads of them,
      And the white skeletons of young men, I saw them,
180   I saw the debris and debris of all the slain soldiers of the war,
      But I saw they were not as was thought,
      They themselves were fully at rest, they suffer'd not,
      The living remain'd and suffer'd, the mother suffer'd,
      And the wife and the child and the musing comrade suffer'd,
185   And the armies that remained suffer'd.

16

Passing the visions, passing the night,
Passing, unloosing the hold of my comrades' hands,
Passing the song of the hermit bird and the tallying song of my soul,
Victorious song, death's outlet song, yet varying, ever-altering song.
190   As low and wailing, yet clear the notes, rising and falling, flooding the night,
Sadly sinking and fainting, as warning and warning, and yet again bursting with joy,
Covering the earth and filling the spread of the heaven,
As that powerful psalm in the night I heard from recesses,
Passing, I leave thee lilac with heart-shaped leaves,
195   I leave thee there in the door-yard, blooming, returning with spring.

I cease from my song for thee,
From my gaze on thee in the west, fronting the west, communing with thee,
O comrade lustrous with silver face in the night.

Yet each to keep and all, retrievements out of the night,
200   The song, the wondrous chant of the gray-brown bird,
And the tallying chant, the echo arous'd in my soul,
With the lustrous and drooping star with the countenance full of woe,
With the holders holding my hand nearing the call of the bird,
Comrades mine and I in the midst, and their memory ever to keep, for the dead I loved so well,
205   For the sweetest, wisest soul of all my days and lands—and this for his dear sake,
Lilac and star and bird twined with the chant of my soul,
There in the fragrant pines and the cedars dusk and dim.

Walt Whitman   (1819 – 1892)

THYRSIS

A Monody, to commemorate the author's friend, Arthur Hugh Clough, who died at Florence, 1861

Thus yesterday, to-day, to-morrow come,
They hustle one another and they pass;
But all our hustling morrows only make
The smooth to-day of God.
        from *Lucretius, An unpublished Tragedy.*

How changed is here each spot man makes or fills!
  In the two Hinkseys nothing keeps the same;
    The village-street its haunted mansion lacks,
  And from the sign is gone Sibylla's name,
5   And from the roofs the twisted chimney-stacks—
      Are ye too changed, ye hills?
  See, 'tis no foot of unfamiliar men
    To-night from Oxford up your pathway strays!
    Here came I often, often, in old days—
10 Thyrsis and I; we still had Thyrsis then.

Runs it not here, the track by Childsworth Farm,
  Past the high wood, to where the elm-tree crowns
    The hill behind whose ridge the sunset flames?
  The signal-elm, that looks on Ilsley Downs,
15   The Vale, the three lone weirs, the youthful Thames?—
      This winter-eve is warm,
  Humid the air! leafless, yet soft as spring,
    The tender purple spray on copse and briers!
    And that sweet city with her dreaming spires,
20 She needs not June for beauty's heightening,

Lovely all times she lies, lovely to-night!—
  Only, methinks, some loss of habit's power
    Befalls me wandering through this upland dim.
  Once pass'd I blindfold here, at any hour;
25   Now seldom come I, since I came with him.
      That single elm-tree bright
  Against the west—I miss it! is it gone?
    We prized it dearly; while it stood, we said,
    Our friend, the Gipsy Scholar, was not dead;
30 While the tree lived, he in these fields lived on.

Too rare, too rare, grow now my visits here,
  But once I knew each field, each flower, each stick;
    And with the country-folk acquaintance made
  By barn in threshing-time, by new-built rick.
35   Here, too, our shepherd-pipes we first assay'd.
      Ah me! this many a year
  My pipe is lost, my shepherd's-holiday!
    Needs must I lose them, needs with heavy heart
    Into the world and wave of men depart;
40 But Thyrsis of his own will went away.

It irk'd him to be here, he could not rest.
  He loved each simple joy the country yields,
    He loved his mates; but yet he could not keep,
  For that a shadow lour'd on the fields,
45   Here with the shepherds and the silly sheep.

Some life of men unblest
He knew, which made him droop, and fill'd his head.
He went; his piping took a troubled sound
Of storms that rage outside our happy ground;
50   He could not wait their passing, he is dead.

So, some tempestuous morn in early June,
When the year's primal burst of bloom is o'er,
Before the roses and the longest day—
When garden-walks and all the grassy floor,
55   With blossoms red and white of fallen May,
And chestnut-flowers are strewn—
So have I heard the cuckoo's parting cry,
From the wet field, through the vext garden-trees,
Come with the volleying rain and tossing breeze:
60   *The bloom is gone, and with the bloom go I!*

Too quick despairer, wherefore wilt thou go?
Soon will the high Midsummer pomps come on,
Soon will the musk carnations break and swell,
Soon shall we have gold-dusted snapdragon,
65   Sweet-William with his homely cottage-smell,
And stocks in fragrant blow;
Roses that down the alleys shine afar,
And open, jasmine-muffled lattices,
And groups under the dreaming garden-trees,
70   And the full moon, and the white evening-star.

He hearkens not! light comer, he is flown!
What matters it? next year he will return,
And we shall have him in the sweet spring-days,
With whitening hedges, and uncrumpling fern,
75   And blue-bells trembling by the forest-ways,
And scent of hay new-mown.
But Thyrsis never more we swains shall see;
See him come back, and cut a smoother reed,
And blow a strain the world at last shall heed—
80   For Time, not Corydon, hath conquer'd thee.

Alack, for Corydon no rival now!—
But when Sicilian shepherds lost a mate,
Some good survivor with his flute would go,
Piping a ditty sad for Bion's fate,
85   And cross the unpermitted ferry's flow,
And relax Pluto's brow,
And make leap up with joy the beauteous head
Of Proserpine, among whose crowned hair
Are flowers, first open'd on Sicilian air;
90   And flute his friend, like Orpheus, from the dead.

O easy access to the hearer's grace,
  When Dorian shepherds sang to Proserpine!
    For she herself had trod Sicilian fields,
  She knew the Dorian water's gush divine,
95   She knew each lily white which Enna yields,
      Each rose with blushing face;
  She loved the Dorian pipe, the Dorian strain.
    But ah, of our poor Thames she never heard!
    Her foot the Cumner cowslips never stirr'd;
100 And we should tease her with our plaint in vain!

Well! wind-dispersed and vain the words will be,
  Yet, Thyrsis, let me give my grief its hour
    In the old haunt, and find our tree-topp'd hill!
  Who, if not I, for questing here hath power?
105   I know the wood which hides the daffodil,
      I know the Fyfield tree,
  I know what white, what purple fritillaries
    The grassy harvest of the river-fields,
    Above by Ensham, down by Sandford, yields,
110   And what sedged brooks are Thames's tributaries;

I know these slopes; who knows them if not I?—
  But many a dingle on the loved hill-side,
    With thorns once studded, old, white-blossom'd trees,
  Where thick the cowslips grew, and, far descried
115   High tower'd the spikes of purple orchises,
      Hath since our day put by
  The coronals of that forgotten time;
    Down each green bank hath gone the ploughboy's team,
    And only in the hidden brookside gleam
120 Primroses, orphans of the flowery prime.

Where is the girl, who, by the boatman's door,
  Above the locks, above the boating throng,
    Unmoor'd our skiff, when, through the Wytham flats,
  Red loosestrife and blond meadow-street among,
125   And darting swallows, and light water-gnats,
      We track'd the shy Thames shore?
  Where are the mowers, who, as the tiny swell
    Of our boat passing heaved the river-grass,
    Stood with suspended scythe to see us pass?—
130 They all are gone, and thou art gone as well.

Yes, thou art gone! and round me too the night
  In ever-nearing circle weaves her shade.
    I see her veil draw soft across the day,
    I feel her slowly chilling breath invade
135   The cheek grown thin, the brown hair sprent with grey;

        I feel her finger light
   Laid pausefully upon life's headlong train; —
     The foot less prompt to meet the morning dew,
     The heart less bounding at emotion new,
140   And hope, once crush'd, less quick to spring again.

   And long the way appears, which seem'd so short
    To the less practised eye of sanguine youth;
     And high the mountain-tops, in cloudy air,
    The mountain-tops where is the throne of Truth,
145   Tops in life's morning-sun so bright and bare.
       Unbreachable the fort
   Of the long-batter'd world uplifts its wall;
    And strange and vain the earthly turmoil grows,
    And near and real the charm of thy repose,
150   And night as welcome as a friend would fall.

   But hush! the upland hath a sudden loss
    Of quiet! — Look, adown the dusk hill-side,
     A troop of Oxford hunters going home,
    As in old days, jovial and talking, ride!
155   From hunting with the Berkshire hounds they come.
       Quick! let me fly, and cross
   Into yon farther field! — 'Tis done; and see,
    Back'd by the sunset, which doth glorify
    The orange and pale violet evening-sky,
160   Bare on its lonely ridge, the Tree! the Tree!

   I take the omen! Eve lets down her veil,
    The white fog creeps from bush to bush about,
     The west unflushes, the high stars grow bright,
    And in the scatter'd farms the lights come out.
165   I cannot reach the signal-tree to-night,
       Yet, happy omen, hail!
   Hear it from thy broad lucent Arno-vale
    (For there thine earth-forgetting eyelids keep
    The morningless and unawakening sleep
170   Under the flowery oleanders pale),

   Hear it, O Thyrsis, still our tree is there! —
    Ah, vain! These English fields, this upland dim,
     These brambles pale with mist engarlanded,
    That lone, sky-pointing tree, are not for him.
175   To a boon southern country he is fled,
       And now in happier air,
   Wandering with the great Mother's train divine
    (And purer or more subtle soul than thee,
    I trow, the mighty Mother doth not see!)
180   Within a folding of the Apennine,

Thou hearest the immortal chants of old! —
  Putting his sickle to the perilous grain,
    In the hot cornfield of the Phrygian king,
  For thee the Lityerses song again
185   Young Daphnis with his silver voice doth sing;
      Sings his Sicilian fold,
  His sheep, his hapless love, his blinded eyes —
    And how a call celestial round him rang,
    And heavenward from the fountain-brink he sprang,
190   And all the marvel of the golden skies.

There thou art gone, and me thou leavest here
  Sole in these fields! yet will I not despair;
    Despair I will not, while I yet descry
  'Neath the mild canopy of English air
195   That lonely tree against the western sky.
      Still, still these slopes, 'tis clear,
  Our Gipsy-Scholar haunts, outliving thee!
    Fields where soft sheep from cages pull the hay,
    Woods with anemonies in flower till May,
200   Know him a wanderer still; then why not me?

A fugitive and gracious light he seeks,
  Shy to illumine; and I seek it too.
    This does not come with houses or with gold,
  With place, with honour, and a flattering crew;
205   'Tis not in the world's market bought and sold —
      But the smooth-slipping weeks
  Drop by, and leave its seeker still untired:
    Out of the heed of mortals he is gone,
    He wends unfollow'd, he must house alone;
210   Yet on he fares, by his own heart inspired.

Thou too, O Thyrsis, on like quest wast bound,
  Thou wanderedst with me for a little hour!
    Men gave thee nothing; but this happy quest,
  If men esteem'd thee feeble, gave thee power,
215   If men procured thee trouble, gave thee rest.
      And this rude Cumner ground,
  Its fir-topped Hurst, its farms, its quiet fields,
    Here cam'st thou in thy jocund youthful time,
    Here was thine height of strength, thy golden prime!
220   And still the haunt beloved a virtue yields.

What though the music of thy rustic flute
  Kept not for long its happy, country tone;
    Lost it too soon, and learnt a stormy note
  Of men contention-tost, of men who groan,
225   Which task'd thy pipe too sore, and tired thy throat —

It fail'd, and thou wast mute!
Yet hadst thou alway visions of our light,
And long with men of care thou couldst not stay,
And soon thy foot resumed its wandering way,
230   Left human haunt, and on alone till night.

Too rare, too rare, grow now my visits here!
'Mid city-noise, not, as with thee of yore,
Thyrsis! in reach of sheep-bells is my home.
—Then through the great town's harsh, heart-wearying roar,
235   Let in thy voice a whisper often come,
To chase fatigue and fear:
Why faintest thou? I wander'd till I died.
Roam on! the light we sought is shining still.
Dost thou ask proof? Our tree yet crowns the hill,
240   *Our Scholar travels yet the loved hill-side.*

Matthew Arnold   (1822 – 1888)

ODE TO THE CONFEDERATE DEAD

Row after row with strict impunity
The headstones yield their names to the element,
The wind whirrs without recollection;
In the riven troughs the splayed leaves
5   Pile up, of nature the casual sacrament
To the seasonal eternity of death,
Then driven by the fierce scrutiny
Of heaven to their business in the vast breath,
They sough the rumor of mortality.

10   Autumn is desolation in the plot
Of a thousand acres, where these memories grow
From the inexhaustible bodies that are not
Dead, but feed the grass row after rich row:
Remember now the autumns that have gone—
15   Ambitious November with the humors of the year,
With a particular zeal for every slab,
Staining the uncomfortable angels that rot
On the slabs, a wing chipped here, an arm there:
The brute curiosity of an angel's stare
20   Turns you like them to stone,
Transforms the heaving air,
Till plunged to a heavier world below
You shift your sea-space blindly,
Heaving, turning like the blind crab.

25   Dazed by the wind, only the wind
        The leaves flying, plunge

        You know who have waited by the wall
        The twilit certainty of an animal;
        Those midnight restitutions of the blood
30   You know—the immitigable pines, the smoky frieze
        Of the sky, the sudden call; you know the rage—
        The cold pool left by the mounting flood—
        The rage of Zeno and Parmenides.
        You who have waited for the angry resolution
35   Of those desires that should be yours tomorrow,
        You know the unimportant shift of death
        And praise the vision
        And praise the arrogant circumstance
        Of those who fall
40   Rank upon rank, hurried beyond decision—
        Here by the sagging gate, stopped by the wall.

        Seeing, seeing only the leaves
        Flying, plunge and expire

        Turn your eyes to the immoderate past
45   Turn to the inscrutable infantry rising
        Demons out of the earth—they will not last.
        Stonewall, Stonewall—and the sunken fields of hemp
        Shiloh, Antietam, Malvern Hill, Bull Run.
        Lost in that orient of the thick and fast
50   You will curse the setting sun

        Cursing only the leaves crying
        Like an old man in a storm

        You hear the shout—the crazy hemlocks point
        With troubled fingers to the silence which
55   Smothers you, a mummy, in time. The hound bitch
        Toothless and dying, in a musty cellar
        Hears the wind only.

        Now that the salt of their blood
        Stiffens the saltier oblivion of the sea,
60   Seals the malignant purity of the flood,
        What shall we, who count our days and bow
        Our heads with a commemorial woe,
        In the ribboned coats of grim felicity,
        What shall we say of the bones, unclean
65   Their verdurous anonymity will grow—
        The ragged arms, the ragged heads and eyes
        Lost in these acres of the insane green?

The grey lean spiders come; they come and go;
In a tangle of willows without light
70 The singular screech-owl's bright
Invisible lyric seeds the mind
With the furious murmur of their chivalry.

We shall say only, the leaves
Flying, plunge and expire

75 We shall say only, the leaves whispering
In the improbable mist of nightfall
That flies on multiple wing:
Night is the beginning and the end.
And in between the ends of distraction
80 Waits mute speculation, the patient curse
That stones the eyes, or like the jaguar leaps
For his own image in a jungle pool, his victim.

What shall we say who have knowledge
Carried to the heart? Shall we take the act
85 To the grave? Shall we, more hopeful, set up the grave
In the house? The ravenous grave?

Leave now

The turnstile and the old stone wall:
The gentle serpent, green in the mulberry bush,
Riots with his tongue through the hush—
90 Sentinel of the grave who counts us all!

Allen Tate   (1899—   )

IN MEMORY OF W. B. YEATS

1

He disappeared in the dead of winter:
The brooks were frozen, the airports almost deserted,
And snow disfigured the public statues;
The mercury sank in the mouth of the dying day.
5 O all the instruments agree
The day of his death was a dark cold day.

Far from his illness
The wolves ran on through the evergreen forests,
The peasant river was untempted by the fashionable quays;
10   By mourning tongues
The death of the poet was kept from his poems.

But for him it was his last afternoon as himself,
An afternoon of nurses and rumours;
The provinces of his body revolted,
15   The squares of his mind were empty,
Silence invaded the suburbs,
The current of his feeling failed: he became his admirers.

Now he is scattered among a hundred cities
And wholly given over to unfamiliar affections;
20   To find his happiness in another kind of wood
And be punished under a foreign code of conscience.
The words of a dead man
Are modified in the guts of the living.

But in the importance and noise of tomorrow
25   When the brokers are roaring like beasts on the floor of the Bourse,
And the poor have the sufferings to which they are fairly accustomed,
And each in the cell of himself is almost convinced of his freedom;
A few thousand will think of this day
As one thinks of a day when one did something slightly unusual.

30   O all the instruments agree
The day of his death was a dark cold day.

2

You were silly like us: your gift survived it all;
The parish of rich women, physical decay,
Yourself; mad Ireland hurt you into poetry.
35   Now Ireland has her madness and her weather still,
For poetry makes nothing happen: it survives
In the valley of its saying where executives
Would never want to tamper; it flows south
From ranches of isolation and the busy griefs,
40   Raw towns that we believe and die in; it survives,
A way of happening, a mouth.

3

Earth, receive an honoured guest;
William Yeats is laid to rest:
Let the Irish vessel lie
45   Emptied of its poetry.

Time that is intolerant
Of the brave and innocent,
And indifferent in a week
To a beautiful physique,

50   Worships language and forgives
Everyone by whom it lives;
Pardons cowardice, conceit,
Lays its honours at their feet.

Time that with this strange excuse
55   Pardoned Kipling and his views,
And will pardon Paul Claudel,
Pardons him for writing well.

In the nightmare of the dark
All the dogs of Europe bark,
60   And the living nations wait,
Each sequestered in its hate;

Intellectual disgrace
Stares from every human face,
And the seas of pity lie
65   Locked and frozen in each eye.

Follow, poet, follow right
To the bottom of the night,
With your unconstraining voice
Still persuade us to rejoice;

70   With the farming of a verse
Make a vineyard of the curse,
Sing of human unsuccess
In a rapture of distress;

In the deserts of the heart
75   Let the healing fountain start,
In the prison of his days
Teach the free man how to praise.

W. H. Auden   (1907 –   )

ELEGY FOR A DEAD SOLDIER

I

A white sheet on the tail-gate of a truck
Becomes an altar; two small candlesticks
Sputter at each side of the crucifix
Laid round with flowers brighter than the blood,
5   Red as the red of our apocalypse,
Hibiscus that a marching man will pluck
To stick into his rifle or his hat,
And great blue morning-glories pale as lips
That shall no longer taste or kiss or swear.
10   The wind begins a low magnificat,
The chaplain chats, the palmtrees swirl their hair,
The columns come together through the mud.

II

We too are ashes as we watch and hear
The psalm, the sorrow, and the simple praise
15   Of one whose promised thoughts of other days
Were such as ours, but now wholly destroyed,
The service record of his youth wiped out,
His dream dispersed by shot, must disappear.
What can we feel but wonder at a loss
20   That seems to point at nothing but the doubt
Which flirts our sense of luck into the ditch?
Reader of Paul who prays beside this fosse,
Shall we believe our eyes or legends rich
With glory and rebirth beyond the void?

III

25   For this comrade is dead, dead in the war,
A young man out of millions yet to live,
One cut away from all that war can give,
Freedom of self and peace to wander free.
Who mourns in all this sober multitude
30   Who did not feel the bite of it before
The bullet found its aim? This worthy flesh,
This boy laid in a coffin and reviewed—
Who has not wrapped himself in this same flag,
Heard the light fall of dirt, his wound still fresh,
35   Felt his eyes closed, and heard the distant brag
Of the last volley of humanity?

IV

By chance I saw him die, stretched on the ground,
A tattooed arm lifted to take the blood
Of someone else sealed in a tin. I stood
40   During the last delirium that stays
The intelligence a tiny moment more,
And then the strangulation, the last sound.
The end was sudden, like a foolish play,
A stupid fool slamming a foolish door,
45   The absurd catastrophe, half-prearranged,
And all the decisive things still left to say.
So we disbanded, angrier and unchanged,
Sick with the utter silence of dispraise.

V

We ask for no statistics of the killed,
50   For nothing political impinges on
This single casualty, or all those gone,
Missing or healing, sinking or dispersed,
Hundreds of thousands counted, millions lost.
More than an accident and less than willed
55   Is every fall, and this one like the rest.
However others calculate the cost,
To us the final aggregate is *one*,
One with a name, one transferred to the blest;
And though another stoops and takes the gun,
60   We cannot add the second to the first.

VI

I would not speak for him who could not speak
Unless my fear were true: he was not wronged,
He knew to which decision he belonged
But let it choose itself. Ripe in instinct,
65   Neither the victim nor the volunteer,
He followed, and the leaders could not seek
Beyond the followers. Much of this he knew;
The journey was a detour that would steer
Into the Lincoln Highway of a land
70   Remorselessly improved, excited, new,
And that was what he wanted. He had planned
To earn and drive. He and the world had winked.

VII

No history deceived him, for he knew
Little of times and armies not his own;
75   He never felt that peace was but a loan,
Had never questioned the idea of gain.
Beyond the headlines once or twice he saw
The gathering of a power by the few
But could not tell their names; he cast his vote,
80   Distrusting all the elected but not the law.
He laughed at socialism; *on mourrait*
Pour les industriels? He shed his coat
And not for brotherhood, but for his pay.
To him the red flag marked the sewer main.

VIII

85   Above all else he loathed the homily,
The slogan and the ad. He paid his bill
But not for Congressmen at Bunker Hill.
Ideals were few and those there were not made
For conversation. He belonged to church
90   But never spoke of God. The Christmas tree,
The Easter egg, baptism, he observed,
Never denied the preacher on his perch,
And would not sign Resolved That or Whereas.
Softness he had and hours and nights reserved
95   For thinking, dressing, dancing to the jazz.
His laugh was real, his manners were home made.

IX

Of all men poverty pursued him least;
He was ashamed of all the down and out,
Spurned the panhandler like an uneasy doubt,
100   And saw the unemployed as a vague mass
Incapable of hunger or revolt.
He hated other races, south or east,
And shoved them to the margin of his mind.
He could recall the justice of the Colt,
105   Take interest in a gang-war like a game.
His ancestry was somewhere far behind
And left him only his peculiar name.
Doors opened, and he recognized no class.

X

His children would have known a heritage,
110   Just or unjust, the richest in the world,
The quantum of all art and science curled
In the horn of plenty, bursting from the horn,
A people bathed in honey, Paris come,
Vienna transferred with the highest wage,
115   A World's Fair spread to Phoenix, Jacksonville,
Earth's capitol, the new Byzantium,
Kingdom of man — who knows? Hollow or firm,
No man can ever prophesy until
Out of our death some undiscovered germ,
120   Whole toleration or pure peace is born.

XI

The time to mourn is short that best becomes
The military dead. We lift and fold the flag,
Lay bare the coffin with its written tag,
And march away. Behind, four others wait
125   To lift the box, the heaviest of loads.
The anesthetic afternoon benumbs,
Sickens our senses, forces back our talk.
We know that others on tomorrow's roads
Will fall, ourselves perhaps, the man beside,
130   Over the world the threatened, all who walk:
And could we mark the grave of him who died
We would write this beneath his name and date:

Epitaph

Underneath this wooden cross there lies
A Christian killed in battle. You who read,
135   Remember that this stranger died in pain;
And passing here, if you can lift your eyes
Upon a peace kept by a human creed,
Know that one soldier has not died in vain.

Karl Shapiro   (1913 –   )

QUESTIONS FOR DISCUSSION AND FURTHER STUDY

TO THE MEMORY OF MY BELOVED THE AUTHOR, MR. WILLIAM SHAKE-SPEARE, AND WHAT HE HATH LEFT US

1. In the poem Jonson mentions the names of numerous writers of enduring fame. What is Shakespeare's rank among them? What reasons does Jonson give for awarding Shakespeare the rank he does?
2. Some people have claimed that Shakespeare was the poet of nature, Jonson, the poet of art. How does Jonson himself feel about this?
3. How does Jonson, himself a most accomplished dramatist, regard his talents in comparison with Shakespeare's?
4. What is the symbolic significance of the "sock" and "buskin"?

AN ELEGY UPON THE DEATH OF DOCTOR DONNE, DEAN OF PAUL'S

1. Compare the language used in this poem with that used in "Elegy for a Dead Soldier" or "In Memory of W. B. Yeats." What does the comparison suggest about the development of English poetry; in other words, what has happened to the level of English poetic diction during the intervening centuries?
2. What kinds of images does Carew use to praise Donne as a poet? In terms of the style of Donne's "metaphysical" poetry, what is especially appropriate about Carew's figures?
3. Unlike Jonson, Carew does not compare his subject with a number of other writers. Rather, he speaks of no one else but Donne. Which elegiac technique do you think is more effective? Why?
4. These two elegies by Jonson and Carew primarily praise Shakespeare and Donne as poets, not as men. Can you find passages in either poem which praise the poets as virtuous men?

LYCIDAS

1. Describe the emotional states through which Milton passes as he eulogizes Edward King. Is there any pattern or consistent movement in the progression of emotions?
2. What part does nature play in this poem? Is nature merely a passive observer, or does it take a more active role in the poem? If nature takes a more active role, what is it?
3. In this poem Milton criticizes the English clergy at the same time he praises his friend. Do you feel that this kind of critical attack is out of place in a poem of praise for the dead? Why or why not?

TO THE MEMORY OF MR. OLDHAM

1. Marcellus was a Roman general and statesman whose dates are 268?–208 B.C. Why does Dryden mention him in connection with Oldham? How is Oldham the "Marcellus of our tongue!"?
2. Does Dryden imply that Oldham had not yet reached full perfection and maturity as a poet? Where? Is there any passage in the poem which praises Oldham as a man?
3. When Dryden writes that he and Oldham were "Cast in the same poetic mold," he is paying the highest compliment to Oldham. Why?

ELEGY TO THE MEMORY OF AN UNFORTUNATE LADY

1. What verse form does Pope use in this elegy? Do you think that this verse form is appropriate for an elegiac poem? Why or why not?
2. Where in the elegy does Pope make any comment about poets and poetry? How does he relate his feelings about poets to the death of the young lady?
3. What is Pope's attitude toward the lady's uncle, her evidently rather cruel guardian? What destiny does Pope predict for this man and his issue? Do you feel Pope's harsh criticism of the uncle is out of place in an elegy to the niece? Why or why not?
4. Does Pope really have anything to praise the lady for, or must he content himself only with feeling sorry for her?

ELEGY WRITTEN IN A COUNTRY CHURCHYARD

1. According to the definition of *elegy* in the glossary, is Gray's poem an elegy? Why or why not?
2. What do you consider to be the poem's theme? Is the epitaph at the end of the poem consistent with the main theme? Explain your answer.
3. You will find that Gray's lines read slowly and quietly. How does he slow the pace of his verse to achieve the somber, lonely, quiet sense of meditation in the poem?

ADONAIS

1. How important is Shelley's grief for Keats in this poem? In other words, who is the more important character, the mourner or the dead man?
2. This suggests another question. Is Shelley concerned only with Keats' tragic death or is the death really a point of departure for

Shelley to discuss other matters of concern to him? What are these other matters?

3. What is Shelley's view of an afterlife? Does he anywhere suggest a personal immortality? The first half of stanza 60 has been called "Shelley's most exalted statement" of the opposition between eternal reality and the illusory physical world (a Platonic doctrine which Shelley embraced). Attempt to explain those five lines.

WHEN LILACS LAST IN THE DOORYARD BLOOM'D

1. Discuss Whitman's use of the poem's three major symbols: the lilac, the western star, and the thrush. What does each symbolize, and how are all three interwoven throughout the poem?

2. In this century numerous American public figures have been assassinated. Would Whitman's elegy be a suitable tribute for John F. Kennedy or Martin Luther King, for example? Why or why not?

3. Discuss Whitman's use of sound patterns in the poem. What kinds of sounds predominate? How does Whitman use sound to create a prayerful, meditative, quiet air?

THYRSIS

1. Like Arnold, Clough was a poet. Does Arnold praise his subject as a poet, a man, or as both? Exactly what does Clough mean to Arnold? Is it fair to say, in this connection, that the poem is as much about Arnold as it is about Clough? Why?

2. What do the Scholar Gipsy, Clough, and the tree symbolize in this poem?

3. On what note does the poem end? Does the ending focus more on Clough than on Arnold? What is Arnold's frame of mind at the poem's end? It has been reported that Arnold did not send a copy of this poem to Clough's widow. Can you think of any reason why Arnold might not have wanted to do this?

ODE TO THE CONFEDERATE DEAD

1. Zeno and Parmenides were both Greek philosophers. Here Tate attributes rage to them. Why? Why does he mention them at all here? What relevance do they have for the poem's subject?

2. Discuss the symbol of the leaves. How does Tate interweave the symbolism of the leaves to unify the poem? What thematic significance is suggested by the leaves?

3. What attitude does Tate wish us to have toward the Confederate dead? What, for example, does Tate mean when he asks, "Shall we, more hopeful, set up the grave / In the house?"

IN MEMORY OF W. B. YEATS

1.   What kinds of images does Auden employ in this poem? Is it fair
     to say that relatively recent discoveries in science have expanded
     the world from which the poet may select images?
2.   In the first part of the poem the death of Yeats is contrasted with
     what? In what language is this comparison sustained?
3.   What view of poetry does Auden present in section two of the
     poem?
4.   What verse form does Auden use to create the incantatory tone
     achieved in section three? Why is this incantation especially ap-
     propriate in an elegy of this kind?

ELEGY FOR A DEAD SOLDIER

1.   Note the number of times the word "one" appears in this poem;
     the word also appears in the epitaph. What does its frequent ap-
     pearance suggest about the poem's theme? Are there other words
     which connote the same idea?
2.   What is the attitude of the speaker toward the dead soldier? How
     involved is the speaker with the death of his fallen comrade? Is
     there a universality conveyed even about the individuality of
     death?
3.   What kind of person was the dead soldier in life? Does the speaker
     discuss the faults as well as the virtues of the dead soldier? Cite
     passages to support your answer.
4.   The last line of the epitaph states, "Know that one soldier has not
     died in vain." How does the total poem seem to justify this final
     statement?

DEATH

Death is man's most universal experience. It is an experience about which sensitive and intelligent men have always speculated. In this anthology, for example, the poets' emotional and intellectual responses to death range all the way from enthusiastic welcome to fierce raging, from loud defiance to quiet acceptance.

"Holy Sonnet X" (Death be not proud), a seventeenth-century poem, states the traditional Christian belief that man's soul is everlasting. Donne says that, paradoxically, by dying we conquer death and are then able to live forever. Donne, himself a clergyman, is the great poet of paradox, as "Holy Sonnet X" clearly shows. In reading this poem the student should note the simple, clear, masculine language with which Donne changes his fear of death into a feeling of triumph.

"Ode to the West Wind," one of Shelley's best lyrics, sees in outer nature a symbol corresponding to the poet's inner mood. As autumn comes, nature ceases to be fertile; Shelley identifies this with a sense of futility and yearns to be productive as a poet and moral teacher. He compares his sense of inner listlessness to the torpor of nature. Yet, the poem ends on an optimistic note. Shelley hopes that he will be as subject to the power of the west wind (nature) as the leaf, the cloud, and the wave are. In fact, he wishes nature to use him as her servant, imparting her message to all mankind—much as the Biblical writers did, not from their own points of view, but from God's. In this poem the "death" involved is a symbolic one, associated with the passage of the seasons—the decay of autumn, the death of winter. But in this cyclical certainty Shelley finds the gloriously optimistic affirmation that decay and death are inexorably followed by rebirth, the new growth of spring.

The point of view from which "Hamatreya" is told makes this poem markedly different from the others in this section. As the poem opens, we learn from the speaker that men who have bragged of their ownership of land are now dead. The point of view then shifts, and we learn from Earth in the "Earth-song" that *she* holds (or owns) men, not the opposite. On hearing this, the speaker of the poem loses his greedy and avaricious desire to be like one of the landlords who boasted of wealth and property.

"Crossing the Bar," like "Holy Sonnet X," expresses a traditional Christian view of life after death. Tennyson accents the word "hope" in this simple but moving poem as he states metaphorically his religious belief. Just as a skilled pilot must guide a ship over the shallow sandbar lying off shore, so must Christ pilot us across the dangerous shallows of death. It was, incidentally, Tennyson's wish that this poem always be printed last in any collection of his works.

Browning's "Epilogue to 'Asolando'" strikes a more positive and assured note concerning life after death than does Tennyson's "Crossing the Bar." The speaker of the poem, close to death, refuses to indulge in self-pity. His life has been vigorous and full, and he has always held to the faith that physical death leads to spiritual rebirth. He will not cringe at the prospect of death; indeed, he will greet it "with a cheer." Christian optimism can hardly be carried further.

On the other hand, "Out of the Cradle Endlessly Rocking" is not a Christian poem at all in the orthodox sense. Here, Whitman expresses once again his belief in a cyclical theory of existence, just as he does in "There Was a Child Went Forth." Conception, birth, growth, maturity, decline, death — each follows the other inevitably, over and over again. Mankind is one, always and everywhere, and the experience of life is unified and repetitious. It is as if we were all parts of some master soul which combines and unifies all our individual fragments.

Emily Dickinson's "Because I Could Not Stop for Death" is told from the point of view of one who is dead. It poses a striking contrast between living activity and death; note, for example, the children playing at school as Death drives the speaker by in his carriage. Probably the most arresting metaphor in the poem is the comparison between the grave and a house, surely a chilling figure of speech.

The emphasis shifts in "Up-Hill" to the universality and inevitability of death. Viewing life as a journey up or down a hill is a common metaphorical device. (Note Robert Burns' "John Anderson, My Jo" in another section.) The intensely religious Christina Rossetti builds her poem around a simple question-answer technique, with God providing calm assurance that there will be a provision in his heavenly inn for all who seek accommodations. The simple, quiet faith presented in this poem differs markedly from the robust assertion of faith in Browning's "Epilogue to 'Asolando.'"

"The Garden of Proserpine" requires a special word of explanation. Proserpine was a mythological goddess who was carried off to Hades by Pluto. The daughter of Ceres (Demeter) and Zeus, Proserpine had to spend six months of each year in Hades, returning to earth only in springtime. Swinburne emphasizes Proserpine's role as the goddess of death or of the final sleep and associates her also with the sea, which becomes a symbol of permanence amid apparent change. Swinburne's attitude toward death differs significantly from the views of Donne, Browning, or Christina Rossetti, for he asserts that man should be thankful that there is no life after death, that instead there is nothing but eternal sleep in an eternal night. However, as in "Up-Hill," there is emphasis on the inevitability and universality of death. Concerning technique, the student should note the unusual and persistent rhythm and meter of the poem.

The key word to be found in the poem "In Tenebris" is "unhope." A stark and disillusioned attitude prevails throughout. It is written from the point of view of one drained of all emotion, one so emptied of all hope and expectation that no event—not even one's own death—will apall or frighten the speaker of the poem. Hardy looks full into the face of destiny and sees nothing but blankness and indifference; the only solace he can find in his lamentations is that one cannot die more than once.

Housman's poem "To an Athlete Dying Young" echoes Hardy's emptiness and disillusionment. The theme of the poem is simple: death is welcome coming at the height of one's powers and abilities, before time and age erode the best of our accomplishments. The student should note the simple language of the poem; in particular, Housman's use of understatement is unparalleled in English literature. When the athlete dies, for example, Housman, instead of stating this fact, tells us that the young man is now the "Townsman of a stiller town."

"Do Not Go Gentle Into That Good Night," which was written by Dylan Thomas to his father, urges that those "on the sad height" of old age—those approaching their end—should rage fiercely against the inevitability of death. In fact, the overwhelming finality of death must be faced, Thomas says, with resistance and stubbornness. The cup of life, as it were, must be drained empty with enthusiasm and determination.

As the poems in this section reveal, man's response to the fact of death has been as varied as it has been universal. Poets, knowing that all men are engulfed finally by death, react to this with emotions ranging from eagerness to rage. Few poetic subjects exhibit more varied attitudes—the result perhaps of each man's personal realization that, in Hamlet's words, "to this end we must come."

HOLY SONNET X (Death be not proud)

Death, be not proud, though some have callèd thee
Mighty and dreadful, for thou art not so,
For those whom thou think'st thou dost overthrow
Die not, poor Death, nor yet canst thou kill me.
5   From rest and sleep, which but thy picture be,
Much pleasure, then from thee much more must flow;
And soonest our best men with thee do go —
Rest of their bones and souls' delivery!
Thou'rt slave to fate, chance, kings and desperate men,
10   And dost with poison, war, and sickness dwell,
And poppy or charms can make us sleep as well,
And better than thy stroke; why swell'st thou then?
One short sleep past, we wake eternally,
And death shall be no more: Death, thou shalt die!

John Donne   (1571? – 1631)

ODE TO THE WEST WIND

1

O wild West Wind, thou breath of Autumn's being,
Thou, from whose unseen presence the leaves dead
Are driven, like ghosts from an enchanter fleeing,

Yellow, and black, and pale, and hectic red,
5   Pestilence-stricken multitudes: O thou,
Who chariotest to their dark wintry bed

The wingéd seeds, where they lie cold and low,
Each like a corpse within its grave, until
Thine azure sister of the Spring shall blow

10   Her clarion o'er the dreaming earth, and fill
(Driving sweet buds like flocks to feed in air)
With living hues and odors plain and hill:

Wild Spirit, which art moving everywhere;
Destroyer and preserver; hear, oh, hear!

2

15 Thou on whose stream, mid the steep sky's commotion,
Loose clouds like earth's decaying leaves are shed,
Shook from the tangled boughs of Heaven and Ocean.

Angels of rain and lightning: there are spread
On the blue surface of thine aëry surge,
20 Like the bright hair uplifted from the head

Of some fierce Maenad, even from the dim verge
Of the horizon to the zenith's height,
The locks of the approaching storm. Thou dirge

Of the dying year, to which this closing night
25 Will be the dome of a vast sepulcher,
Vaulted with all thy congregated might

Of vapors, from whose solid atmosphere
Black rain, and fire, and hail will burst: oh, hear!

3

Thou who didst waken from his summer dreams
30 The blue Mediterranean, where he lay,
Lulled by the coil of his crystalline streams,

Beside a pumice isle in Baiae's bay,
And saw in sleep old palaces and towers
Quivering within the wave's intenser day,

35 All overgrown with azure moss and flowers
So sweet, the sense faints picturing them! Thou
For whose path the Atlantic's level powers

Cleave themselves into chasms, while far below
The sea-blooms and the oozy woods which wear
40 The sapless foliage of the ocean, know

Thy voice, and suddenly grow gray with fear,
And tremble and despoil themselves: oh, hear!

4

If I were a dead leaf thou mightest bear,
If I were a swift cloud to fly with thee;
45 A wave to pant beneath thy power, and share

The impulse of thy strength, only less free
Than thou, O uncontrollable! If even
I were as in my boyhood, and could be

The comrade of thy wanderings over Heaven,
50   As then, when to outstrip thy skyey speed
Scarce seemed a vision; I would ne'er have striven

As thus with thee in prayer in my sore need.
Oh, lift me as a wave, a leaf, a cloud!
I fall upon the thorns of life! I bleed!

55   A heavy weight of hours has chained and bowed
One too like thee: tameless, and swift, and proud.

5

Make me thy lyre, even as the forest is:
What if my leaves are falling like its own!
The tumult of thy mighty harmonies

60   Will take from both a deep, autumnal tone,
Sweet though in sadness. Be thou, Spirit fierce,
My spirit! Be thou me, impetuous one!

Drive my dead thoughts over the universe
Like withered leaves to quicken a new birth!
65   And, by the incantation of this verse,

Scatter, as from an unextinguished hearth
Ashes and sparks, my words among mankind!
Be through my lips to unawakened earth

The trumpet of a prophecy! O Wind,
70   If Winter comes, can Spring be far behind?

Percy Bysshe Shelley   (1792 – 1822)

HAMATREYA

Bulkeley, Hunt, Willard, Hosmer, Meriam, Flint
Possessed the land which rendered to their toil
Hay, corn, roots, hemp, flax, apples, wool and wood.
Each of these landlords walked amidst his farm,
5   Saying, " 'Tis mine, my children's and my name's.

How sweet the west wind sounds in my own trees!
How graceful climb those shadows on my hill!
I fancy these pure waters and the flags
Know me, as does my dog: we sympathize;
10 And, I affirm, my actions smack of the soil.''

Where are these men? Asleep beneath their grounds:
And strangers, fond as they, their furrows plough.
Earth laughs in flowers, to see her boastful boys
Earth-proud, proud of the earth which is not theirs;
15 Who steer the plough, but cannot steer their feet
Clear of the grave.
They added ridge to valley, brook to pond,
And sighed for all that bounded their domain;
"This suits me for a pasture; that's my park;
20 We must have clay, lime, gravel, granite-ledge,
And misty lowland, where to go for peat.
The land is well, — lies fairly to the south.
'Tis good, when you have crossed the sea and back,
To find the sitfast acres where you left them."
25 Ah! the hot owner sees not Death, who adds
Him to his land, a lump of mould the more.
Hear what the Earth says: —

   Earth-song

   "Mine and yours;
30   Mine, not yours.
   Earth endures;
   Stars abide —
   Shine down in the old sea;
   Old are the shores;
35   But where are old men?
   I who have seen much,
   Such have I never seen.

   "The lawyer's deed
   Ran sure,
40   In tail,
   To them, and to their heirs
   Who shall succeed,
   Without fail,
   Forevermore.

45   "Here is the land,
   Shaggy with wood,
   With its old valley,
   Mound and flood.
   But the heritors? —

50   Fled like the flood's foam.
         The lawyer, and the laws,
         And the kingdom,
         Clean swept herefrom.

         "They called me theirs,
55   Who so controlled me;
         Yet every one
         Wished to stay, and is gone,
         How am I theirs,
         If they cannot hold me,
60   But I hold them?"

When I heard the Earth-song
I was no longer brave;
My avarice cooled
Like lust in the chill of the grave.

         Ralph Waldo Emerson   (1803 – 1882)

CROSSING THE BAR

Sunset and evening star,
    And one clear call for me!
And may there be no moaning of the bar,
    When I put out to sea,

5   But such a tide as moving seems asleep,
        Too full for sound and foam,
    When that which drew from out the boundless deep
        Turns again home.

Twilight and evening bell,
10   And after that the dark!
    And may there be no sadness of farewell,
        When I embark;

    For tho' from out our bourne of Time and Place
        The flood may bear me far,
15   I hope to see my Pilot face to face
        When I have crost the bar.

         Alfred, Lord Tennyson   (1809 – 1892)

EPILOGUE TO "ASOLANDO"

At the midnight in the silence of the sleeptime,
   When you set your fancies free,
Will they pass to where — by death, fools think, imprisoned —
Low he lies who once so loved you, whom you loved so,
5   — Pity me?

Oh to love so, be so loved, yet so mistaken!
   What had I on earth to do
With the slothful, with the mawkish, the unmanly?
Like the aimless, helpless, hopeless, did I drivel
10   — Being — who?

One who never turned his back but marched breast forward,
   Never doubted clouds would break,
Never dreamed, though right were worsted, wrong would triumph,
Held we fall to rise, are baffled to fight better,
15   Sleep to wake.

No, at noonday in the bustle of man's worktime
   Greet the unseen with a cheer!
Bid him forward, breast and back as either should be,
   'Strive and thrive!' cry 'Speed, — fight on, fare ever
20   There as here!'

Robert Browning (1812 – 1889)

OUT OF THE CRADLE ENDLESSLY ROCKING

Out of the cradle endlessly rocking,
Out of the mocking-bird's throat, the musical shuttle,
Out of the Ninth-month midnight,
Over the sterile sands and the fields beyond, where the child leaving
   his bed wander'd alone, bareheaded, barefoot,
5 Down from the shower'd halo,
Up from the mystic play of shadows twining and twisting as if they
   were alive,
Out from the patches of briers and blackberries,
From the memories of the bird that chanted to me,
From your memories sad brother, from the fitful risings and fallings I
   heard,

From under that yellow half-moon late-risen and swollen as if with
10   tears,
From those beginning notes of yearning and love there in the mist,
From the thousand responses of my heart never to cease,
From the myriad thence-arous'd words,
From the word stronger and more delicious than any,
15   From such as now they start the scene revisiting,
As a flock, twittering, rising, or overhead passing,
Borne hither, ere all eludes me, hurriedly,
A man, yet by these tears a little boy again,
Throwing myself on the sand, confronting the waves,
20   I, chanter of pains and joys, uniter of here and hereafter,
Taking all hints to use them, but swiftly leaping beyond them,
A reminiscence sing.

Once Paumanok,
When the lilac-scent was in the air and Fifth-month grass was growing,
25   Up this seashore in some briers,
Two feather'd guests from Alabama, two together,
And their nest, and four light-green eggs spotted with brown,
And every day the he-bird to and fro near at hand,
And every day the she-bird crouch'd on her nest, silent, with bright
              eyes,
30   And every day I, a curious boy, never too close, never disturbing them,
Cautiously peering, absorbing, translating.

Shine! shine! shine!
Pour down your warmth, great sun!
While we bask, we two together.

35   *Two together!*
Winds blow south, or winds blow north,
Day come white, or night come black,
Home, or rivers and mountains from home,
Singing all time, minding no time,
40   *While we two keep together.*

Till of a sudden,
May-be kill'd, unknown to her mate,
One forenoon the she-bird crouch'd not on the nest,
Nor return'd that afternoon, nor the next,
45   Nor ever appear'd again.

And thenceforward all summer in the sound of the sea,
And at night under the full of the moon in calmer weather,
Over the hoarse surging of the sea,
Or flitting from brier to brier by day,
50   I saw, I heard at intervals the remaining one, the he-bird,
The solitary guest from Alabama.

Blow! blow! blow!
Blow up sea-winds along Paumanok's shore;
I wait and I wait till you blow my mate to me.

55   Yes, when the stars glisten'd,
        All night long on the prong of a moss-scallop'd stake,
        Down almost amid the slapping waves,
        Sat the lone singer wonderful causing tears.

        He call'd on his mate,
60   He pour'd forth the meanings which I of all men know.

        Yes my brother I know,
        The rest might not, but I have treasur'd every note,
        For more than once dimly down to the beach gliding,
        Silent, avoiding the moonbeams, blending myself with the shadows,
65   Recalling now the obscure shapes, the echoes, the sounds and sights
            after their sorts,
        The white arms out in the breakers tirelessly tossing,
        I, with bare feet, a child, the wind wafting my hair,
        Listen'd long and long.

        Listen'd to keep, to sing, now translating the notes,
70   Following you my brother.

        Soothe! soothe! soothe!
        Close on its wave soothes the wave behind,
        And again another behind embracing and lapping, every one close,
        But my love soothes not me, not me.

75   *Low hangs the moon, it rose late,*
        It is lagging—O I think it is heavy with love, with love.

        O madly the sea pushes upon the land,
        With love, with love.
        O night! do I not see my love fluttering out among the breakers?
80   *What is that little black thing I see there in the white?*

        Loud! loud! loud!
        Loud I call to you, my love!

        High and clear I shoot my voice over the waves,
        Surely you must know who is here, is here,
85   *You must know whom I am, my love.*

        Low-hanging moon!
        What is that dusky spot in your brown yellow?
        O it is the shape, the shape of my mate!
        O moon do not keep her from me any longer.

90   *Land! land! O land!*
         Whichever way I turn, O I think you could give me my mate back
                 again if you only would,
         For I am almost sure I see her dimly whichever way I look.

         O rising stars!
         Perhaps the one I want so much will rise, will rise with some of you.

95   *O throat! O trembling throat!*
         Sound clearer through the atmosphere!
         Pierce the woods, the earth,
         Somewhere listening to catch you must be the one I want.

         Shake out carols!
100   *Solitary here, the night's carols!*
         Carols of lonesome love! death's carols!
         Carols under that lagging, yellow, waning moon!
         O under that moon where she droops almost down into the sea!
         O reckless despairing carols.

105   *But soft! sink low!*
         Soft! let me just murmur,
         And do you wait a moment you husky-nois'd sea,
         For somewhere I believe I heard my mate responding to me,
         So faint, I must be still, be still to listen,
110   *But not altogether still, for then she might not come immediately to*
                 me.

         Hither my love!
         Here I am! here!
         With this just-sustain'd note I announce myself to you,
         This gentle call is for you my love, for you.

115   *Do not be decoy'd elsewhere,*
         That is the whistle of the wind, it is not my voice,
         That is the fluttering, the fluttering of the spray,
         Those are the shadows of leaves.

         O darkness! O in vain!
120   *O I am very sick and sorrowful.*

         O brown halo in the sky near the moon, drooping upon the sea!
         O troubled reflection in the sea!
         O throat! O throbbing heart!
         And I singing uselessly, uselessly all the night.

125   *O past! O happy life! O songs of joy!*
      In the air, in the woods, over fields,
      Loved! loved! loved! loved! loved!
      But my mate no more, no more with me!
      We two together no more.

130   The aria sinking,
      All else continuing, the stars shining,
      The winds blowing, the notes of the bird continuous echoing,
      With angry moans the fierce old mother incessantly moaning,
      On the sands of Paumanok's shore gray and rustling,
135   The yellow half-moon enlarged, sagging down, drooping, the face of
            the sea almost touching,
      The boy ecstatic, with his bare feet the waves, with his hair the atmos-
            phere dallying,
      The love in the heart long pent, now loose, now at last tumultuously
            bursting,
      The aria's meaning, the ears, the soul, swiftly depositing,
      The strange tears down the cheeks coursing,
140   The colloquy there, the trio, each uttering,
      The undertone, the savage old mother incessantly crying,
      To the boy's soul's questions sullenly timing, some drown'd secret
            hissing,
      To the outsetting bard.

      Demon or bird! (said the boy's soul,)
145   Is it indeed toward your mate you sing? or is it really to me?
      For I, that was a child, my tongue's use sleeping, now I have heard
            you,
      Now in a moment I know what I am for, I awake,
      And already a thousand singers, a thousand songs, clearer, louder and
            more sorrowful than yours,
      A thousand warbling echoes have started to life within me, never to
            die.

150   O you singer solitary, singing by yourself, projecting me,
      O solitary me listening, never more shall I cease perpetuating you,
      Never more shall I escape, never more the reverberations,
      Never more the cries of unsatisfied love be absent from me,
      Never again leave me to be the peaceful child I was before what there
            in the night,
155   By the sea under the yellow and sagging moon,
      The messenger there arous'd, the fire, the sweet hell within,
      The unknown want, the destiny of me.

      O give me the clew! (it lurks in the night here somewhere,)
      O if I am to have so much, let me have more!

160   A word then, (for I will conquer it,)
    The word final, superior to all,
    Subtle, sent up — what is it? — I listen;
    Are you whispering it, and have been all the time, you sea waves?
    Is that it from your liquid rims and wet sands?

165   Whereto answering, the sea,
    Delaying not, hurrying not,
    Whisper'd me through the night, and very plainly before daybreak,
    Lisp'd to me the low and delicious word death,
    And again death, death, death, death,
170   Hissing melodious, neither like the bird nor like my arous'd child's
       heart,
    But edging near as privately for me rustling at my feet,
    Creeping thence steadily up to my ears and laving me softly all over,
    Death, death, death, death, death.

    Which I do not forget,
175   But fuse the song of my dusky demon and brother,
    That he sang to me in the moonlight on Paumanok's gray beach,
    With the thousand responsive songs at random,
    My own songs awaked from that hour,
    And with them the key, the word up from the waves,
180   The word of the sweetest song and all songs,
    That strong and delicious word which, creeping to my feet,
    (Or like some old crone rocking the cradle, swathed in sweet gar-
       ments, bending aside,)
    The sea whisper'd me.

Walt Whitman (1819 – 1892)

BECAUSE I COULD NOT STOP FOR DEATH

    Because I could not stop for Death,
    He kindly stopped for me;
    The carriage held but just ourselves
    And Immortality.

5   We slowly drove, he knew no haste,
    And I had put away
    My labor, and my leisure too,
    For his civility.

10   We passed the school where children played
      At wrestling in a ring;
      We passed the fields of gazing grain,
      We passed the setting sun.

      We paused before a house that seemed
      A swelling of the ground;
15   The roof was scarcely visible,
      The cornice but a mound.

      Since then 'tis centuries; but each
      Feels shorter than the day
      I first surmised the horses' heads
20   Were toward eternity.

                    Emily Dickinson   (1830 – 1886)

UPHILL

      Does the road wind uphill all the way?
          Yes, to the very end.
      Will the day's journey take the whole long day?
          From morn to night, my friend.

5   But is there for the night a resting-place?
          A roof for when the slow dark hours begin.
      May not the darkness hide it from my face?
          You cannot miss that inn.

      Shall I meet other wayfarers at night?
10   Those who have gone before.
      Then must I knock, or call when just in sight?
          They will not keep you standing at that door.

      Shall I find comfort, travel-sore and weak?
          Of labor you shall find the sum.
15   Will there be beds for me and all who seek?
          Yea, beds for all who come.

                    Christina Rossetti   (1830 – 1894)

THE GARDEN OF PROSERPINE

Here, where the world is quiet;
  Here, where all trouble seems
Dead winds' and spent waves' riot
  In doubtful dreams of dreams;
5 I watch the green field growing
For reaping folk and sowing,
For harvest-time and mowing,
  A sleepy world of streams.

I am tired of tears and laughter,
10   And men that laugh and weep;
Of what may come hereafter
  For men that sow to reap:
I am weary of days and hours,
Blown buds of barren flowers
15 Desires and dreams and powers
  And everything but sleep.

Here life has death for neighbour,
  And far from eye or ear
Wan waves and wet winds labour,
20   Weak ships and spirits steer;
They drive adrift, and whither
They wot not who make thither;
But no such winds blow hither,
  And no such things grow here.

25 No growth of moor or coppice,
  No heather-flower or vine,
But bloomless buds of poppies,
  Green grapes of Proserpine,
Pale beds of blowing rushes
30 Where no leaf blooms or blushes
Save this whereout she crushes
  For dead men deadly wine.

Pale, without name or number,
  In fruitless fields of corn,
35 They bow themselves and slumber
  All night till light is born;
And like a soul belated,
In hell and heaven unmated,
By cloud and mist abated
40   Comes out of darkness morn.

Though one were strong as seven,
    He too with death shall dwell,
Nor wake with wings in heaven,
    Nor weep for pains in hell;
45   Though one were fair as roses,
His beauty clouds and closes;
And well though love reposes,
    In the end it is not well.

Pale, beyond porch and portal,
50   Crowned with calm leaves, she stands
Who gathers all things mortal
    With cold immortal hands;
Her languid lips are sweeter
Than love's who fears to greet her
55   To men that mix and meet her
    From many times and lands.

She waits for each and other,
    She waits for all men born;
Forgets the earth her mother,
60   The life of fruits and corn;
And spring and seed and swallow
Take wing for her and follow
Where summer song rings hollow
    And flowers are put to scorn.

65   There go the loves that wither,
    The old loves with wearier wings;
And all dead years draw thither,
    And all disastrous things;
Dead dreams of days forsaken,
70   Blind buds that snows have shaken,
Wild leaves that winds have taken,
    Red strays of ruined springs.

We are not sure of sorrow,
    And joy was never sure;
75   To-day will die to-morrow;
    Time stoops to no man's lure;
And love, grown faint and fretful,
With lips but half regretful
Sighs, and with eyes forgetful
80   Weeps that no loves endure.

From too much love of living,
    From hope and fear set free,

We thank with brief thanksgiving
  Whatever gods may be
85 That no life lives for ever;
That dead men rise up never;
That even the weariest river
  Winds somewhere safe to sea.

Then star nor sun shall waken,
90   Nor any change of light:
Nor sound of waters shaken,
  Nor any sound or sight:
Nor wintry leaves nor vernal,
Nor days nor things diurnal;
95 Only the sleep eternal
  In an eternal night.

A. C. Swinburne   (1837 – 1909)

IN TENEBRIS I

  Wintertime nighs;
But my bereavement-pain
It cannot bring again:
  Twice no one dies.

5   Flower-petals flee;
But, since it once hath been,
No more that severing scene
  Can harrow me.

  Birds faint in dread:
10 I shall not lose old strength
In the lone frost's black length:
  Strength long since fled!

  Leaves freeze to dun;
But friends cannot turn cold
15 This season as of old
  For him with none.

  Tempests may scath;
But love cannot make smart
Again this year his heart
20   Who no heart hath.

Black is night's cope;
But death will not appal
One who, past doubtings all,
 Waits in unhope.

Thomas Hardy   (1840–1928)

TO AN ATHLETE DYING YOUNG

The time you won your town the race
We chaired you through the market-place;
Man and boy stood cheering by,
And home we brought you shoulder-high.

5 Today, the road all runners come,
Shoulder high we bring you home,
And set you at your threshold down,
Townsman of a stiller town.

Smart lad, to slip betimes away
10 From fields where glory does not stay,
And early though the laurel grows
It withers quicker than the rose.

Eyes the shady night has shut
Cannot see the record cut,
15 And silence sounds no worse than cheers
After earth has stopped the ears:

Now you will not swell the rout
Of lads that wore their honors out,
Runners whom renown outran
20 And the name died before the man.

So set, before its echoes fade,
The fleet foot on the sill of shade,
And hold to the low lintel up
The still-defended challenge-cup.

25 And round that early-laureled head
Will flock to gaze the strengthless dead,
And find unwithered on its curls
The garland briefer than a girl's.

A. E. Housman   (1859–1936)

DO NOT GO GENTLE INTO THAT GOOD NIGHT

Do not go gentle into that good night,
Old age should burn and rave at close of day;
Rage, rage against the dying of the light.

Though wise men at their end know dark is right,
5   Because their words had forked no lightning they
Do not go gentle into that good night.

Good men, the last wave by, crying how bright
Their frail deeds might have danced in a green bay,
Rage, rage against the dying of the light.

10   Wild men who caught and sang the sun in flight,
And learn, too late, they grieved it on its way,
Do not go gentle into that good night.

Grave men, near death, who see with blinding sight
Blind eyes could blaze like meteors and be gay,
15   Rage, rage against the dying of the light.

And you, my father, there on the sad height,
Curse, bless, me now with your fierce tears, I pray.
Do not go gentle into that good night.
Rage, rage against the dying of the light.

Dylan Thomas   (1914–1953)

QUESTIONS FOR DISCUSSION AND FURTHER STUDY

HOLY SONNET X (DEATH BE NOT PROUD)

1. This poem depends largely on personification for its effect. How does Donne convey the impression that death is not an abstraction but a personality?
2. How would you characterize Donne's language in this poem? Is it blunt, forceful, weak, vague, specific, or what? Relate the language to the meaning of the poem. For example, if you think the language is forceful, how is that sense of force related to Donne's affirmation of an afterlife?
3. What images other than the personification of death appear in this poem?

ODE TO THE WEST WIND

1. The stanzaic form used by Shelley in this poem is called *terza rima*. Note that the middle rhyme of each stanza becomes the first rhyme of the next stanza. What sound effect does this produce? Does the technique help produce unity?
2. What, specifically, does Shelley ask the west wind to do for him? Why could this poem also have been included in the "Poetry and Literature" section?
3. In Greek mythology the Maenads were nymphs who attended Dionysus; since they participated in Bacchanalian rituals, they became known as fierce or raging women. Why does Shelley mention them here?
4. The last two lines of this poem are often quoted as an expression of optimism. In what way can they be considered such? In what way are they consistent with the rest of the poem?

HAMATREYA

1. What is Emerson's view of property, as might be inferred from this poem? What roles do law and farming play in Emerson's theme?
2. What is compared in the poem with the brevity of man's life (and the inevitability of his death)?
3. How effective is the shift in the narrative point of view which occurs in this poem?

CROSSING THE BAR

1.   What images does Tennyson use to describe the literal fact of death? How does the evident simplicity of imagery enhance the total effect of the poem?
2.   Do you feel that this poem is sentimental, perhaps excessively so? Why or why not?
3.   Who is the Pilot in the last stanza? In actual nautical practice a pilot is needed when a ship leaves the harbor, for he guides it through the bars found near harbor entrances. Normally the pilot leaves the ship once it has crossed the bars. How is Tennyson's metaphor inaccurate? How does the inaccuracy affect the poem's meaning?

EPILOGUE TO "ASOLANDO"

1.   This poem is normally printed at the end of selections from Browning's poetry. Why do you suppose that editors do this?
2.   In what emotional and physical condition is the speaker in the poem? What images does Browning use to mark man's progress through life?
3.   Do you feel that Browning is being foolishly optimistic when he writes "Greet the unseen with a cheer!"? Is there any passage in the poem which indicates that the speaker has earned – through suffering and doubt – the right to make such a statement?

OUT OF THE CRADLE ENDLESSLY ROCKING

1.   What images does Whitman use to suggest the cyclical theory of existence in which he believed? How does the title itself present such an image?
2.   This is a philosophical poem, and it has been said that philosophical poetry is always doomed to failure, the idea being that philosophy is abstract and poetry concrete. Whitman's poem is written in free verse. Why might it be that a free-verse philosophical poem could serve the purposes of both disciplines?
3.   Why are some sections of the poem in italics, while some are in normal Roman type?

BECAUSE I COULD NOT STOP FOR DEATH

1.   Death is spoken of here as being kind and civil. Does Emily Dickinson mean this ironically or literally? How can you support your answer?

2.   What effect is gained by contrasting the journey into eternity with the children's play in the schoolyard?
3.   Identify specifically the figure of speech used in the fourth stanza to describe a grave.

UPHILL

1.   What rhetorical technique does Christina Rossetti use to narrate her poem? In this connection, how many speakers are there in the poem? Who are they?
2.   What view of life is implied by the title? What notion of an afterlife is at least suggested in the poem?
3.   The poem depends largely on one sustained metaphor. Describe this metaphor. What details are to be found in it which lend concreteness and power to the poem's central idea?

THE GARDEN OF PROSERPINE

1.   What is Swinburne's attitude toward death? Does he approach it reluctantly or with gratitude? In what stanza of the poem is there an almost direct answer to this question?
2.   Describe the rhyme scheme used in this poem. What effect does Swinburne achieve by using both one- and two-syllable rhymes?
3.   What is the poet's attitude toward an afterlife? What lines in the poem specifically indicate his attitude? How is his boredom with this life related to his feelings about an afterlife?

IN TENEBRIS I

1.   Hardy's poem shares much in common with "The Garden of Proserpine." What are the main points of similarity?
2.   Note the number of negative words used in this poem. Why is negative language especially appropriate and effective in a poem with this theme?
3.   The line length is brief, the rhymes are of one syllable, and the language is simple. Again, in terms of theme, how do these elements contribute to the poem as a whole?

TO AN ATHLETE DYING YOUNG

1.   Characterize Housman's language. As you note its simplicity, try to analyze the reasons why this plain, simple language is more effective in a bleak poem like this than ornate, heightened language would have been.

2.   What is Housman's view of life? Does he suggest that it is without meaning entirely? Is there no compensation for existence in
his mind? Also, what is his view of an afterlife? Do you find any
suggestion that consciousness endures after death?

3.   How do you feel about the poem's central statement, that is, that
it is better to die young in the midst of one's triumph than to live
long enough to become an object of pity or scorn? Can you think
of any public figures in recent times who outlived their glory and
others who died at or near the height of their careers?

DO NOT GO GENTLE INTO THAT GOOD NIGHT

1.   What is significant about the first and last rhymes of each stanza?
What of the rhyme in each stanza's second line? What effect does
this technique have on the structure of the poem?

2.   To what does the basic metaphor in this poem compare a man's
life?

3.   Imagery of light occurs often in the poem. How does it support the
central metaphor and, indeed, the theme of the poem?

DESPAIR

Despair, when it is treated in poetry, seems to arise from one of two causes: some biographical incident, like the death of a loved one, or some more abstract, philosophical notion, such as the conviction that there is no God. The two categories overlap, of course, and often a poem will treat both personal and philosophical reasons for the poet's despondency.

Of the poems in which despair is caused primarily by philosophical belief rather than personal suffering, the earliest represented in this collection is the "Ode on Melancholy" by John Keats. Keats is conscious of his own personal despair. He wanted but two things in life, the love of Fanny Brawne and poetic success; because of tuberculosis he knew he was to get neither. This ode explores in general terms the relation between joy and despair. In the first stanza, Keats tells us not to seek melancholy among the settings or stage properties usually associated with it. "But when the melancholy fit shall fall," he tells us in the second stanza, we should seek out and contemplate beautiful things. The third stanza provides us with the cause of Keats' despair: beauty is transitory and must die; joy will always depart. Within all beauty, joy, pleasure, and delight there dwells the realization that it will pass—melancholy indeed dwells with its opposite.

In Arthur Hugh Clough's more religiously oriented poem "Where Lies the Land to Which the Ship Would Go?" despair is caused by doubt replacing faith. In one of his poems, Matthew Arnold, a close friend of Clough, writes that his generation is "Wandering between two worlds, one dead, / The other powerless to be born." In other words, man's faith has been weakened or destroyed, but nothing has replaced it. This is also the theme of Clough's poem, and he expresses the idea in a sustained metaphor; there is literally no place for man to anchor his hope. Note that this brief but striking poem opens and closes on the same questioning note.

Like Clough's poem, "Dover Beach" depends on an extended metaphor. As the poem opens, Arnold is looking across the English Channel, which is receding as the tide goes out. This suggests to Arnold that the sea of faith too was once full but is now emptying out. (Note the similarity in theme to Clough's poem.) Addressing his love, Arnold's audience in the poem, the poet goes on to say that, since there is no certainty about any absolute truth, all we can do as lovers is to be true to one another. Since the lack of certitude permeates all things, even love itself, Arnold looks upon the world with an existential bleakness. The reader should note the many images of darkness through which the poet describes an existence void of all hope.

"There's a Certain Slant of Light" by Emily Dickinson delicately suggests that despair might even come from heaven. At a certain time of day in winter, the poem states, a slant or beam of light sends rays of despair to us. Unaccountably, all the earth seems to become still and the look of death accompanies the light's going. Certainly the very simple language used in this chilling little poem contributes substantially to its effectiveness.

"Last Poems IX" (The chestnut casts his flambeaux) is one of Housman's most perfect lyrics. The setting of the poem is particularly remarkable. Storms have ruined the season of spring; the two youths drinking in the tavern are acutely conscious of just how few springs are given to them, and they are bitter at time's quick passage. Note the almost blasphemous statement that God is a "black guard" and life a "fool's-errand." Our troubles are permanent; our lives are not. All men of all times share as companions the same sorrows of life. The speaker feels our only compensations are alcohol and friendship. Although despair is caused by life's meaninglessness, the poem ends on a tone of stoicism – we *can* bear our lives, so we must.

The most fascinating thing about E. A. Robinson's "Richard Cory" is that the entire poem is a celebration of Cory's success – until the last line. Men are deceived by appearances, and all are jealous of Cory's success until his suicide. The surprising, climactic ending startles and shocks us, especially since we never really know just what did cause Cory's despair – a despair powerful enough to lead to suicide. The deceptively conversational tone of this poem is a major factor contributing to the effectiveness of the ending.

In "The Hollow Men" T. S. Eliot writes that the barrenness, emptiness, and sterility of modern life cause despair – we are indeed hollow. The language of this poem is admittedly difficult, but images constantly repeated suggest emptiness, barrenness, sterility, aridity, death, decay, and chaos. All is "broken," and the fragmented quotes from "The Lord's Prayer" suggest that modern man has succeeded in alienating himself from the traditions of his past. One could even suggest that T. S. Eliot is addressing the people who inherited the despair of Arnold and Clough two or three generations before. Note especially the two little jingling rhymes denoting barrenness. Instead of a mulberry bush we go round a "prickly pear"; the world ends not with a bang but a whimper.

Cecil Hemley's "If He Were Anywhere," the most recent of the philosophically oriented poems about despair, is a brief statement denying God's reality: "He is nameless, nothing, and nowhere." The poet wishes there were a God to serve, but he is convinced there is not. Here, the poet's despair is caused by the total lack of any evidence supporting the possibility of God's existence.

Coleridge's "Dejection: An Ode" provides a good transitional poem between those in which despair is primarily philosophical and those in which it is primarily biographical. Written during a period of despair over his own unhappy marriage and his unfulfilled love for Sara Hutchinson—the "Lady" to whom the poem was originally addressed—he attempts to delineate the loss of poetic power ("This beautiful and beauty-making power") that he experienced during his thirtieth year. Incidentally, the poem was first published on the day that his friend Wordsworth married Mary Hutchinson, Sara's sister. In many respects the poem resembles the despair of the first four stanzas of Wordsworth's "Ode: Intimations of Immortality," which Coleridge had probably seen in manuscript. In his earlier years Coleridge had believed that nature could inspire the poet to write, but now he realizes that one's internal powers are necessary to give "life" to nature. He can see things, but cannot feel them; his "shaping spirit of Imagination" has been numbed. The paradox, of course, is that Coleridge's poetic powers were rarely better than in this poem—in which he laments their loss.

Personal circumstances are also much in evidence in "Stanzas Written in Dejection, Near Naples." Shelley's life, it seemed, was reduced to chaos. His first wife, Harriet, had died a suicide, he was deprived of seeing their children, his baby Clara (by his second wife, Mary Godwin Shelley) had died, his love for Mary had cooled, and his poetry had failed to gain the large audience he wanted so desperately—only because he believed that poetry was the greatest moral teacher. Shelley's despair, then, is caused by personal and professional misfortunes, and he turns to despondency, to thoughts of his own death, and even to the possibility of suicide.

Tennyson's "Tears, Idle Tears" captures the mood of quiet melancholy which characterized much of his life and poetry. Here, the poet luxuriates in a kind of "divine despair," thinking of "the days that are no more." In simple but beautiful images the poem speaks of death, the loss of loved ones, and the transitoriness of life.

The last of the poems with a personal orientation is "Carrion Comfort" by Gerard Manley Hopkins. A deeply religious man and a Jesuit priest, he records in this poem a period of horrifying religious doubt and despair. The poem was written after a night of suffering nightmares. The octave describes in dramatic form the poet's battle with religious doubt, while the sestet employs a strategy of self-detachment to reveal to the poet the horror and blasphemy of his struggle with God. In its total impact the poem celebrates a victory over religious despair, though the intensity of the struggle makes that victory a somber one.

Clearly, then, some poets despair because of intellectual conviction, others because of personal misfortune; perhaps some combination of the two, however slight, is always involved.

DEJECTION: AN ODE

[written April 4, 1802]

Late, late yestreen I saw the new Moon,
With the old Moon in her arms;
And I fear, I fear, my Master dear!
We shall have a deadly storm.

Ballad of Sir Patrick Spence

I

Well! If the Bard was weather-wise, who made
   The grand old ballad of Sir Patrick Spence,
    This night, so tranquil now, will not go hence
Unroused by winds, that ply a busier trade
Than those which mould yon cloud in lazy flakes,
Or the dull sobbing draft, that moans and rakes
Upon the strings of this Aeolian lute,
    Which better far were mute.
    For lo! the New-moon winter-bright!
    And overspread with phantom light,
    (With swimming phantom light o'erspread
    But rimmed and circled by a silver thread)
I see the old Moon in her lap, foretelling
    The coming-on of rain and squally blast.
And oh! that even now the gust were swelling,
    And the slant night-shower driving loud and fast!
Those sounds which oft have raised me, whilst they awed,
    And sent my soul abroad,
Might now perhaps their wonted impulse give,
Might startle this dull pain, and make it move and live!

II

A grief without a pang, void, dark, and drear,
   A stifled, drowsy, unimpassioned grief,
   Which finds no natural outlet, no relief,
    In word, or sigh, or tear—
O Lady! in this wan and heartless mood,
To other thoughts by yonder throstle woo'd,
   All this long eve, so balmy and serene,
Have I been gazing on the western sky,
   And its peculiar tint of yellow green:
And still I gaze—and with how blank an eye!
And those thin clouds above, in flakes and bars,
That give away their motion to the stars;
Those stars, that glide behind them or between,
Now sparkling, now bedimmed, but always seen:

5

10

15

20

25

30

35   Yon crescent Moon, as fixed as if it grew
    In its own cloudless, starless lake of blue;
    I see them all so excellently fair,
    I see, not feel, how beautiful they are!

    III

     My genial spirits fail;
40   And what can these avail
    To lift the smothering weight from off my breast?
      It were a vain endeavour,
      Though I should gaze for ever
    On that green light that lingers in the west:
45   I may not hope from outward forms to win
    The passion and the life, whose fountains are within.

    IV

    O Lady! we receive but what we give,
    And in our life alone does Nature live:
    Ours is her wedding garment, ours her shroud!
50   And would we aught behold, of higher worth,
    Than that inanimate cold world allowed
    To the poor loveless ever-anxious crowd,
     Ah! from the soul itself must issue forth
    A light, a glory, a fair luminous cloud
55   Enveloping the Earth—
    And from the soul itself must there be sent
     A sweet and potent voice, of its own birth,
    Of all sweet sounds the life and element!

    V

    O pure of heart! thou need'st not ask of me
60   What this strong music in the soul may be!
    What, and wherein it doth exist,
    This light, this glory, this fair luminous mist,
    This beautiful and beauty-making power.
     Joy, virtuous Lady! Joy that ne'er was given,
65   Save to the pure, and in their purest hour,
    Life, and Life's effluence, cloud at once and shower,
    Joy, Lady! is the spirit and the power,
    Which wedding Nature to us gives in dower
     A new Earth and new Heaven,
70   Undreamt of by the sensual and the proud—
    Joy is the sweet voice, Joy the luminous cloud—
     We in ourselves rejoice!
    And thence flows all that charms or ear or sight,
     All melodies the echoes of that voice,
75   All colours a suffusion from that light.

VI

There was a time when, though my path was rough,
   This joy within me dallied with distress,
And all misfortunes were but as the stuff
   Whence Fancy made me dreams of happiness:
80   For hope grew round me, like the twining vine,
And fruits, and foliage, not my own, seemed mine.
But now afflictions bow me down to earth:
Nor care I that they rob me of my mirth;
     But oh! each visitation
85 Suspends what nature gave me at my birth,
   My shaping spirit of Imagination.
For not to think of what I needs must feel,
   But to be still and patient, all I can;
And haply by abstruse research to steal
90   From my own nature all the natural man—
   This was my sole resource, my only plan:
Till that which suits a part infects the whole,
And now is almost grown the habit of my soul.

VII

Hence, viper thoughts, that coil around my mind,
95   Reality's dark dream!
I turn from you, and listen to the wind,
   Which long has raved unnoticed. What a scream
Of agony by torture lengthened out
That lute sent forth! Thou Wind, that rav'st without,
100   Bare crag, or mountain-tairn, or blasted tree,
Or pine-grove whither woodman never clomb,
Or lonely house, long held the witches' home,
   Methinks were fitter instruments for thee,
Mad Lutanist! who in this month of showers,
105 Of dark-brown gardens, and of peeping flowers,
Mak'st Devils' yule, with worse than wintry song,
The blossoms, buds, and timorous leaves among.
   Thou Actor, perfect in all tragic sounds!
Thou mighty Poet, e'en to frenzy bold!
110   What tell'st thou now about?
    'Tis of the rushing of an host in rout,
   With groans, of trampled men, with smarting wounds—
At once they groan with pain, and shudder with the cold!
But hush! there is a pause of deepest silence!
115   And all that noise, as of a rushing crowd,
With groans, and tremulous shudderings—all is over—
   It tells another tale, with sounds less deep and loud!
    A tale of less affright,
    And tempered with delight,

120   As Otway's self had framed the tender lay, —
          'Tis of a little child
          Upon a lonesome wild,
      Not far from home, but she hath lost her way:
      And now moans low in bitter grief and fear,
125   And now screams loud, and hopes to make her mother hear.

      VIII

      'Tis midnight, but small thoughts have I of sleep:
      Full seldom may my friend such vigils keep!
      Visit her, gentle Sleep! with wings of healing,
          And may this storm be but a mountain-birth,
130   May all the stars hang bright above her dwelling,
          Silent as though they watched the sleeping Earth!
              With light heart may she rise,
              Gay fancy, cheerful eyes,
      Joy lift her spirit, joy attune her voice;
135   To her may all things live, from pole to pole,
      Their life the eddying of her living soul!
          O simple spirit, guided from above,
      Dear Lady! friend devoutest of my choice,
      Thus mayest thou ever, evermore rejoice.

                          Samuel Taylor Coleridge   (1772 – 1834)

STANZAS WRITTEN IN DEJECTION, NEAR NAPLES

      The sun is warm, the sky is clear,
          The waves are dancing fast and bright,
      Blue isles and snowy mountains wear
          The purple noon's transparent might,
5   The breath of the moist earth is light,
      Around its unexpanded buds;
          Like many a voice of one delight,
      The winds, the birds, the ocean floods,
      The City's voice itself, is soft like Solitude's.

10   I see the Deep's untrampled floor
          With green and purple seaweeds strown;
      I see the waves upon the shore,
          Like light dissolved in star-showers, thrown:
              I sit upon the sands alone, —
15   The lightning of the noontide ocean
              Is flashing round me, and a tone
      Arises from its measured motion,
      How sweet! did any heart now share in my emotion.

Alas! I have nor hope nor health,
20   Nor peace within nor calm around,
Nor that content surpassing wealth
        The sage in meditation found,
        And walked with inward glory crowned—
Nor fame, nor power, nor love, nor leisure.
25   Others I see whom these surround—
Smiling they live, and call life pleasure;—
To me that cup has been dealt in another measure.

Yet now despair itself is mild,
        Even as the winds and waters are;
30   I could lie down like a tired child,
        And weep away the life of care
        Which I have borne and yet must bear,
Till death like sleep might steal on me,
        And I might feel in the warm air
35   My cheek grow cold, and hear the sea
Breathe o'er my dying brain its last monotony.

Some might lament that I were cold,
        As I, when this sweet day is gone,
Which my lost heart, too soon grown old,
40   Insults with this untimely moan;
They might lament—for I am one
Whom men love not,—and yet regret,
        Unlike this day, which, when the sun
        Shall on its stainless glory set,
45   Will linger, though enjoyed, like joy in memory yet.

Percy Bysshe Shelley   (1792–1822)

ODE ON MELANCHOLY

No, no, go not to Lethe, neither twist
        Wolf's-bane, tight-rooted, for its poisonous wine;
Nor suffer thy pale forehead to be kissed
        By nightshade, ruby grape of Proserpine;
5   Make not your rosary of yew-berries,
        Nor let the beetle, nor the death-moth be
        Your mournful Psyche, nor the downy owl
A partner in your sorrow's mysteries;
        For shade to shade will come too drowsily,
10   And drown the wakeful anguish of the soul.

But when the melancholy fit shall fall
  Sudden from heaven like a weeping cloud,
That fosters the droop-headed flowers all,
  And hides the green hill in an April shroud;
15   Then glut thy sorrow on a morning rose,
    Or on the rainbow of the salt sand-wave,
      Or on the wealth of globèd peonies;
Or if thy mistress some rich anger shows,
    Emprison her soft hand, and let her rave,
20   And feed deep, deep upon her peerless eyes.

She dwells with Beauty — Beauty that must die,
  And Joy, whose hand is ever at his lips
Bidding adieu; and aching Pleasure nigh,
  Turning to poison while the bee-mouth sips:
25   Ay, in the very temple of delight
    Veiled Melancholy has her sovran shrine,
      Though seen of none save him whose strenuous tongue
Can burst Joy's grape against his palate fine;
  His soul shall taste the sadness of her might,
30   And be among her cloudy trophies hung.

John Keats   *(1795 – 1821)*

TEARS, IDLE TEARS

  Tears, idle tears, I know not what they mean,
Tears from the depth of some divine despair
Rise in the heart, and gather to the eyes,
In looking on the happy Autumn-fields,
5   And thinking of the days that are no more.

  Fresh as the first beam glittering on a sail,
That brings our friends up from the underworld,
Sad as the last which reddens over one
That sinks with all we love below the verge;
10   So sad, so fresh, the days that are no more.

  Ah, sad and strange as in dark summer dawns
The earliest pipe of half-awaken'd birds
To dying ears, when unto dying eyes
The casement slowly grows a glimmering square;
15   So sad, so strange, the days that are no more.

Dear as remember'd kisses after death,
And sweet as those by hopeless fancy feign'd
On lips that are for others; deep as love,
Deep as first love, and wild with all regret;
20   O Death in Life, the days that are no more.

Alfred, Lord Tennyson   (1809 – 1892)

WHERE LIES THE LAND TO WHICH THE SHIP WOULD GO?

Where lies the land to which the ship would go?
Far, far ahead, is all her seamen know.
And where the land she travels from? Away,
Far, far behind, is all that they can say.

5   On sunny noons upon the deck's smooth face,
Linked arm in arm, how pleasant here to pace;
Or, o'er the stern reclining, watch below
The foaming wake far widening as we go.

On stormy nights when wild north-westers rave,
10   How proud a thing to fight with wind and wave!
The dripping sailor on the reeling mast
Exults to bear, and scorns to wish it past.

Where lies the land to which the ship would go?
Far, far ahead, is all her seamen know.
15   And where the land she travels from? Away,
Far, far behind, is all that they can say.

Arthur Hugh Clough   (1819 – 1861)

DOVER BEACH

The sea is calm to-night.
The tide is full, the moon lies fair
Upon the straits; — on the French coast the light
Gleams and is gone; the cliffs of England stand,
5   Glimmering and vast, out in the tranquil bay.
Come to the window, sweet is the night-air!

Only, from the long line of spray
Where the sea meets the moon-blanch'd land,
Listen! you hear the grating roar
10   Of pebbles which the waves draw back, and fling,
At their return, up the high strand,
Begin, and cease, and then again begin,
With tremulous cadence slow, and bring
The eternal note of sadness in.

15   Sophocles long ago
Heard it on the Aegean, and it brought
Into his mind the turbid ebb and flow
Of human misery; we
Find also in the sound a thought,
20   Hearing it by this distant northern sea.

The Sea of Faith
Was once, too, at the full, and round earth's shore
Lay like the folds of a bright girdle furl'd.
But now I only hear
25   Its melancholy, long, withdrawing roar,
Retreating, to the breath
Of the night-wind, down the vast edges drear
And naked shingles of the world.

Ah, love, let us be true
30   To one another! for the world, which seems
To lie before us like a land of dreams,
So various, so beautiful, so new,
Hath really neither joy, nor love, nor light,
Nor certitude, nor peace, nor help for pain;
35   And we are here as on a darkling plain
Swept with confused alarms of struggle and flight,
Where ignorant armies clash by night.

                    Matthew Arnold   (1822 – 1888)

THERE'S A CERTAIN SLANT OF LIGHT

There's a certain slant of light,
On winter afternoons,
That oppresses, like the weight
Of cathedral tunes.

5   Heavenly hurt it gives us;
     We can find no scar,
     But internal difference
     Where the meanings are.

     None may teach it anything,
10   'Tis the seal, despair, —
     An imperial affliction
     Sent us of the air.

     When it comes, the landscape listens,
     Shadows hold their breath;
15   When it goes, 'tis like the distance
     On the look of death.

                   Emily Dickinson   (1830 – 1886)

CARRION COMFORT

     Not, I'll not, carrion comfort, Despair, not feast on thee;
     Not untwist — slack they may be — these last strands of man
     In me, ór, most weary, cry *I can no more.* I can;
     Can something, hope, wish day come, not choose not to be.
5   But ah, but O thou terrible, why wouldst thou rude on me
     Thy wring-world right foot rock? lay a lionlimb against me? scan
     With darksome devouring eyes my bruisèd bones? and fan,
     O in turns of tempest, me heaped there; me frantic to avoid thee and
          flee?

     Why? That my chaff might fly; my grain lie, sheer and clear.
10   Nay in all that toil, that coil, since (seems) I kissed the rod,
     Hand rather, my heart lo! lapped strength, stole joy, would laugh,
          chéer.
     Cheer whom though? the hero whose heaven-handling flung me, fóot
          tród
     Me? or me that fought him? O which one? is it each one? That night,
          that year
     Of now done darkness I wretch lay wrestling with (my God!) my God.

                   Gerard Manley Hopkins   (1844 – 1889)

THE CHESTNUT CASTS HIS FLAMBEAUX

The chestnut casts his flambeaux, and the flowers
    Stream from the hawthorn on the wind away,
The doors clap to, the pane is blind with showers.
    Pass me the can, lad; there's an end of May.

5   There's one spoilt spring to scant our mortal lot,
    One season ruined of our little store.
May will be fine next year as like as not:
    Oh, ay, but then we shall be twenty-four.

We for a certainty are not the first
10   Have sat in taverns while the tempest hurled
Their hopeful plans to emptiness, and cursed
    Whatever brute and blackguard made the world.

It is in truth iniquity on high
    To cheat our sentenced souls of aught they crave,
15   And mar the merriment as you and I
    Fare on our long fool's-errand to the grave.

Iniquity it is; but pass the can.
    My lad, no pair of kings our mothers bore;
Our only portion is the estate of man:
20   We want the moon, but we shall get no more.

If here to-day the cloud of thunder lours
    To-morrow it will hie on far behests;
The flesh will grieve on other bones than ours
    Soon, and the soul will mourn in other breasts.

25   The troubles of our proud and angry dust
    Are from eternity, and shall not fail.
Bear them we can, and if we can we must.
    Shoulder the sky, my lad, and drink your ale.

A. E. Housman (1859 – 1936)

RICHARD CORY

Whenever Richard Cory went down town,
We people on the pavement looked at him:
He was a gentleman from sole to crown,
Clean favored, and imperially slim.

5   And he was always quietly arrayed,
        And he was always human when he talked;
        But still he fluttered pulses when he said,
        "Good-morning," and he glittered when he walked.

        And he was rich—yes, richer than a king—
10   And admirably schooled in every grace:
        In fine, we thought that he was everything
        To make us wish that we were in his place.

        So on we worked, and waited for the light,
        And went without the meat, and cursed the bread;
15   And Richard Cory, one calm summer night,
        Went home and put a bullet through his head.

                        Edwin Arlington Robinson   (1869 – 1935)

THE HOLLOW MEN

A penny for the Old Guy

        I

        We are the hollow men
        We are the stuffed men
        Leaning together
        Headpiece filled with straw. Alas!
5   Our dried voices, when
        We whisper together
        Are quiet and meaningless
        As wind in dry grass
        Or rats' feet over broken glass
10   In our dry cellar.

        Shape without form, shade without color,
        Paralyzed force, gesture without motion;

        Those who have crossed
        With direct eyes, to death's other Kingdom
15   Remember us—if at all—not as lost
        Violent souls, but only
        As the hollow men
        The stuffed men.

II

Eyes I dare not meet in dreams
20   In death's dream kingdom
These do not appear:
There, the eyes are
Sunlight on a broken column
There, is a tree swinging
25   And voices are
In the wind's singing
More distant and more solemn
Than a fading star.

Let me be no nearer
30   In death's dream kingdom
Let me also wear
Such deliberate disguises
Rat's skin, crowskin, crossed staves
In a field
35   Behaving as the wind behaves
No nearer —

Not that final meeting
In the twilight kingdom.

III

This is the dead land
40   This is cactus land
Here the stone images
Are raised, here they receive
The supplication of a dead man's hand
Under the twinkle of a fading star.

45   Is it like this
In death's other kingdom
Waking alone
At the hour when we are
Trembling with tenderness
50   Lips that would kiss
Form prayers to broken stone.

IV

The eyes are not here
There are no eyes here
In this valley of dying stars
55   In this hollow valley
This broken jaw of our lost kingdoms

In this last of meeting places
We grope together
And avoid speech
60   Gathered on this beach of the tumid river

Sightless, unless
The eyes reappear
As the perpetual star
Multifoliate rose
65   Of death's twilight kingdom
The hope only
Of empty men.

V

Here we go round the prickly pear
Prickly pear prickly pear
70   *Here we go round the prickly pear*
At five o'clock in the morning.

Between the idea
And the reality
Between the motion
75   And the act
Falls the Shadow

                        For Thine is the Kingdom

Between the conception
And the creation
80   Between the emotion
And the response
Falls the Shadow

                              Life is very long

Between the desire
85   And the spasm
Between the potency
And the existence
Between the essence
And the descent
90   Falls the Shadow

                        For Thine is the Kingdom

For Thine is
Life is
For Thine is the

95 *This is the way the world ends*
    This is the way the world ends
    This is the way the world ends
    Not with a bang but a whimper.

                              T. S. Eliot   (1888 – 1965)

IF HE WERE ANYWHERE

I would be His if He were anywhere;
If He were anything He would appear.

If He had any name the name I give
Would find Him in the night and make Him live.

5   But He is nameless, nothing, and nowhere,
    Beyond concern with me and my despair.

And, naming Him, I only name my wish:
To break from bone and live in spirit's flesh.

And, seeking Him, still trammeled in the mind,
10 I dare not leave my selfish name behind.

That which is actual does not endure;
He will not have me till I forfeit more.

                  Cecil Hemley   (1914 –   )

QUESTIONS FOR DISCUSSION AND FURTHER STUDY

DEJECTION: AN ODE

1. This poem has often been compared and contrasted with Wordsworth's "Ode: Intimations of Immortality," which is also included in this anthology. What similarities and differences can you find between the two poems?
2. Coleridge prefaces the poem with a stanza from the "Ballad of Sir Patrick Spence." What relevance does that stanza have to his poem?
3. What reasons does Coleridge give for his dejection? What does he mean in stanza four when he says that "in our life alone does Nature live"?

STANZAS WRITTEN IN DEJECTION, NEAR NAPLES

1. Describe the poetic foot and line length for this poem. Do you feel that these elements ever threaten to become too regular, monotonous, and jogging? Why or why not? Does Shelley do anything to achieve variety?
2. Part of the poem's effectiveness rests with the contrast between Shelley's dejected state and the state of nature. How does Shelley describe nature? Does he imagine nature to share his troubles, or is she indifferent to them?
3. This poem has sometimes been criticized as a maudlin expression of self-pity. Do you agree? Have you ever indulged in moods similar to Shelley's?

ODE ON MELANCHOLY

1. Lethe is the river of forgetfulness, in Hades. Proserpine is the wife of Pluto; hence, the queen of Hades. Nightshade and wolfsbane are poisons; Psyche is another word for soul. In effect, what is Keats recommending that the reader should not do?
2. In the second stanza Keats mentions a number of joy-giving experiences. Yet he says that we should seek these experiences when the melancholy fit has fallen upon us. Why?
3. The first line of stanza three holds the key to the poem. What is the theme of the poem? Is the theme related to the *carpe diem* poetry contained in the "Love" section? How?

TEARS, IDLE TEARS

1. At what point in life would you judge the speaker of the poem to be? Why?
2. The poem depends greatly on simile. Discuss the effectiveness of Tennyson's similes here. Do they share a consistent strain or are they miscellaneous? How do the similes help the poem to achieve its deep, meditative, quiet tone?
3. Note that the refrain changes slightly in every stanza. Why is this more effective than if it had been exactly the same throughout? What specifically is "Death in Life"? How is that related to the refrain?

WHERE LIES THE LAND TO WHICH THE SHIP WOULD GO?

1. Clough uses the metaphor of a journey by sea to express his despair with life. Note that stanzas one and four ask rather profound rhetorical questions which approach the poem's theme, but stanzas two and three describe momentary pleasure and glory to be experienced on board the ship. What view of life is reflected in the poem's symmetrical contrast?
2. The last line of stanza two contains some splendid alliteration. Why is the alliteration particularly appropriate in terms of the line's literal meaning?
3. Does the poem go so far as to say that there are no ultimate values in life which can be known with certainty? Why or why not?

DOVER BEACH

1. This poem, like Coleridge's "Dejection: An Ode," uses the phenomena of nature as a point of departure for the poet's discussion of despair. Discuss the physical setting of Arnold's poem. With whom is the speaker talking?
2. The poem has been variously interpreted as a love poem, a work about religious doubt, and an expression of profound personal despair. Do you think the poem could justifiably have been placed in the sections on "Belief and Doubt" or "Love" as well as in this section on "Despair"? How can poems communicate on more than one level of meaning?
3. Discuss the tone of the poem's ending. Is there no compensation in life; is the tone one of complete despair? If there is some faint note of optimism, however slight, wherein does it lie?

THERE'S A CERTAIN SLANT OF LIGHT

1. Why should "cathedral tunes" depress us? Why is the phrase "ca-
    thedral tunes" an arresting one within itself? In the second stanza,
    the phrase "Heavenly hurt" also is fresh and unusual. Can you
    identify the figure of speech exemplified by this phrase?
2. Stanza three contains still another unusual and seemingly contra-
    dictory phrase. Can you find it?
3. What is the theme of this poem? What is the poet's attitude to-
    ward the slant of light? In what way is her attitude paradoxical?

CARRION COMFORT

1. Discuss Hopkins' use of alliteration. Note that in order to gain the
    greatest effects from alliteration, he often may omit words of rela-
    tively minor grammatical importance.
2. Hopkins' dates are 1844–1889; yet he is usually considered a
    modern poet and studied in the context of modern poetry. What
    elements in his poetry account for this?
3. What emotional stages must the speaker of the poem endure be-
    fore he wins his victory against God? Is his victory complete or
    only a partial one? Give reasons for your answer.

THE CHESTNUT CASTS HIS FLAMBEAUX

1. What is the speaker's attitude toward God? How is this attitude
    related to his sense of despair? If the speaker feels as he does
    about God, how can the "troubles of our proud and angry dust" be
    from eternity?
2. What philosophy is advocated in the poem, particularly in the last
    two lines? Evaluate the philosophy as a pattern to be followed.
    What dangers does it have?
3. Do you think the young narrator has a reasonably good sense of
    values, or do you think there is a strain of selfishness or immaturity
    in his statements? Defend your answer.

RICHARD CORY

1. Suppose that the speaker of Housman's "The Chestnut Casts His
    Flambeaux" had received in life what he wished. He would have
    been someone rather like Richard Cory. Yet Cory commits suicide.
    What does this say about life as viewed by these two poets? Do
    you think they are correct?

2. What level of language does Robinson use in this poem—ornate, complex, simple, exuberant, restrained? Try to describe the tone of his language; then explain why he chooses to use that particular kind of language.
3. A contrast is made between Cory and the other townspeople. When Cory shoots himself, the implication is that the townspeople are better off than they might think. Could this poem be considered a poem about jealousy?

THE HOLLOW MEN

1. Discuss the images used by Eliot to suggest his feelings toward modern man. What do these images have in common?
2. What effects do the fragments of prayer and the mutilated nursery rhyme have upon the structure of the poem? Do these elements tend to set up a contrast with the rest of the poem?
3. Does Eliot suggest or imply why we are hollow men? If so, how? The fragments of language in italics have already been mentioned. Are there other ways he does this?

IF HE WERE ANYWHERE

1. What, fundamentally, causes Hemley's despair? Is this a sufficient reason for despair?
2. What is the meaning of the last couplet? How is it related to the rest of the poem? What must the speaker of the poem forfeit? What is the speaker's attitude toward having to do this?
3. Why does the poet regard his own name as "selfish"? If God is "nameless, nothing, and nowhere," how can the poet address Him in the last line as if He existed?

ISOLATION

The theme of isolation or alienation has appeared in lyric poetry throughout the ages, yet it has asserted itself with particular urgency in recent years. Man, basically a gregarious creature, generally seeks the companionship of others on both the physical and spiritual level. When he feels cut off from others, he becomes an outsider, alienated from his fellow human beings. Artists, because they tend to perceive things more acutely than do most other people and because the production of art (whether a painting or a lyric poem) is essentially a personal experience, often feel thus set off from the crowd. In fact, one modern critic has argued that any artist is by nature an outsider, feeling the pain of his isolated position and seeking through his art to have others join him.

Yet one need not seek esoteric or complex explanations for the popularity of poems dealing with isolation. All humans, artists or otherwise, have experienced the pain of isolation in one form or another; indeed, many humans have welcomed it. One need not be an artist to know the exhilaration of being totally alone on a mountain top or in a trout stream or on a deserted city street at dawn. It is perhaps one of the great paradoxes of our advanced and overpopulated civilization that man finds himself more prone to spiritual alienation and at the same time less able to enjoy the pleasures of solitude.

The poems in this section differ widely. Some sing the praises of isolation or solitude; others comment on the sadness, fear, or regret associated with it. Among the first group of poems, those which welcome isolation, the earliest is "To Althea, from Prison" by Richard Lovelace. In this often-quoted lyric, Lovelace suggests that our minds can set us free, regardless of physical circumstances which restrict freedom. The power of the mind, he says, is so great that it can create its own world of the imagination. The utterance which passed into the language as a cliché, "Stone walls do not a prison make, / Nor iron bars a cage," expresses the theme of the poem.

Alexander Pope's "Ode on Solitude" is another celebration of isolation. Written when the brilliant eighteenth-century poet was twelve, this poem praises isolation, linking it to the pleasures of a quiet, contemplative, rural life. The relatively simple language of the poem makes eloquent the notion that "innocence" and "meditation" are joined together when one retreats from the world.

"This Lime-Tree Bower My Prison" is still another enumeration of the compensations afforded by solitude. In June of 1797, some friends of Coleridge, including Charles Lamb, visited the great Romantic poet. Unable to walk because of an accident, Coleridge was confined to his scenic retreat while his guests went for a hike. Not only does Coleridge participate imaginatively in the walk his friends are taking, but he also discovers much to soothe him within the relatively narrow confinement of his lime-tree bower. With great power the poem states that "Nature ne'er deserts the wise and pure; / No plot so narrow, be but Nature there." In other words, nature's tonic, healing effects are always available to us, even when we are alone, deprived of companionship and movement.

The tone of the two stanzas from *Childe Harold's Pilgrimage* differs from that of most other poems on isolation. Proud, haughty, disdainful, the arrogant but talented Lord Byron boasts in stanza 113 that he has always stood apart from the mob. In his challenge to the world, Byron scornfully declaims that he may have been in the world, but he was never of it. The tone changes somewhat in stanza 114. Here Byron tries to show that, however disillusioned he might appear, he is not a complete misanthrope. It is possible "That two, or one, are almost what they seem / That goodness is no name, and happiness no dream."

Matthew Arnold's "The Scholar-Gipsy" contrasts solitude with the scholarly life. The background of the poem is simple. Arnold refers to the legend of an Oxford student who joins a band of wandering Gypsies after he is forced to leave his studies because of poverty. Isolated from his own cultural heritage, the young man learns the value of peace, harmony, tranquility, and solitude. Indeed, the poem suggests through a series of splendid images that there is more to be learned from the Gypsies' way of life than from formal academic training. The scholar Gypsy has found the secret of belief and hope. With "*one* aim, *one* business, *one* desire," he has escaped the modern curse of divided purpose and light half-belief "of our casual creeds." The poem suggests by implication that our whole modern, complex, industrial culture is far inferior to simple, older, "Iberian" values.

In this collection, the most recent poem which treats isolation optimistically is "The Return of Odysseus" by Edwin Muir. Again, as in "The Scholar-Gipsy," the background of this poem is important. Muir makes use of the legend of Penelope's web, which comes from Homer's epic *The Odyssey*. According to this legend, Penelope, the wife of Odysseus, is being wooed by suitors who have taken over Odysseus' home. Odysseus has been gone so long that most believe him dead, but Penelope clings to the hope that he is alive. In order to stall her suitors, Penelope promises to choose one for her future husband after she has finished the garment she is weaving. Each night she secretly rips apart what she has woven during the day. Penelope continues in her devotion to love and duty even though she does *not* know that Odysseus is returning to her. Read analogically, the poem affirms the importance of love, duty, work – activity of all kinds – even when the reason for adhering to these values is unclear.

The other six poems in this section reflect the more commonly experienced sorrow of isolation. William Blake's "The Book of Thel," a late eighteenth-century poem, suggests that Thel's refusal to endure the experience of life causes loneliness and lack of involvement on her part. According to Blake, the human personality should progress through the state of innocence (symbolized by heaven, childhood, joy, and virginity) to the state of experience (symbolized by hell, adulthood, knowledge of sorrow, and indulgence). Though she feels the need for participation in the world of experience, Thel is not ready to make the transition, and she flees back to the vales of Har. This refusal of hers to perfect herself through suffering causes her sense of alienation.

Charles Lamb's poem "The Old Familiar Faces" is a less philosophical poem than Blake's, but it is much more poignant. Lamb's sister was subject to fits of madness; during one of these fits she stabbed her mother. Rather than commit his sister to an asylum (such places were grim indeed in early nineteenth-century England), Lamb gave his life to looking after her, even though this meant he had to forsake his own love for Ann Simmons. In the poem Lamb sees the world as a desert through which he must travel. His sense of isolation and loss – his sorrow at not seeing the familiar faces he once loved – is caused by the loss of loved ones and by the tragic circumstances of his life.

The word *impercipient* means "one who does not know." In "The Impercipient" Thomas Hardy sees his isolation being caused by his inability to find cause for optimism in this life. With ironic acidity, he laments his own lack of vision; what others seem to see and understand, he cannot. Unable to share the hope and religious faith of those around him, he feels set apart, isolated from them.

"Mr. Flood's Party," by Edwin Arlington Robinson, is somewhat similar to "The Old Familiar Faces." Here we meet a lonely but determined old man who is saddened by the fact that he has outlived his contemporaries. For solace Mr. Flood must turn to the bottle, which, at least temporarily, brings him comfort. So he indulges in a little drinking party with his only remaining friend – himself. Readers of the French epic *The Song of Roland* will recognize the allusion to that work in this poem as Mr. Flood is likened to Roland warning his fellow warriors by blowing on his horn.

"Desert Places" shares the meditative, conversational tone of "Mr. Flood's Party." Loneliness is close by; it is internal as well as external. Again there is a contrast between Frost's loneliness and the companionship he feels that "all animals" have while they are "smothered in their lairs." Read analogically or symbolically, the poem suggests that man is a wayfarer doomed to loneliness and isolation. As old age and fear of death inevitably close about us, we feel more and more a sense of internal loneliness. The external setting of the poem then becomes a symbol of this internal sense of isolation.

Richard Eberhart's poem "The Human Being Is a Lonely Creature" is the most recent poem in this collection which cites the inevitability of loneliness. The only consolations we have, according to the poem, are love and harmony. These are scant consolations, and the terror of loneliness is never quite obliterated by them. Even so, the poem ends on the faintest note of affirmation, suggesting that love and harmony are all we have worth seeking.

The twelve poems in this section all treat some aspect of isolation from other human beings. In them the individual poets attempt to communicate an intensely personal emotional experience, yet the universality of the feeling that each individual is essentially alone lends poignancy to their unique messages.

TO ALTHEA, FROM PRISON

When love with unconfinèd wings
    Hovers within my gates,
And my divine Althea brings
    To whisper at the grates;
5   When I lie tangled in her hair,
    And fettered to her eye,
The gods that wanton in the air
    Know no such liberty.

When flowing cups run swiftly round
10   With no allaying Thames,
Our careless heads with roses bound,
    Our hearts with loyal flames;
When thirsty grief in wine we steep,
    When healths and draughts go free,
15   Fishes that tipple in the deep
    Know no such liberty.

When, like committed linnets, I
    With shriller throat shall sing
The sweetness, mercy, majesty,
20   And glories of my King;
When I shall voice aloud how good
    He is, how great should be,
Enlargèd winds that curl the flood
    Know no such liberty.

25   Stone walls do not a prison make,
    Nor iron bars a cage;
Minds innocent and quiet take
    That for an hermitage;
If I have freedom in my love,
30   And in my soul am free,
Angels alone that soar above
    Enjoy such liberty.

        Richard Lovelace (1618 – 1658)

ODE ON SOLITUDE

Happy the man whose wish and care
    A few paternal acres bound,
Content to breathe his native air,
    In his own ground.

5   Whose herds with milk, whose fields with bread,
             Whose flocks supply him with attire,
         Whose trees in summer yield him shade,
             In winter fire.

         Blest, who can unconcern'dly find
10   Hours, days, and years slide soft away,
         In health of body, peace of mind,
             Quiet by day,

         Sound sleep by night; study and ease,
             Together mix'd; sweet recreation;
15   And Innocence, which most does please
             With meditation.

         Thus let me live, unseen, unknown,
             Thus unlamented let me die,
         Steal from the world, and not a stone
20   Tell where I lie.

                    Alexander Pope   (1688 – 1744)

THE BOOK OF THEL

Thel's Motto

Does the Eagle know what is in the pit?
Or wilt thou go ask the Mole?
Can Wisdom be put in a silver rod?
Or Love in a golden bowl?

I

The daughters of the Seraphim led round their sunny flocks,
All but the youngest: she in paleness sought the secret air,
To fade away like morning beauty from her mortal day:
Down by the river of Adona her soft voice is heard,
5   And thus her gentle lamentation falls like morning dew:

"O life of this our spring! why fades the lotus of the water,
Why fade these children of the spring, born but to smile & fall?
Ah! Thel is like a wat'ry bow, and like a parting cloud;
Like a reflection in a glass; like shadows in the water;
10   Like dreams of infants, like a smile upon an infant's face;

Like the dove's voice; like transient day; like music in the air.
Ah! gentle may I lay me down, and gentle rest my head,
And gentle sleep the sleep of death, and gentle hear the voice
Of him that walketh in the garden in the evening time."

15   The Lilly of the valley, breathing in the humble grass,
Answer'd the lovely maid and said: "I am a wat'ry weed,
And I am very small and love to dwell in lowly vales;
So weak, the gilded butterfly scarce perches on my head.
Yet I am visited from heaven, and he that smiles on all
20   Walks in the valley and each morn over me spreads his hand,
Saying, 'Rejoice, thou humble grass, thou new-born lilly flower,
Thou gentle maid of silent valleys and of modest brooks;
For thou shalt be clothed in light, and fed with morning manna,
Till summer's heat melts thee beside the fountains and the springs
25   To flourish in eternal vales.' Then why should Thel complain?
Why should the mistress of the vales of Har utter a sigh?"

She ceas'd & smil'd in tears, then sat down in her silver shrine.

Thel answer'd: "O thou little virgin of the peaceful valley,
Giving to those that cannot crave, the voiceless, the o'ertired;
30   Thy breath doth nourish the innocent lamb, he smells thy milky
            garments,
He crops thy flowers while thou sittest smiling in his face,
Wiping his mild and meekin mouth from all contagious taints.
Thy wine doth purify the golden honey; thy perfume,
Which thou dost scatter on every little blade of grass that springs,
35   Revives the milked cow, & tames the fire-breathing steed.
But Thel is like a faint cloud kindled at the rising sun:
I vanish from my pearly throne, and who shall find my place?"

"Queen of the vales," the Lilly answer'd, "ask the tender cloud,
And it shall tell thee why it glitters in the morning sky,
40   And why it scatters its bright beauty thro' the humid air.
Descend, O little Cloud, & hover before the eyes of Thel."

The Cloud descended, and the Lilly bow'd her modest head
And went to mind her numerous charge among the verdant grass.

II

"O little Cloud," the virgin said, "I charge thee tell to me
45   Why thou complainest not when in one hour thou fade away:
Then we shall seek thee, but not find. Ah! Thel is like to thee:
I pass away: yet I complain, and no one hears my voice."
The Cloud then shew'd his golden head & his bright form emerg'd,
Hovering and glittering on the air before the face of Thel.

50   "O virgin, know'st thou not our steeds drink of the golden springs
      Where Luvah doth renew his horses? Look'st thou on my youth,
      And fearest thou, because I vanish and am seen no more,
      Nothing remains? O maid, I tell thee, when I pass away
      It is to tenfold life, to love, to peace and raptures holy:
55   Unseen descending, weigh my light wings upon balmy flowers,
      And court the fair-eyed dew to take me to her shining tent:
      The weeping virgin, trembling kneels before the risen sun,
      Till we arise link'd in a golden band and never part,
      But walk united, bearing food to all our tender flowers."

60   "Dost thou, O little Cloud? I fear that I am not like thee,
      For I walk thro' the vales of Har, and smell the sweetest flowers,
      But I feed not the little flowers; I hear the warbling birds,
      But I feed not the warbling birds; they fly and seek their food:
      But Thel delights in these no more, because I fade away;
65   And all shall say, 'Without a use this shining woman liv'd,
      Or did she only live to be at death the food of worms?' "
      The Cloud reclin'd upon his airy throne and answer'd thus:

      "Then if thou art the food of worms, O virgin of the skies,
      How great thy use, how great thy blessing! Every thing that lives
70   Lives not alone nor for itself. Fear not, and I will call
      The weak worm from its lowly bed, and thou shalt hear its voice.
      Come forth, worm of the silent valley, to thy pensive queen."

      The helpless worm arose, and sat upon the Lilly's leaf,
      And the bright Cloud sail'd on, to find his partner in the vale.

      III

75   Then Thel astonish'd view'd the Worm upon its dewy bed.

      "Art thou a Worm? Image of weakness, art thou but a Worm?
      I see thee like an infant wrapped in the Lilly's leaf.
      Ah! weep not, little voice, thou canst not speak, but thou canst weep.
      Is this a Worm? I see thee lay helpless & naked, weeping,
80   And none to answer, none to cherish thee with mother's smiles."

      The Clod of Clay heard the Worm's voice & rais'd her pitying head:
      She bow'd over the weeping infant, and her life exhal'd
      In milky fondness: then on Thel she fix'd her humble eyes.

      "O beauty of the vales of Har! we live not for ourselves.
85   Thou seest me the meanest thing, and so I am indeed.
      My bosom of itself is cold, and of itself is dark;
      But he, that loves the lowly, pours his oil upon my head,
      And kisses me, and binds his nuptial bands around my breast,

90 And says: 'Thou mother of my children, I have loved thee
And I have given thee a crown that none can take away.'
But how this is, sweet maid, I know not, and I cannot know;
I ponder, and I cannot ponder; yet I live and love."

The daughter of beauty wip'd her pitying tears with her white veil,
And said: "Alas! I knew not this, and therefore did I weep.
95 That God would love a Worm I knew, and punish the evil foot
That wilful bruis'd its helpless form; but that he cherish'd it
With milk and oil I never knew, and therefore did I weep;
And I complain'd in the mild air, because I fade away,
And lay me down in thy cold bed, and leave my shining lot."

100 "Queen of the vales," the matron Clay answer'd, "I heard thy sighs,
And all thy moans flew o'er my roof, but I have call'd them down.
Wilt thou, O Queen, enter my house? 'Tis given thee to enter
And to return: fear nothing, enter with thy virgin feet."

IV

The eternal gates' terrific porter lifted the northern bar:
105 Thel enter'd in & saw the secrets of the land unknown.
She saw the couches of the dead, & where the fibrous roots
Of every heart on earth infixes deep its restless twists:
A land of sorrows & of tears where never smile was seen.

She wander'd in the land of clouds thro' valleys dark, list'ning
110 Dolours & lamentations; waiting oft beside a dewy grave
She stood in silence, list'ning to the voices of the ground,
Till to her own grave plot she came, & there she sat down,
And heard this voice of sorrow breathed from the hollow pit.

"Why cannot the Ear be closed to its own destruction?
115 Or the glist'ning Eye to the poison of a smile?
Why are Eyelids stor'd with arrows ready drawn,
Where a thousand fighting men in ambush lie?
Or an Eye of gifts & graces show'ring fruits & coined gold?
Why a Tongue impress'd with honey from every wind?
120 Why an Ear, a whirlpool fierce to draw creations in?
Why a Nostril wide inhaling terror, trembling, & affright?
Why a tender curb upon the youthful burning boy?
Why a little curtain of flesh on the bed of our desire?"

The Virgin started from her seat, & with a shriek
125 Fled back unhinder'd till she came into the vales of Har.

William Blake   (1757 – 1827)

THIS LIME-TREE BOWER MY PRISON

[*Addressed to Charles Lamb, of the India House, London*]

In the June of 1797 some long-expected friends paid a visit to the author's cottage; and on the morning of their arrival, he met with an accident, which disabled him from walking during the whole time of their stay. One evening, when they had left him for a few hours, he composed the following lines in the garden-bower.

Well, they are gone, and here must I remain,
This lime-tree bower my prison! I have lost
Beauties and feelings, such as would have been
Most sweet to my remembrance even when age
5   Had dimm'd mine eyes to blindness! They, meanwhile,
Friends, whom I never more may meet again,
On springy heath, along the hill-top edge,
Wander in gladness, and wind down, perchance,
To that still roaring dell, of which I told;
10   The roaring dell, o'erwooded, narrow, deep,
And only speckled by the mid-day sun;
Where its slim trunk the ash from rock to rock
Flings arching like a bridge;—that branchless ash,
Unsunn'd and damp, whose few poor yellow leaves
15   Ne'er tremble in the gale, yet tremble still,
Fann'd by the water-fall! and there my friends
Behold the dark green file of long lank weeds,
That all at once (a most fantastic sight!)
Still nod and drip beneath the dripping edge
20   Of the blue clay-stone.

                Now, my friends emerge
Beneath the wide wide Heaven—and view again
The many-steepled tract magnificent
Of hilly fields and meadows, and the sea,
With some fair bark, perhaps, whose sails light up
25   The slip of smooth clear blue betwixt two Isles
Of purple shadow! Yes! they wander on
In gladness all; but thou, methinks, most glad,
My gentle-hearted Charles! for thou hast pined
And hunger'd after Nature, many a year,
30   In the great City pent, winning thy way
With sad yet patient soul, through evil and pain
And strange calamity! Ah! slowly sink
Behind the western ridge, thou glorious Sun!

Shine in the slant beams of the sinking orb,
35   Ye purple heath-flowers! richlier burn, ye clouds!
Live in the yellow light, ye distant groves!
And kindle, thou blue Ocean! So my friend
Struck with deep joy may stand, as I have stood,
Silent with swimming sense; yea, gazing round
40   On the wide landscape, gaze till all doth seem
Less gross than bodily; and of such hues
As veil the Almighty Spirit, when yet he makes
Spirits perceive his presence.

                         A delight
Comes sudden on my heart, and I am glad
45   As I myself were there! Nor in this bower,
This little lime-tree bower, have I not mark'd
Much that has sooth'd me. Pale beneath the blaze
Hung the transparent foliage; and I watch'd
Some broad and sunny leaf, and lov'd to see
50   The shadow of the leaf and stem above
Dappling its sunshine! And that walnut-tree
Was richly ting'd, and a deep radiance lay
Full on the ancient ivy, which usurps
Those fronting elms, and now, with blackest mass
55   Makes their dark branches gleam a lighter hue
Through the late twilight: and though now the bat
Wheels silent by, and not a swallow twitters,
Yet still the solitary humble-bee
Sings in the bean-flower! Henceforth I shall know
60   That Nature ne'er deserts the wise and pure;
No plot so narrow, be but Nature there,
No waste so vacant, but may well employ
Each faculty of sense, and keep the heart
Awake to Love and Beauty! and sometimes
65   'Tis well to be bereft of promis'd good,
That we may lift the soul, and contemplate
With lively joy the joys we cannot share.
My gentle-hearted Charles! when the last rook
Beat its straight path along the dusky air
70   Homewards, I blest it! deeming its black wing
(Now a dim speck, now vanishing in light)
Had cross'd the mighty Orb's dilated glory,
While thou stood'st gazing; or, when all was still,
Flew creeking o'er thy head, and had a charm
75   For thee, my gentle-hearted Charles, to whom
No sound is dissonant which tells of Life.

Samuel Taylor Coleridge   (1772 – 1834)

THE OLD FAMILIAR FACES

Where are they gone, the old familiar faces?

I had a mother, but she died, and left me,
Died prematurely in a day of horrors —
All, all are gone, the old familiar faces.

5   I have had playmates, I have had companions,
In my days of childhood, in my joyful school-days —
All, all are gone, the old familiar faces.

I have been laughing, I have been carousing,
Drinking late, sitting late, with my bosom cronies —
10   All, all are gone, the old familiar faces.

I loved a love once, fairest among women.
Closed are her doors on me, I must not see her —
All, all are gone, the old familiar faces.

I have a friend, a kinder friend has no man.
15   Like an ingrate, I left my friend abruptly;
Left him, to muse on the old familiar faces.

Ghost-like, I paced round the haunts of my childhood.
Earth seemed a desert I was bound to traverse,
Seeking to find the old familiar faces.

20   Friend of my bosom, thou more than a brother!
Why wert not thou born in my father's dwelling?
So might we talk of the old familiar faces.

For some they have died, and some they have left me,
And some are taken from me; all are departed;
25   All, all are gone, the old familiar faces.

                    Charles Lamb   (1775 – 1834)

from CHILDE HAROLD'S PILGRIMAGE (Canto III)

113

I have not loved the world, nor the world me;
I have not flattered its rank breath, nor bowed
To its idolatries a patient knee,

5   Nor coined my cheek to smiles, nor cried aloud
In worship of an echo; in the crowd
They could not deem me one of such; I stood
Amongst them, but not of them; in a shroud
Of thoughts which were not their thoughts, and still could,
Had I not filed my mind, which thus itself subdued.

114

10   I have not loved the world, nor the world me, —
But let us part fair foes; I do believe,
Though I have found them not, that there may be
Words which are things, hopes which will not deceive,
And virtues which are merciful, nor weave
15   Snares for the failing; I would also deem
O'er others' griefs that some sincerely grieve;
That two, or one, are almost what they seem,
That goodness is no name, and happiness no dream.

George Noel Gordon, Lord Byron   *(1788 – 1824)*

THE SCHOLAR-GIPSY

Go, for they call you, shepherd, from the hill;
Go, shepherd, and untie the wattled cotes!
No longer leave thy wistful flock unfed,
Nor let thy bawling fellows rack their throats,
5   Nor the cropp'd herbage shoot another head.
But when the fields are still,
And the tired men and dogs all gone to rest,
And only the white sheep are sometimes seen
Cross and recross the strips of moon-blanch'd green,
10   Come, shepherd, and again begin the quest!

Here, where the reaper was at work of late —
In this high field's dark corner, where he leaves
His coat, his basket, and his earthen cruse,
And in the sun all morning binds the sheaves,
15   Then here, at noon, comes back his stores to use —
Here will I sit and wait,
While to my ear from uplands far away
The bleating of the folded flocks is borne,
With distant cries of reapers in the corn —
20   All the live murmur of a summer's day.

Screen'd is this nook o'er the high, half-reap'd field,
And here till sun-down, shepherd! will I be.
 Through the thick corn the scarlet poppies peep,
And round green roots and yellowing stalks I see
25 Pale pink convolvulus in tendrils creep;
 And air-swept lindens yield
Their scent, and rustle down their perfumed showers
 Of bloom on the bent grass where I am laid,
 And bower me from the August sun with shade;
30 And the eye travels down to Oxford's towers.

And near me on the grass lies Glanvil's book—
 Come, let me read the oft-read tale again!
 The story of the Oxford scholar poor,
Of pregnant parts and quick inventive brain,
35 Who, tired of knocking at preferment's door,
 One summer-morn forsook
His friends, and went to learn the gipsy-lore,
 And roam'd the world with that wild brotherhood,
 And came, as most men deem'd, to little good,
40 But came to Oxford and his friends no more.

But once, years after, in the country-lanes,
 Two scholars, whom at college erst he knew,
 Met him, and of his way of life enquired;
Whereat he answer'd, that the gipsy-crew,
45 His mates, had arts to rule as they desired
 The workings of men's brains,
And they can bind them to what thoughts they will.
 'And I,' he said, 'the secret of their art,
 When fully learn'd, will to the world impart;
50 But it needs heaven-sent moments for this skill.'

This said, he left them, and return'd no more.—
 But rumours hung about the country-side,
 That the lost Scholar long was seen to stray,
Seen by rare glimpses, pensive and tongue-tied,
55 In hat of antique shape, and cloak of grey,
 The same the gipsies wore.
Shepherds had met him on the Hurst in spring;
 At some lone alehouse in the Berkshire moors,
 On the warm ingle-bench, the smock-frock'd boors
60 Had found him seated at their entering,

But, 'mid their drink and clatter, he would fly.
 And I myself seem half to know thy looks,
 And put the shepherds, wanderer! on thy trace;
 And boys who in lone wheatfields scare the rocks
65 I ask if thou hast pass'd their quiet place;

Or in my boat I lie
Moor'd to the cool bank in the summer-heats,
'Mid wide grass meadows which the sunshine fills,
And watch the warm, green-muffled Cumner hills,
70 And wonder if thou haunt'st their shy retreats.

For most, I know, thou lov'st retired ground!
Thee at the ferry Oxford riders blithe,
Returning home on summer-nights, have met
Crossing the stripling Thames at Bab-lock-hithe,
75 Trailing in the cool stream thy fingers wet,
As the punt's rope chops round;
And leaning backward in a pensive dream,
And fostering in thy lap a heap of flowers
Pluck'd in shy fields and distant Wychwood bowers,
80 And thine eyes resting on the moonlit stream.

And then they land, and thou art seen no more! —
Maidens, who from the distant hamlets come
To dance around the Fyfield elm in May,
Oft through the darkening fields have seen thee roam,
85 Or cross a stile into the public way.
Oft thou hast given them store
Of flowers - the frail-leaf'd, white anemony,
Dark bluebells drench'd with dews of summer eves,
And purple orchises with spotted leaves —
90 But none hath words she can report of thee.

And, above Godstow Bridge, when hay-time's here
In June, and many a scythe in sunshine flames,
Men who through those wide fields of breezy grass
Where black-wing'd swallows haunt the glittering Thames,
95 To bathe in the abandon'd lasher pass,
Have often pass'd near
Sitting upon the river bank o'ergrown;
Mark'd thine outlandish garb, thy figure spare,
Thy dark vague eyes, and soft abstracted air —
100 But, when they came from bathing, thou wast gone!

At some lone homestead in the Cumner hills,
Where at her open door the housewife darns,
Thou hast been seen, or hanging on a gate
To watch the threshers in the mossy barns.
105 Children, who early range these slopes and late
For cresses from the rills,
Have known thee eying, all an April-day,
The springing pastures and the feeding kine;
And mark'd thee, when the stars come out and shine,
110 Through the long dewy grass move slow away.

In autumn, on the skirts of Bagley Wood—
  Where most the gipsies by the turf-edged way
    Pitch their smoked tents, and every bush you see
  With scarlet patches tagg'd and shreds of grey,
115   Above the forest-ground called Thessaly—
    The blackbird, picking food,
  Sees thee, nor stops his meal, nor fears at all;
    So often has he known thee past him stray,
    Rapt, twirling in thy hand a wither'd spray,
120 And waiting for the spark from heaven to fall.

And once, in winter, on the causeway chill
  Where home through flooded fields foot-travellers go,
    Have I not pass'd thee on the wooden bridge,
  Wrapt in thy cloak and battling with the snow,
125   Thy face tow'rd Hinksey and its wintry ridge?
    And thou hast climb'd the hill,
  And gain'd the white brow of the Cumner range;
    Turn'd once to watch, while thick the snowflakes fall,
    The line of festal light in Christ-Church hall—
130 Then sought thy straw in some sequester'd grange.

But what—I dream! Two hundred years are flown
  Since first thy story ran through Oxford halls,
    And the grave Glanvil did the tale inscribe
  That thou wert wander'd from the studious walls
135   To learn strange arts, and join a gipsy-tribe;
    And thou from earth art gone
  Long since, and in some quiet churchyard laid—
    Some country-nook, where o'er thy unknown grave
    Tall grasses and white flowering nettles wave,
140 Under a dark, red-fruited yew-tree's shade.

—No, no, thou hast not felt the lapse of hours!
  For what wears out the life of mortal men?
    'Tis that from change to change their being rolls;
  'Tis that repeated shocks, again, again,
145   Exhaust the energy of strongest souls
    And numb the elastic powers.
  Till having used our nerves with bliss and teen,
    And tired upon a thousand schemes our wit,
    To the just-pausing Genius we remit
150 Our worn-out life, and are — what we have been.

Thou hast not lived, why should'st thou perish, so?
  Thou hadst *one* aim, *one* business, *one* desire;
    Else wert thou long since number'd with the dead!
  Else hadst thou spent, like other men, thy fire!
155   The generations of thy peers are fled,

And we ourselves shall go;
And we imagine thee exempt from age
But thou possessest an immortal lot,
And living as thou liv'st on Glanvil's page,
160 Because thou hadst — what we, alas! have not.

For early didst thou leave the world, with powers
Fresh, undiverted to the world without,
Firm to their mark, not spent on other things;
Free from the sick fatigue, the languid doubt,
165 Which much to have tried, in much been baffled, brings.
O life unlike to ours!
Who fluctuate idly without term or scope,
Of whom each strives, nor knows for what he strives,
And each half lives a hundred different lives;
170 Who wait like thee, but not, like thee, in hope.

Thou waitest for the spark from heaven! and we,
Light half-believers of our casual creeds,
Who never deeply felt, nor clearly will'd,
Whose insight never has borne fruit in deeds,
175 Whose vague resolves never have been fulfill'd;
For whom each year we see
Breeds new beginnings, disappointments new;
Who hesitate and falter life away,
And lose to-morrow the ground won to-day —
180 Ah! do not we, wanderer! await it too?

Yes, we await it! — but it still delays,
And then we suffer! and amongst us one,
Who most has suffer'd, takes dejectedly
His seat upon the intellectual throne;
185 And all his store of sad experience he
Lays bare of wretched days;
Tells us his misery's birth and growth and signs,
And how the dying spark of hope was fed,
And how the breast was soothed, and how the head,
190 And all his hourly varied anodynes.

This for our wisest! and we others pine,
And wish the long unhappy dream would end,
And waive all claim to bliss, and try to bear;
With close-lipp'd patience for our only friend,
195 Sad patience, too near neighbour to despair —
But none has hope like thine!
Thou through the fields and through the woods dost stray,
Roaming the country-side, a truant boy,
Nursing thy project in unclouded joy,
200 And every doubt long blown by time away.

O born in days when wits were fresh and clear,
   And life ran gaily as the sparkling Thames;
      Before this strange disease of modern life,
    With its sick hurry, its divided aims,
205   Its heads o'ertax'd, its palsied hearts, was rife—
      Fly hence, our contact fear!
   Still fly, plunge deeper in the bowering wood!
      Averse, as Dido did with gesture stern
      From her false friend's approach in Hades turn,
210   Wave us away, and keep thy solitude!

Still nursing the unconquerable hope,
   Still clutching the inviolable shade,
      With a free, onward impulse brushing through,
    By night, the silver'd branches of the glade —
215   Far on the forest-skirts, where none pursue,
      On some mild pastoral slope
   Emerge, and resting on the moonlit pales
      Freshen thy flowers as in former years
      With dew, or listen with enchanted ears,
220   From the dark dingles, to the nightingales!

But fly our paths, our feverish contact fly!
   For strong the infection of our mental strife,
      Which, though it gives no bliss, yet spoils for rest;
    And we should win thee from thy own fair life,
225   Like us distracted, and like us unblest.
      Soon, soon thy cheer would die,
   Thy hopes grow timorous, and unfix'd thy powers,
      And thy clear aims be cross and shifting made;
      And then thy glad perennial youth would fade,
230   Fade, and grow old at last, and die like ours.

Then fly our greetings, fly our speech and smiles!
   —As some grave Tyrian trader, from the sea,
      Descried at sunrise an emerging prow
    Lifting the cool-hair'd creepers stealthily,
235   The fringes of a southward-facing brow
      Among the Aegaean isles;
   And saw the merry Grecian coaster come,
      Freighted with amber grapes, and Chian wine,
      Green, bursting figs, and tunnies steep'd in brine—
240   And knew the intruders on his ancient home,

The young light-hearted masters of the waves—
   And snatch'd his rudder, and shook out more sail;
      And day and night held on indignantly
    O'er the blue Midland waters with the gale,
245   Betwixt the Syrtes and soft Sicily,

To where the Atlantic raves
Outside the western straits; and unbent sails
   There, where down cloudy cliffs, through sheets of foam,
   Shy traffickers, the dark Iberians come;
250   And on the beach undid his corded bales.

Matthew Arnold   (1822 – 1888)

THE IMPERCIPIENT

(At a Cathedral Service)

That with this bright believing band
   I have no claim to be,
That faiths by which my comrades stand
   Seem fantasies to me,
5   And mirage-mists their Shining Land,
   Is a strange destiny.

Why thus my soul should be consigned
   To infelicity,
Why always I must feel as blind
10   To sights my brethren see,
Why joys they've found I cannot find,
   Abides a mystery.

Since heart of mine knows not that ease
   Which they know; since it be
15   That He who breathes All's Well to these
   Breathes no All's-Well to me,
My lack might move their sympathies
   And Christian charity!

I am like a gazer who should mark
20   An inland company
Standing upfingered, with, "Hark! hark!
   The glorious distant sea!"
And feel, "Alas, 'tis but yon dark
   And wind-swept pine to me!"

25   Yet I would bear my shortcomings
             With meet tranquillity,
         But for the charge that blessed things
             I'd liefer not have be.
         O, doth a bird deprived of wings
30   Go earthbound wilfully!

         .   .   .   .

         Enough. As yet disquiet clings
             About us. Rest shall we.

                         Thomas Hardy   (1840 – 1928)

MR. FLOOD'S PARTY

         Old Eben Flood, climbing alone one night
         Over the hill between the town below
         And the forsaken upland hermitage
         That held as much as he should ever know
5   On earth again of home, paused warily.
         The road was his with not a native near;
         And Eben, having leisure, said aloud,
         For no man else in Tilbury Town to hear:

         "Well, Mr. Flood, we have the harvest moon
10   Again, and we may not have many more;
         The bird is on the wing, the poet says,
         And you and I have said it here before.
         Drink to the bird." He raised up to the light
         The jug that he had gone so far to fill,
15   And answered huskily: "Well, Mr. Flood,
         Since you propose it, I believe I will."

         Alone, as if enduring to the end
         A valiant armor of scarred hopes outworn,
         He stood there in the middle of the road
20   Like Roland's ghost winding a silent horn.
         Below him, in the town among the trees,
         Where friends of other days had honored him,
         A phantom salutation of the dead
         Rang thinly till old Eben's eyes were dim.

25 Then, as a mother lays her sleeping child
 Down tenderly, fearing it may awake,
 He set the jug down slowly at his feet
 With trembling care, knowing that most things break;
 And only when assured that on firm earth
30 It stood, as the uncertain lives of men
 Assuredly did not, he paced away,
 And with his hand extended paused again:

 "Well, Mr. Flood, we have not met like this
 In a long time; and many a change has come
35 To both of us, I fear, since last it was
 We had a drop together. Welcome home!"
 Convivially returning with himself,
 Again he raised the jug to the light;
 And with an acquiescent quaver said:
40 "Well, Mr. Flood, if you insist, I might.

 "Only a very little, Mr. Flood—
 For auld lang syne. No more, sir; that will do."
 So, for the time, apparently it did,
 And Eben evidently thought so too;
45 For soon amid the silver loneliness
 Of night he lifted up his voice and sang,
 Secure, with only two moons listening,
 Until the whole harmonious landscape rang—

 "For auld lang syne." The weary throat gave out,
50 The last word wavered; and the song being done,
 He raised again the jug regretfully
 And shook his head, and was again alone.
 There was not much that was ahead of him,
 And there was nothing in the town below—
55 Where strangers would have shut the many doors
 That many friends had opened long ago.

Edwin Arlington Robinson   (1869 – 1935)

DESERT PLACES

Snow falling and night falling fast oh fast
In a field I looked into going past,
And the ground almost covered smooth in snow,
But a few weeds and stubble showing last.

5   The woods around it have it—it is theirs.
       All animals are smothered in their lairs.
       I am too absent-spirited to count;
       The loneliness includes me unawares.

       And lonely as it is that loneliness
10   Will be more lonely ere it will be less—
       A blanker whiteness of benighted snow
       With no expression, nothing to express.

       They cannot scare me with their empty spaces
       Between stars—on stars where no human race is.
15   I have it in me so much nearer home
       To scare myself with my own desert places.

                    Robert Frost   (1874 – 1963)

THE RETURN OF ODYSSEUS

       The doors flapped open in Odysseus' house,
       The lolling latches gave to every hand,
       Let traitor, babbler, tout and bargainer in.
       The rooms and passages resounded
5   With ease and chaos of a public market,
       The walls mere walls to lean on as you talked,
       Spat on the floor, surveyed some newcomer
       With an absent eye. There you could be yourself.
       Dust in the nooks, weeds nodding in the yard,
10   The thick walls crumbling. Even the cattle came
       About the doors with mild familiar stare
       As if this were their place.
       All round the island stretched the clean blue sea.

       Sole at the house's heart Penelope
15   Sat at her chosen task, endless undoing
       Of endless doing, endless weaving, unweaving,
       In the clean chamber. Still her loom ran empty
       Day after day. She thought: "Here I do nothing
       Or less than nothing, making an emptiness
20   Amid disorder, weaving, unweaving the lie
       The day demands. Odysseus, this is duty,
       To do and undo, to keep a vacant gate
       Where order and right and hope and peace can enter.
       Oh will you ever return? Or are you dead,

25 And this wrought emptiness my ultimate emptiness?"
    She wove and unwove and wove and did not know
    That even then Odysseus on the long
    And winding road of the world was on his way.

                    Edwin Muir   (1887 – 1959)

THE HUMAN BEING IS A LONELY CREATURE

    It is borne in upon me that pain
    Is essential. The bones refuse to act.
    Recalcitrancy is life's fine flower.
    The human being is a lonely creature.

5   Fear is of the essence. You do not fear?
    I say you lie. Fear is the truth of time.
    If it is not now, it will come hereafter.
    Death is waiting for the human creature.

    Praise to harmony and love.
10 They are best, all else is false.
    Yet even in love and harmony
    The human being is a lonely creature.

    The old sloughed off, the new new-born,
    What fate and what high hazards join
15 As life tries out the soul's enterprise.
    Time is waiting for the human creature.

    Life is daring all our human stature.
    Death looks, and waits for each bright eye.
    Love and harmony are our best nurture.
20 The human being is a lonely creature.

                    Richard Eberhart   (1904 –   )

QUESTIONS FOR DISCUSSION AND FURTHER STUDY

TO ALTHEA, FROM PRISON

1. Basically, this poem contrasts elements external to the individual with internal ones. Where does Lovelace feel true liberty lies? Do you agree with him?
2. The first two lines of the last stanza of this poem are often quoted out of context and have indeed become an "old saying." What qualities do you find in these lines which would endear them to people?
3. In some versions of this poem, line eight reads "The gods that wanton in the air"; in other versions the word *god* is replaced by the word *birds*. Which version do you prefer? Why?

ODE ON SOLITUDE

1. Compare and/or contrast the attitudes of Lovelace and Pope on the subject of isolation. Are the poets saying something similar? If not, how do they differ?
2. This poem uses more abstract language than is to be found in many lyric poems. What is your opinion of its language?
3. Why does the speaker wish to die unlamented?

THE BOOK OF THEL

1. Name the beings with whom Thel converses. What does she learn from each?
2. What is the basis of Thel's complaint? Can you find evidence to agree (or disagree) with one scholar's statement that this poem deals with the "mutual interdependence of all things"?
3. What is the theme of this poem? What is Blake's attitude toward escapism?

THIS LIME-TREE BOWER MY PRISON

1. Does Coleridge feel that external nature or one's own internal view of nature is more important as a healing force?
2. What is Coleridge's attitude toward the city?
3. What role does Charles Lamb play in the poem? How is his presence related to the theme?

THE OLD FAMILIAR FACES

1. How effective is Lamb's frequent repetition of the title phrase?
2. The language of this poem is almost prose-like. What effects does Lamb gain by using such a quiet, conversational level of language? Is his language appropriate to this theme?
3. Study of the standard biography of Charles Lamb would reveal the details behind certain lines of the poem (e.g., the mother who died "in a day of horrors," the "fairest among women," the kind friend whom he left "abruptly"). Do you think that the knowledge of these details would add measurably to the impact of the poem?

CHILDE HAROLD'S PILGRIMAGE, (CANTO III)

1. This poem (as well as Shelley's *Adonais*, in another section) employs a stanzaic form called the Spenserian stanza, which consists of eight lines of iambic pentameter followed by an alexandrine and rhyming *a b a b b c b c c*. Examining both poems, can you suggest the purpose or the value of using an alexandrine at the end?
2. On the basis of these two stanzas, do you consider Byron a misanthrope? Does he hold out any hope that some human relationships might be sincere?
3. Can you explain the phrase "coined my cheek to smiles"? What is the meaning and effect of the line, "That two, or one, are almost what they seem"?

THE SCHOLAR-GIPSY

1. What is Arnold's attitude toward human society in general and modern life in particular?
2. Why does Arnold, toward the end of the poem, contrast our society with an older, primitive, Mediterranean one?
3. Could this poem be considered anti-intellectual? Why or why not?

THE IMPERCIPIENT

1. Do you feel that the combination of long and short lines in this poem is effective? Give the line length for both types of lines used by Hardy.
2. What is Hardy's attitude toward God and religion? What is the meaning of the last two lines in the poem?
3. If Hardy's lack of faith makes him unhappy, why doesn't he simply begin to believe in God so that he can be happy?

MR. FLOOD'S PARTY

1.   Who are the speaker and audience in this poem? Is the word *party* appropriate for the title? Why or why not?
2.   Why are there *two* moons listening to Mr. Flood? What are these two moons? Can you identify the allusion in the third line of the second stanza?
3.   What is your opinion of the simile used in stanza four to suggest the way Mr. Flood sets down his jug?

DESERT PLACES

1.   What are these desert places of Frost's own which he mentions? How are they related to the poem's theme?
2.   How do this poem and "The Darkling Thrush" compare in theme?
3.   How do this poem and "Stopping by Woods on a Snowy Evening" compare? Is Frost consistent in his themes?

THE RETURN OF ODYSSEUS

1.   What attitude toward duty does Muir hold?
2.   Who is the important character in the poem, Odysseus or Penelope? Does she ever become the poem's speaker? Where?
3.   This is certainly a poem about isolation. Could it also be read as a poem about fidelity?
4.   What if Odysseus had been killed on his journey home? Would Penelope have been foolish to remain loyal and dutiful to him?

THE HUMAN BEING IS A LONELY CREATURE

1.   What do you think Eberhart has in mind when he says that "pain/Is essential" and "Fear is of the essence"?
2.   What is the theme of this poem? How are love and harmony related to this theme?
3.   Note Eberhart's reliance on forms of the verb *to be*. What effects are produced by this technique?

LOVE

No anthology of lyric poetry could be complete without a generous sampling of poems dealing with that richly complex emotion, love between the sexes. Always a favorite subject of lyric poets—indeed, of most human beings—the emotion of love has inspired some of the greatest poets to their noblest efforts.

The range of love poetry is very wide, going from simple statements of physical desire to elaborate comments on the philosophical implications of love, extending to descriptions of the joy as well as the tragedy that love can bring. The twelve poems included in this section illustrate that range.

The first love lyric here anthologized, as well as those by Herrick and Marvell, can properly be called a *carpe diem* poem. Such poems all suggest in one way or another that youth should "seize the day" (the literal meaning of *carpe diem*). In actual fact, all *carpe diem* poems are didactic; they persuade, cajole, or reason with a lover to enjoy the pleasures of love *now*. Youth is fleeting, time's course is swift, the grave is final, there is time enough in old age for prudence and purity—these are the conventional ideas associated with *carpe diem* poetry. Christopher Marlowe's "The Passionate Shepherd to His Love" is a pastoral poem which suggests rather traditionally the pleasures of love in a rural setting. It persuades by setting before the potential lover a series of pleasant, warm, soft images.

John Donne's "A Valediction: Forbidding Mourning" is the earliest of the several poems dealing with married life. Written as he was preparing to leave his beloved wife so that he might undertake a diplomatic mission for his monarch, James I, Donne tries to calm his wife's fears about their impending separation. In doing so, the poet uses unusual and arresting imagery to suggest the notion that true lovers are always united, even when physically apart.

"To the Virgins, to Make Much of Time" is another *carpe diem* lyric. Robert Herrick's approach, unlike Marlowe's, is impersonal. He makes no pleas to a specific individual; rather, he advocates a view of life which urges young women not to waste the passion of their youth, and he reminds them that their beauty is certain to fade. The popularity of the poem over the years can be measured in part by the fact that its first line has become a kind of cliché for the expression of the *carpe diem* sentiment.

Still another *carpe diem* lyric is Andrew Marvell's "To His Coy Mistress." Starting with ingenious flattery, Marvell then reminds his lover of the passage of time and the chilling imminence of the grave. He builds his argument carefully and forcefully, reaching toward the urgent conclusion that his reserved mistress should capitulate to his entreaties.

The next poem, William Blake's "The Garden of Love," suggests a preference for free and uninhibited love over that sanctioned by the church. Blake's well-known arguments against restraints of any kind carry over in this poem to an attack upon the institution of marriage itself. In another poem he speaks of the "marriage hearse"; in this one he equates the "Thou shalt not" restrictions of religious marriage with graves and tombstones.

Robert Burns' "John Anderson My Jo," on the other hand, provides a very favorable view of marriage. Very few poems deal with love among the elderly, and those few that do often tend toward excessive sentimentality. This poem, however, avoids that extreme. It deals with a married couple well past the first fires of their love, who nevertheless are still companions and partners filled with a sincere and profound affection for each other which goes far beyond the physical vigor of the young. They remember their "canty" days and find a peaceful solace in their recollections.

Percy Bysshe Shelley's "Epipsychidion" is the longest and, in some ways, the most complex poem included in this section on love. Highly philosophical, and at the same time highly autobiographical, the poem was inspired by Shelley's spiritual love for a young Italian girl, Emilia Viviani, who was at the time imprisoned in a convent. The poem is about both an idealized, perfect principle of beauty and Shelley's tragically unsuccessful attempts to find that perfect, eternal beauty in one human being.

Another poem treating of love's disenchantment is "La Belle Dame Sans Merci" (the beautiful woman without mercy) by John Keats. Ecstasy, the poet seems to say, cannot sustain itself; climax results in an inevitable return to reality—to the "cold hillside." Keats relies in part upon medieval legend, as the poem shows us a knight enchanted by the charms of a beautiful temptress, the *femme fatale*, who is supernatural and possibly Satanic. Although the story was old when Keats found it, his rendering of it is fresh and engaging.

Shortly after their marriage, Elizabeth Barrett Browning presented her husband with a sequence of sonnets celebrating their love, and he used her nickname (the Portuguese) to give the group of poems its title, *Sonnets from the Portuguese*. The one included here contains a somewhat rhetorical statement of a woman's love for her husband, yet the elements of sincerity and affection are so genuinely and obviously present that the poem escapes embarrassing, tear-jerking sentimentality.

The next poem is also part of a larger sequence dealing with matrimony, but in this case the marriage is about to break up. Throughout the series of experimental sixteen-line sonnets, George Meredith reflects upon his disastrous marriage to Mary Nicolls. *Modern Love* is a work known for its psychological realism. In this particular poem, the first in the sequence, Meredith states honestly and bluntly the anguish a married couple suffers when their marriage is breaking up. Of particular note is the fact that Meredith so accurately delineates his wife's anguish while he is still in the throes of his own suffering.

A different kind of disillusionment is revealed in A. E. Housman's "When I Was One and Twenty." The young narrator has been told that suffering and sorrow inevitably follow love, but with the self-assuredness of youth does not heed the advice. After experiencing his first love, however, the now cynical narrator testifies to the wisdom of the advice he had rejected a year earlier. What appeals to us in this poem is not so much the theme (though its playful cynicism contains more than a little wisdom), but the exact yet simple technique with which Housman chisels his words.

T. S. Eliot's "The Love Song of J. Alfred Prufrock" shares the psychological realism of Meredith. Cast as a dramatic monologue, the poem deals with two characters (the "you and I" of the first line) who are actually two separate personalities within the same person. The poem describes a situation in which the middle-aged Prufrock confronts both himself and his meaningless, monotonous life. Anxiety, fear, and feelings of inferiority prevent the consummation of physical love and force the narrator into recognizing his own limitations.

The variety in the selections chosen for this section should suggest to the student the wide range of attitudes expressed in the poetry of love. Certainly no other emotion has more persistently and more variously been the inspiration for great lyric poetry.

THE PASSIONATE SHEPHERD TO HIS LOVE

Come live with me and be my Love,
And we will all the pleasures prove
That valleys, groves, hills and fields,
Woods or steepy mountain yields.

5   And we will sit upon the rocks
Seeing the shepherds feed their flocks,
By shallow rivers, to whose falls
Melodious birds sing madrigals.

And I will make thee beds of roses
10   And a thousand fragrant posies,
A cap of flowers, and a kirtle
Embroidered all with leaves of myrtle.

A gown made of the finest wool,
Which from our pretty lambs we pull,
15   Fair linèd slippers for the cold,
With buckles of the purest gold.

A belt of straw and ivy buds,
With coral clasps and amber studs:
And if these pleasures may thee move,
20   Come live with me and be my Love.

The shepherd swains shall dance and sing
For thy delight each May-morning:
If these delights thy mind may move,
Then live with me and be my Love.

Christopher Marlowe   (1564 – 1593)

A VALEDICTION: FORBIDDING MOURNING

As virtuous men pass mildly away,
   And whisper to their souls, to go,
Whilst some of their sad friends do say,
   The breath goes now, and some say, no:

5   So let us melt, and make no noise
   No tear-floods, nor sigh-tempests move;
'Twere profanation of our joys
   To tell the laity our love.

10
Moving of th' earth brings harms and fears,
    Men reckon what it did and meant,
But trepidation of the spheres,
    Though greater far, is innocent.

15
Dull sublunary lovers' love
    (Whose soul is sense) cannot admit
Absence, because it doth remove
    Those things which elemented it.

20
But we by a love so much refined
    That our selves know not what it is,
Inter-assured of the mind,
    Care less, eyes, lips, and hands to miss.

Our two souls therefore, which are one,
    Though I must go, endure not yet
A breach, but an expansion,
    Like gold to airy thinness beat.

25
If they be two, they are two so
    As stiff twin compasses are two;
Thy soul, the fixed foot, makes no show
    To move, but doth, if th' other do.

30
And though it in the center sit,
    Yet when the other far doth roam,
It leans, and hearkens after it,
    And grows erect, as that comes home.

35
Such wilt thou be to me, who must
    Like th' other foot, obliquely run;
Thy firmness makes my circle just,
    And makes me end, where I begun.

John Donne   (1571?–1631)

TO THE VIRGINS, TO MAKE MUCH OF TIME

Gather ye rose-buds while ye may,
    Old Time is still a-flying:
And this same flower that smiles today,
    Tomorrow will be dying.

5   The glorious lamp of heaven, the Sun,
        The higher he's a-getting
     The sooner will his race be run,
        And nearer he's to setting.

     That age is best which is the first,
10   When youth and blood are warmer;
     But being spent, the worse, and worst
        Times, still succeed the former.

     Then be not coy, but use your time;
        And while ye may, go marry:
15   For having lost but once your prime,
        You may for ever tarry.

                    Robert Herrick   (1591 – 1674)

TO HIS COY MISTRESS

     Had we but world enough, and time,
     This coyness, lady, were no crime.
     We would sit down, and think which way
     To walk, and pass our long love's day.
5   Thou by the Indian Ganges' side
     Should'st rubies find: I by the tide
     Of Humber would complain. I would
     Love you ten years before the Flood,
     And you should, if you please, refuse
10   Till the conversion of the Jews.
     My vegetable love should grow
     Vaster than empires, and more slow.
     An hundred years should go to praise
     Thine eyes, and on thy forehead gaze:
15   Two hundred to adore each breast:
     But thirty thousand to the rest;
     An age at least to every part,
     And the last age should show your heart.
     For, lady, you deserve this state,
20   Nor would I love at lower rate.
        But at my back I always hear
     Time's wingèd chariot hurrying near:
     And yonder all before us lie
     Deserts of vast eternity.
25   Thy beauty shall no more be found;

Nor, in thy marble vault, shall sound
My echoing song: then worms shall try
That long-preserved virginity,
And your quaint honor turn to dust,
30   And into ashes all my lust.
The grave's a fine and private place,
But none, I think, do there embrace.
    Now, therefore, while the youthful hue
Sits on thy skin like morning dew,
35   And while thy willing soul transpires
At every pore with instant fires,
Now let us sport us while we may;
And now, like amorous birds of prey,
Rather at once our Time devour,
40   Than languish in his slow-chapt power.
Let us roll all our strength and all
Our sweetness up into one ball,
And tear our pleasures with rough strife
Through the iron gates of life.
45   Thus, though we cannot make our sun
Stand still, yet we will make him run.

Andrew Marvell   (1621 – 1678)

THE GARDEN OF LOVE

I went to the Garden of Love,
And saw what I never had seen:
A Chapel was built in the midst,
Where I used to play on the green.

5   And the gates of this Chapel were shut,
And "Thou shalt not" writ over the door;
So I turn'd to the Garden of Love
That so many sweet flowers bore;

And I saw it was fillèd with graves,
10   And tomb-stones where flowers should be;
And Priests in black gowns were walking their rounds,
And binding with briars my joys & desires.

William Blake   (1757 – 1827)

JOHN ANDERSON, MY JO

John Anderson, my jo, John,
    When we were first acquent,
Your locks were like the raven,
    Your bonie brow was brent;
5   But now your brow is beld, John,
    Your locks are like the snaw,
But blessings on your frosty pow,
    John Anderson, my jo!

John Anderson, my jo, John,
10   We clamb the hill thegither,
And monie a cantie day, John,
    We've had wi' ane anither;
Now we maun totter down, John,
    And hand in hand we'll go,
15 And sleep thegither at the foot,
    John Anderson, my jo!

Robert Burns   (1759 – 1796)

(Gloss: brent, smooth; beld, bald; pow, head; cantie, happy)

EPIPSYCHIDION

Sweet Spirit! Sister of that orphan one,
Whose empire is the name thou weepest on,
In my heart's temple I suspend to thee
These votive wreaths of withered memory.

5   Poor captive bird! who, from thy narrow cage,
Pourest such music, that it might assuage
The ruggèd hearts of those who prisoned thee,
Were they not deaf to all sweet melody;
This song shall be thy rose: its petals pale
10 Are dead, indeed, my adored Nightingale!
But soft and fragrant is the faded blossom,
And it has no thorn left to wound thy bosom.

High, spirit-wingèd Heart! who dost for ever
Beat thine unfeeling bars with vain endeavour,
15   Till those bright plumes of thought, in which arrayed
It over-soared this low and worldly shade,

Lie shattered; and thy panting, wounded breast
Stains with dear blood its unmaternal nest!
I weep vain tears: blood would less bitter be,
20   Yet poured forth gladlier, could it profit thee.

    Seraph of Heaven! too gentle to be human,
Veiling beneath that radiant form of Woman
All that is insupportable in thee
Of light, and love, and immortality!
25   Sweet Benediction in the eternal Curse!
Veiled Glory of this lampless Universe!
Thou Moon beyond the clouds! Thou living Form
Among the Dead! Thou Star above the Storm!
Thou Wonder, and thou Beauty, and thou Terror!
30   Thou Harmony of Nature's art! Thou Mirror
In whom, as in the splendour of the Sun,
All shapes look glorious which thou gazest on!
Ay, even the dim words which obscure thee now
Flash, lightning-like, with unaccustomed glow;
35   I pray thee that thou blot from this sad song
All of its much mortality and wrong,
With those clear drops, which start like sacred dew
From the twin lights thy sweet soul darkens through,
Weeping, till sorrow becomes ecstasy:
40   Then smile on it, so that it may not die.

    I never thought before my death to see
Youth's vision thus made perfect. Emily,
I love thee; though the world by no thin name
Will hide that love from its unvalued shame.
45   Would we two had been twins of the same mother!
Or, that the name my heart lent to another
Could be a sister's bond for her and thee,
Blending two beams of one eternity!
Yet were one lawful and the other true,
50   These names, though dear, could paint not, as is due,
How beyond refuge I am thine. Ah me!
I am not thine: I am a part of *thee*.

    Sweet Lamp! my moth-like Muse has burned its wings
Or, like a dying swan who soars and sings,
55   Young Love should teach Time, in his own gray style,
All that thou art. Art thou not void of guile,
A lovely soul formed to be blessed and bless?
A well of sealed and secret happiness,
Whose waters like blithe light and music are,
60   Vanquishing dissonance and gloom? A Star
Which moves not in the moving heavens, alone?
A Smile amid dark frowns? a gentle tone

Amid rude voices? a belovèd light?
A Solitude, a Refuge, a Delight?
65   A Lute, which those whom Love has taught to play
Make music on, to soothe the roughest day
And lull fond Grief asleep? a buried treasure?
A cradle of young thoughts of wingless pleasure?
A violet-shrouded grave of Woe?—I measure
70   The world of fancies, seeking one like thee,
And find—alas! mine own infirmity.

She met me, Stranger, upon life's rough way,
And lured me towards sweet Death; as Night by Day,
Winter by Spring, or Sorrow by swift Hope,
75   Led into light, life, peace. An antelope,
In the suspended impulse of its lightness,
Were less aethereally light: the brightness
Of her divinest presence trembles through
Her limbs, as underneath a cloud of dew
80   Embodied in the windless heaven of June
Amid the splendour-wingèd stars, the Moon
Burns, inextinguishably beautiful:
And from her lips, as from a hyacinth full
Of honey-dew, a liquid murmur drops,
85   Killing the sense with passion; sweet as stops
Of planetary music heard in trance.
In her mild lights the starry spirits dance,
The sunbeams of those wells which ever leap
Under the lightnings of the soul—too deep
90   For the brief fathom-line of thought or sense.
The glory of her being, issuing thence,
Stains the dead, blank, cold air with a warm shade
Of unentangled intermixture, made
By Love, of light and motion: one intense
95   Diffusion, one serene Omnipresence,
Whose flowing outlines mingle in their flowing,
Around her cheeks and utmost fingers glowing
With the unintermitted blood, which there
Quivers, (as in a fleece of snow-like air
100   The crimson pulse of living morning quiver,)
Continuously prolonged, and ending never,
Till they are lost, and in that Beauty furled
Which penetrates and clasps and fills the world;
Scarce visible from extreme loveliness.
105   Warm fragrance seems to fall from her light dress
And her loose hair; and where some heavy tress
The air of her own speed has disentwined,
The sweetness seems to satiate the faint wind;
And in the soul a wild odour is felt,
110   Beyond the sense, like fiery dews that melt

Into the bosom of a frozen bud. —
See where she stands! a mortal shape indued
With love and life and light and deity,
And motion which may change but cannot die;
115   An image of some bright Eternity;
A shadow of some golden dream; a Splendour
Leaving the third sphere pilotless; a tender
Reflection of the eternal Moon of Love
Under whose motions life's dull billows move;
120   A Metaphor of Spring and Youth and Morning;
A Vision like incarnate April, warning,
With smiles and tears, Frost the Anatomy
Into his summer grave.
                    Ah, woe is me!
What have I dared? where am I lifted? how
125   Shall I descend, and perish not? I know
That Love makes all things equal: I have heard
By mine own heart this joyous truth averred:
The spirit of the worm beneath the sod
In love and worship, blends itself with God.

130   Spouse! Sister! Angel! Pilot of the Fate
Whose course has been so starless! O too late
Belovéd! O too soon adored, by me!
For in the fields of Immortality
My spirit should at first have worshipped thine,
135   A divine presence in a place divine;
Or should have moved beside it on this earth,
A shadow of that substance, from its birth;
But not as now: — I love thee; yes, I feel
That on the fountain of my heart a seal
140   Is set, to keep its waters pure and bright
For thee, since in those *tears* thou hast delight.
We — are we not formed, as notes of music are,
For one another, though dissimilar;
Such difference without discord, as can make
145   Those sweetest sounds, in which all spirits shake
As trembling leaves in a continuous air?

Thy wisdom speaks in me, and bids me dare
Beacon the rocks on which high hearts are wrecked.
I never was attached to that great sect,
150   Whose doctrine is, that each one should select
Out of the crowd a mistress or a friend,
And all the rest, though fair and wise, commend
To cold oblivion, though it is in the code
Of modern morals, and the beaten road
155   Which those poor slaves with weary footsteps tread,
Who travel to their home among the dead

By the broad highway of the world, and so
With one chained friend, perhaps a jealous foe,
The dreariest and the longest journey go.

160   True Love in this differs from gold and clay,
That to divide is not to take away.
Love is like understanding, that grows bright,
Gazing on many truths; 'tis like thy light,
Imagination! which from earth and sky,

165   And from the depths of human fantasy,
As from a thousand prisms and mirrors, fills
The Universe with glorious beams, and kills
Error, the worm, with many a sun-like arrow
Of its reverberated lightning. Narrow

170   The heart that loves, the brain that contemplates,
The life that wears, the spirit that creates
One object, and one form, and builds thereby
A sepulchre for its eternity.

      Mind from its object differs most in this:

175   Evil from good; misery from happiness;
The baser from the nobler; the impure
And frail, from what is clear and must endure.
If you divide suffering and dross, you may
Diminish till it is consumed away;

180   If you divide pleasure and love and thought,
Each part exceeds the whole; and we know not
How much, while any yet remains unshared,
Of pleasure may be gained, of sorrow spared:
This truth is that deep well, whence sages draw

185   The unenvied light of hope; the eternal law
By which those live, to whom this world of life
Is as a garden ravaged, and whose strife
Tills for the promise of a later birth
The wilderness of this Elysian earth.

190   There was a Being whom my spirit oft
Met on its visioned wanderings, far aloft,
In the clear golden prime of my youth's dawn,
Upon the fairy isles of sunny lawn,
Amid the enchanted mountains, and the caves

195   Of divine sleep, and on the air-like waves
Of wonder-level dream, whose tremulous floor
Paved her light steps;—on an imagined shore,
Under the gray beak of some promontory
She met me, robed in such exceeding glory,

200   That I beheld her not. In solitudes
Her voice came to me through the whispering woods,
And from the fountains, and the odours deep

Of flowers, which, like lips murmuring in their sleep
Of the sweet kisses which had lulled them there,
205 Breathed but of *her* to the enamoured air;
And from the breezes whether low or loud,
And from the rain of every passing cloud,
And from the singing of the summer-birds,
And from all sounds, all silence. In the words
210 Of antique verse and high romance, — in form,
Sound, colour — in whatever checks that Storm
Which with the shattered present chokes the past;
And in that best philosophy, whose taste
Makes this cold common hell, our life, a doom
215 As glorious as a fiery martyrdom;
Her Spirit was the harmony of truth. —

Then, from the caverns of my dreamy youth
I sprang, as one sandalled with plumes of fire,
And towards the lodestar of my one desire,
220 I flitted, like a dizzy moth, whose flight
Is as a dead leaf's in the owlet light,
When it would seek in Hesper's setting sphere
A radiant death, a fiery sepulchre,
As if it were a lamp of earthly flame. —
225 But She, whom prayers or tears then could not tame,
Passed, like a God throned on a wingèd planet,
Whose burning plumes to tenfold swiftness fan it,
Into the dreary cone of our life's shade;
And as a man with mighty loss dismayed,
230 I would have followed, though the grave between
Yawned like a gulf whose spectres are unseen:
When a voice said: — 'O thou of hearts the weakest,
The phantom is beside thee whom thou seekest.'
Then I — 'Where?' — the world's echo answered 'where?'
235 And in that silence, and in my despair,
I questioned every tongueless wind that flew
Over my tower of mourning, if it knew
Whither 'twas fled, this soul out of my soul;
And murmured names and spells which have control
240 Over the sightless tyrants of our fate;
But neither prayer nor verse could dissipate
The night which closed on her; nor uncreate
That world within this Chaos, mine and me,
Of which she was the veiled Divinity,
245 The world I say of thoughts that worshipped her:
And therefore I went forth, with hope and fear
And every gentle passion sick to death,
Feeding my course with expectation's breath,
Into the wintry forest of our life;
250 And struggling through its error with vain strife,

And stumbling in my weakness and my haste,
And half bewildered by new forms, I passed,
Seeking among those untaught foresters
If I could find one form resembling hers,
255   In which she might have masked herself from me.
There, — One, whose voice was venomed melody
Sate by a well, under blue nightshade bowers;
The breath of her false mouth was like faint flowers,
Her touch was as electric poison, — flame
260   Out of her looks into my vitals came,
And from her living cheeks and bosom flew
A killing air, which pierced like honey-dew
Into the core of my green heart, and lay
Upon its leaves; until, as hair grown gray
265   O'er a young brow, they hid its unblown prime
With ruins of unseasonable time.

In many mortal forms I rashly sought
The shadow of that idol of my thought.
And some were fair — but beauty dies away:
270   Others were wise — but honeyed words betray:
And One was true — oh! why not true to me?
Then, as a hunted deer that could not flee,
I turned upon my thoughts, and stood at bay,
Wounded and weak and panting; the cold day
275   Trembled, for pity of my strife and pain.
When, like a noonday dawn, there shone again
Deliverance. One stood on my path who seemed
As like the glorious shape which I had dreamed
As is the Moon, whose changes ever run
280   Into themselves, to the eternal Sun;
The cold chaste Moon, the Queen of Heaven's bright isles,
Who makes all beautiful on which she smiles,
That wandering shrine of soft yet icy flame
Which ever is transformed, yet still the same,
285   And warms not but illumines. Young and fair
As the descended Spirit of that sphere,
She hid me, as the Moon may hide the night
From its own darkness, until all was bright
Between the Heaven and Earth of my calm mind,
290   And, as a cloud charioted by the wind,
She led me to a cave in that wild place,
And sate beside me, with her downward face
Illumining my slumbers, like the Moon
Waxing and waning o'er Endymion.
295   And I was laid asleep, spirit and limb,
And all my being became bright or dim
As the Moon's image in a summer sea,
According as she smiled or frowned on me;

And there I lay, within a chaste cold bed:
300   Alas, I then was nor alive nor dead: —
For at her silver voice came Death and Life,
Unmindful each of their accustomed strife,
Masked like twin babes, a sister and a brother,
The wandering hopes of one abandoned mother,
305   And through the cavern without wings they flew,
And cried 'Away, he is not of our crew.'
I wept, and though it be a dream, I weep.

What storms then shook the ocean of my sleep,
Blotting that Moon, whose pale and waning lips
310   Then shrank as in the sickness of eclipse; —
And how my soul was as a lampless sea,
And who was then its Tempest; and when She,
The Planet of that hour, was quenched, what frost
Crept o'er those waters, till from coast to coast
315   The moving billows of my being fell
Into a death of ice, immovable; —
And then — what earthquakes made it gape and split,
The white Moon smiling all the while on it,
These words conceal: — If not, each word would be
320   The key of staunchless tears. Weep not for me!

At length, into the obscure Forest came
The Vision I had sought through grief and shame.
Athwart that wintry wilderness of thorns
Flashed from her motion splendour like the Morn's,
325   And from her presence life was radiated
Through the gray earth and branches bare and dead;
So that her way was paved, and roofed above
With flowers as soft as thoughts of budding love;
And music from her respiration spread
330   Like light, — all other sounds were penetrated
By the small, still, sweet spirit of that sound,
So that the savage winds hung mute around;
And odours warm and fresh fell from her hair
Dissolving the dull cold in the frore air:
335   Soft as an Incarnation of the Sun,
When light is changed to love, this glorious One
Floated into the cavern where I lay,
And called my Spirit, and the dreaming clay
Was lifted by the thing that dreamed below
340   As smoke by fire, and in her beauty's glow
I stood, and felt the dawn of my long night
Was penetrating me with living light:
I knew it was the Vision veiled from me
So many years — that it was Emily.

345   Twin Spheres of light who rule this passive Earth,
       This world of love, this *me*; and into birth
       Awaken all its fruits and flowers, and dart
       Magnetic might into its central heart;
       And lift its billows and its mists, and guide
350   By everlasting laws, each wind and tide
       To its fit cloud, and its appointed cave;
       And lull its storms, each in the craggy grave
       Which was its cradle, luring to faint bowers
       The armies of the rainbow-wingèd showers;
355   And, as those married lights, which from the towers
       Of Heaven look forth and fold the wandering globe
       In liquid sleep and splendour, as a robe;
       And all their many-mingled influence blend,
       If equal, yet unlike, to one sweet end; —
360   So ye, bright regents, with alternate sway
       Govern my sphere of being, night and day!
       Thou, not disdaining even a borrowed might;
       Thou, not eclipsing a remoter light;
       And, through the shadow of the seasons three,
365   From Spring to Autumn's sere maturity,
       Light it into the Winter of the tomb,
       Where it may ripen to a brighter bloom.
       Thou too, O Comet beautiful and fierce,
       Who drew the heart of this frail Universe
370   Towards thine own; till, wrecked in that convulsion,
       Alternating attraction and repulsion,
       Thine went astray and that was rent in twain;
       Oh, float into our azure heaven again!
       Be there Love's folding-star at thy return;
375   The living Sun will feed thee from its urn
       Of golden fire; the Moon will veil her horn
       In thy last smiles; adoring Even and Morn
       Will worship thee with incense of calm breath
       And lights and shadows; as the star of Death
380   And Birth is worshipped by those sisters wild
       Called Hope and Fear — upon the heart are piled
       Their offerings, — of this sacrifice divine
       A World shall be the altar.
                        Lady mine,
       Scorn not these flowers of thought, the fading birth
385   Which from its heart of hearts that plant puts forth
       Whose fruit, made perfect by thy sunny eyes,
       Will be as of the trees of Paradise.

       The day is come, and thou wilt fly with me.
       To whatsoe'er of dull mortality
390   Is mine, remain a vestal sister still;
       To the intense, the deep, the imperishable,

Not mine but me, henceforth be thou united
Even as a bride, delighting and delighted.
The hour is come: — the destined Star has risen
395   Which shall descend upon a vacant prison.
The walls are high, the gates are strong, thick set
The sentinels — but true Love never yet
Was thus constrained: it overleaps all fence:
Like lightning, with invisible violence
400   Piercing its continents; like Heaven's free breath,
Which he who grasps can hold not; liker Death,
Who rides upon a thought, and makes his way
Through temple, tower, and palace, and the array
Of arms: more strength has Love than he or they;
405   For it can burst his charnel, and make free
The limbs in chains, the heart in agony,
The soul in dust and chaos.
                                Emily,
A ship is floating in the harbour now,
A wind is hovering o'er the mountain's brow;
410   There is a path on the sea's azure floor,
No keel has ever ploughed that path before;
The halcyons brood around the foamless isles;
The treacherous Ocean has forsworn its wiles;
The merry mariners are bold and free:
415   Say, my heart's sister, wilt thou sail with me?
Our bark is as an albatross, whose nest
Is a far Eden of the purple East;
And we between her wings will sit, while Night,
And Day, and Storm, and Calm, pursue their flight,
420   Our ministers, along the boundless Sea,
Treading each other's heels, unheededly.
It is an isle under Ionian skies,
Beautiful as a wreck of Paradise,
And, for the harbours are not safe and good,
425   This land would have remained a solitude
But for some pastoral people native there,
Who from the Elysian, clear, and golden air
Draw the last spirit of the age of gold,
Simple and spirited; innocent and bold.
430   The blue Aegean girds this chosen home,
With ever-changing sound and light and foam,
Kissing the sifted sands, and caverns hoar;
And all the winds wandering along the shore
Undulate with the undulating tide:
435   There are thick woods where sylvan forms abide;
And many a fountain, rivulet, and pond,
As clear as elemental diamond,
Or serene morning air; and far beyond,
The mossy tracks made by the goats and deer

440 (Which the rough shepherd treads but once a year)
Pierce into glades, caverns, and bowers, and halls
Built round with ivy, which the waterfalls
Illumining, with sound that never fails
Accompany the noonday nightingales;
445 And all the place is peopled with sweet airs;
The light clear element which the isle wears
Is heavy with the scent of lemon-flowers,
Which floats like mist laden with unseen showers,
And falls upon the eyelids like faint sleep;
450 And from the moss violets and jonquils peep,
And dart their arrowy odour through the brain
Till you might faint with that delicious pain.
And every motion, odour, beam, and tone,
With that deep music is in unison:
455 Which is a soul within the soul—they seem
Like echoes of an antenatal dream.—
It is an isle 'twixt Heaven, Air, Earth, and Sea,
Cradled, and hung in clear tranquillity;
Bright as that wandering Eden Lucifer,
460 Washed by the soft blue Oceans of young air.
It is a favoured place. Famine or Blight,
Pestilence, War and Earthquake, never light
Upon its mountain-peaks; blind vultures, they
Sail onward far upon their fatal way:
465 The wingèd storms, chanting their thunder-psalm
To other lands, leave azure chasms of calm
Over this isle, or weep themselves in dew,
From which its fields and woods ever renew
Their green and golden immortality.
470 And from the sea there rise, and from the sky
There fall, clear exhalations, soft and bright,
Veil after veil, each hiding some delight,
Which Sun or Moon or zephyr draw aside,
Till the isle's beauty, like a naked bride
475 Glowing at once with love and loveliness,
Blushes and trembles at its own excess:
Yet, like a buried lamp, a Soul no less
Burns in the heart of this delicious isle,
An atom of th' Eternal, whose own smile
480 Unfolds itself, and may be felt, not seen
O'er the gray rocks, blue waves, and forests green,
Filling their bare and void interstices.—
But the chief marvel of the wilderness
Is a lone dwelling, built by whom or how
485 None of the rustic island-people know:
'Tis not a tower of strength, though with its height
It overtops the woods; but, for delight,
Some wise and tender Ocean-King, ere crime

Had been invented, in the world's young prime,
490   Reared it, a wonder of that simple time,
An envy of the isles, a pleasure-house
Made sacred to his sister and his spouse.
It scarce seems now a wreck of human art,
But, as it were Titanic; in the heart
495   Of Earth having assumed its form, then grown
Out of the mountains, from the living stone,
Lifting itself in caverns light and high:
For all the antique and learnèd imagery
Has been erased, and in the place of it
500   The ivy and the wild-vine interknit
The volumes of their many-twining stems;
Parasite flowers illume with dewy gems
The lampless halls, and when they fade, the sky
Peeps through their winter-woof of tracery
505   With moonlight patches, or star atoms keen,
Or fragments of the day's intense serene; —
Working mosaic on their Parian floors.
And, day and night, aloof, from the high towers
And terraces, the Earth and Ocean seem
510   To sleep in one another's arms, and dream
Of waves, flowers, clouds, woods, rocks, and all that we
Read in their smiles, and call reality.

This isle and house are mine, and I have vowed
Thee to be lady of the solitude. —
515   And I have fitted up some chambers there
Looking towards the golden Eastern air,
And level with the living winds, which flow
Like waves above the living waves below. —
I have sent books and music there, and all
520   Those instruments with which high Spirits call
The future from its cradle, and the past
Out of its grave, and make the present last
In thoughts and joys which sleep, but cannot die,
Folded within their own eternity.
525   Our simple life wants little, and true taste
Hires not the pale drudge Luxury, to waste
The scene it would adorn, and therefore still,
Nature with all her children haunts the hill.
The ring-dove, in the embowering ivy, yet
530   Keeps up her love-lament, and the owls flit
Round the evening tower, and the young stars glance
Between the quick bats in their twilight dance;
The spotted deer bask in the fresh moonlight
Before our gate, and the slow, silent night
535   Is measured by the pants of their calm sleep.
Be this our home in life, and when years heap

Their withered hours, like leaves, on our decay,
Let us become the overhanging day,
The living soul of this Elysian isle,
540   Conscious, inseparable, one. Meanwhile
We two will rise, and sit, and walk together,
Under the roof of blue Ionian weather,
And wander in the meadows, or ascend
The mossy mountains, where the blue heavens bend
545   With lightest winds, to touch their paramour;
Or linger, where the pebble-paven shore,
Under the quick, faint kisses of the sea
Trembles and sparkles as with ecstasy,—
Possessing and possessed by all that is
550   Within that calm circumference of bliss,
And by each other, till to love and live
Be one:—or, at the noontide hour, arrive
Where some old cavern hoar seems yet to keep
The moonlight of the expired night asleep,
555   Through which the awakened day can never peep;
A veil for our seclusion, close as night's,
Where secure sleep may kill thine innocent lights;
Sleep, the fresh dew of languid love, the rain
Whose drops quench kisses till they burn again.
560   And we will talk, until thought's melody
Become too sweet for utterance, and it die
In words, to live again in looks, which dart
With thrilling tone into the voiceless heart,
Harmonizing silence without a sound.
565   Our breath shall intermix, our bosoms bound,
And our veins beat together; and our lips
With other eloquence than words, eclipse
The soul that burns between them, and the wells
Which boil under our being's inmost cells,
570   The fountains of our deepest life, shall be
Confused in Passion's golden purity,
As mountain-springs under the morning sun.
We shall become the same, we shall be one
Spirit within two frames, oh! wherefore two?
575   One passion in twin-hearts, which grows and grew,
Till like two meteors of expanding flame,
Those spheres instinct with it become the same,
Touch, mingle, are transfigured; ever still
Burning, yet ever inconsumable:
580   In one another's substance finding food,
Like flames too pure and light and unimbued
To nourish their bright lives with baser prey,
Which point to Heaven and cannot pass away:
One hope within two wills, one will beneath
585   Two overshadowing minds, one life, one death,

One Heaven, one Hell, one immortality,
And one annihilation. Woe is me!
The wingèd words on which my soul would pierce
Into the height of Love's rare Universe,
590 Are chains of lead around its flight of fire—
I pant, I sink, I tremble, I expire!

————————

Weak Verses, go, kneel at your Sovereign's feet,
And say:—'We are the masters of thy slave;
What wouldest thou with us and ours and thine?'
595 Then call your sisters from Oblivion's cave,
All singing loud: 'Love's very pain is sweet,
But its reward is in the world divine
Which, if not here, it builds beyond the grave.'
So shall ye live when I am there. Then haste
600 Over the hearts of men, until ye meet
Marina, Vanna, Primus, and the rest,
And bid them love each other and be blessed:
And leave the troop which errs, and which reproves,
And come and be my guest,—for I am Love's.

Percy Bysshe Shelley   (1792 – 1822)

LA BELLE DAME SANS MERCI

O what can ail thee, knight-at-arms,
    Alone and palely loitering?
The sedge has withered from the lake,
    And no birds sing.

5   O what can ail thee, knight-at-arms,
    So haggard and so woe-begone?
The squirrel's granary is full,
    And the harvest's done.

I see a lily on thy brow
10   With anguish moist and fever dew,
And on thy cheeks a fading rose
    Fast withereth too.

I met a lady in the meads,
    Full beautiful—a faery's child,
15   Her hair was long, her foot was light,
    And her eyes were wild.

I made a garland for her head,
  And bracelets too, and fragrant zone;
She looked at me as she did love,
20   And made sweet moan.

I set her on my pacing steed
  And nothing else saw all day long,
For sidelong would she bend, and sing
  A faery's song.

25   She found me roots of relish sweet,
  And honey wild, and manna dew,
And sure in language strange she said—
  "I love thee true!"

She took me to her elfin grot,
30   And there she wept and sighed full sore,
And there I shut her wild, wild eyes
  With kisses four.

And there she lulléd me asleep,
  And there I dreamed—ah, woe betide!
35   The latest dream I ever dreamed
  On the cold hill side.

I saw pale kings, and princes too,
  Pale warriors, death-pale were they all;
They cried—"La Belle Dame sans Merci
40   Thee hath in thrall!"

I saw their starved lips in the gloam,
  With horrid warning gapéd wide,
And I awoke and found me here,
  On the cold hill's side.

45   And this is why I sojourn here,
  Alone and palely loitering,
Though the sedge is withered from the lake,
  And no birds sing.

John Keats   (1795–1821)

SONNETS FROM THE PORTUGUESE XLIII (How do I
  love thee?)

famous

How do I love thee? Let me count the ways.
I love thee to the depth and breadth and height

My soul can reach, when feeling out of sight
For the ends of Being and ideal Grace.
5   I love thee to the level of every day's
Most quiet need, by sun and candlelight.
I love thee freely, as men strive for Right;
I love thee purely, as they turn from Praise;
I love thee with the passion put to use
10   In my old griefs, and with my childhood's faith.
I love thee with a love I seemed to lose
With my lost saints,—I love thee with the breath,
Smiles, tears, of all my life!—and, if God choose,
I shall but love thee better after death.

Elizabeth Barrett Browning   (1806 – 1861)

MODERN LOVE: I (By this he knew she wept with waking eyes)

By this he knew she wept with waking eyes:
That, at his hand's light quiver by her head,
The strange low sobs that shook their common bed
Were called into her with a sharp surprise,
5   And strangled mute, like little gaping snakes,
Dreadfully venomous to him. She lay
Stone-still, and the long darkness flowed away
With muffled pulses. Then, as midnight makes
Her giant heart of Memory and Tears
10   Drink the pale drug of silence, and so beat
Sleep's heavy measure, they from head to feet
Were moveless, looking through their dead black years,
By vain regret scrawled over the blank wall.
Like sculptured effigies they might be seen
15   Upon their marriage-tomb, the sword between;
Each wishing for the sword that severs all.

George Meredith   (1828 – 1909)

A SHROPSHIRE LAD XIII (When I was one-and-twenty)

When I was one-and-twenty
  I heard a wise man say,
"Give crowns and pounds and guineas
  But not your heart away;

5   Give pearls away and rubies
          But keep your fancy free.''
      But I was one-and-twenty,
          No use to talk to me.

      When I was one-and-twenty
10   I heard him say again,
      ''The heart out of the bosom
          Was never given in vain;
      'Tis paid with sighs a-plenty
          And sold for endless rue.''
15   And I am two-and-twenty,
          And oh, 'tis true, 'tis true.

                 A. E. Housman   (1859 – 1936)

THE LOVE SONG OF J. ALFRED PRUFROCK

S'io credesse che mia risposta fosse
a persona che mai tornasse al mondo,
questa fiamma staria senza più scosse.
Ma per ciò che giammai di questo fondo
non tornò vivo alcun, s'i' odo il vero,
*senza tema d'infamia ti rispondo.**

      Let us go then, you and I,
      When the evening is spread out against the sky
      Like a patient etherized upon a table;
      Let us go, through certain half-deserted streets,
5   The muttering retreats
      Of restless nights in one-night cheap hotels
      And sawdust restaurants with oyster-shells:
      Streets that follow like a tedious argument
      Of insidious intent
10   To lead you to an overwhelming question . . .
      Oh, do not ask, ''What is it?''
      Let us go and make our visit.

      In the room the women come and go
      Talking of Michelangelo.

*Translation of epigraph from Dante's *Inferno*, Canto XXVII: If I thought my reply were made to one who ever could return again to the world, this flame would remain motionless. But since none from this depth ever returned alive, if I hear the truth, I answer without fear of infamy.

15 The yellow fog that rubs its back upon the window-panes,
   The yellow smoke that rubs its muzzle on the window-panes,
   Licked its tongue into the corners of the evening,
   Lingered upon the pools that stand in drains,
   Let fall upon its back the soot that falls from chimneys,
20 Slipped by the terrace, made a sudden leap,
   And seeing that it was a soft October night,
   Curled once about the house, and fell asleep.

   And indeed there will be time
   For the yellow smoke that slides along the street
25 Rubbing its back upon the window-panes;
   There will be time, there will be time
   To prepare a face to meet the faces that you meet;
   There will be time to murder and create,
   And time for all the works and days of hands
30 That lift and drop a question on your plate;
   Time for you and time for me,
   And time yet for a hundred indecisions,
   And for a hundred visions and revisions,
   Before the taking of a toast and tea.

35 In the room the women come and go
   Talking of Michelangelo.

   And indeed there will be time
   To wonder, "Do I dare?" and, "Do I dare?"
   Time to turn back and descend the stair,
40 With a bald spot in the middle of my hair —
   (They will say: "How his hair is growing thin!")
   My morning coat, my collar mounting firmly to the chin,
   My necktie rich and modest, but asserted by a simple pin —
   (They will say: "But how his arms and legs are thin!")
45 Do I dare
   Disturb the universe?
   In a minute there is time
   For decisions and revisions which a minute will reverse.

   For I have known them all already, known them all—
50 Have known the evenings, mornings, afternoons,
   I have measured out my life with coffee spoons;
   I know the voices dying with a dying fall
   Beneath the music from a farther room.
       So how should I presume?

55 And I have known the eyes already, known them all—
   The eyes that fix you in a formulated phrase,
   And when I am formulated, sprawling on a pin,
   When I am pinned and wriggling on the wall,

Then how should I begin
60 To spit out all the butt-ends of my days and ways?
      And how should I presume?

And I have known the arms already, known them all —
Arms that are braceleted and white and bare
(But in the lamplight, downed with light brown hair!)
65 Is it perfume from a dress
That makes me so digress?
Arms that lie along a table, or wrap about a shawl.
      And should I then presume?
      And how should I begin?
                      .   .   .   .   .
70 Shall I say, I have gone at dusk through narrow streets
And watched the smoke that rises from the pipes
Of lonely men in shirt-sleeves, leaning out of windows? . . .

I should have been a pair of ragged claws
Scuttling across the floors of silent seas.
                      .   .   .   .   .
75 And the afternoon, the evening, sleeps so peacefully!
Smoothed by long fingers,
Asleep . . . tired . . . or it malingers,
Stretched on the floor, here beside you and me.
Should I, after tea and cakes and ices,
80 Have the strength to force the moment to its crisis?
But though I have wept and fasted, wept and prayed,
Though I have seen my head (grown slightly bald) brought in upon a
        platter,
I am no prophet — and here's no great matter;
I have seen the moment of my greatness flicker,
85 And I have seen the eternal Footman hold my coat, and snicker,
And in short, I was afraid.

And would it have been worth it, after all,
After the cups, the marmalade, the tea,
Among the porcelain, among some talk of you and me,
90 Would it have been worth while,
To have bitten off the matter with a smile,
To have squeezed the universe into a ball
To roll it toward some overwhelming question,
To say: "I am Lazarus, come from the dead,
95 Come back to tell you all, I shall tell you all" —
If one, settling a pillow by her head,
      Should say: "That is not what I meant at all.
      That is not it, at all."

And would it have been worth it, after all,
100 Would it have been worth while,

After the sunsets and the dooryards and the sprinkled streets,
After the novels, after the teacups, after the skirts that trail along the
    floor—
And this, and so much more?—
It is impossible to say just what I mean!
105   But as if a magic lantern threw the nerves in patterns on a screen:
Would it have been worth while
If one, settling a pillow or throwing off a shawl,
And turning toward the window, should say:
    "That is not it at all,
110   That is not what I meant, at all."

          .   .   .   .   .

No! I am not Prince Hamlet, nor was meant to be;
Am an attendant lord, one that will do
To swell a progress, start a scene or two,
Advise the prince; no doubt, an easy tool,
115   Deferential, glad to be of use,
Politic, cautious, and meticulous;
Full of high sentence, but a bit obtuse;
At times, indeed, almost ridiculous—
Almost, at times, the Fool.

120   I grow old . . . I grow old . . .
I shall wear the bottoms of my trousers rolled.

Shall I part my hair behind? Do I dare to eat a peach?
I shall wear white flannel trousers, and walk upon the beach.
I have heard the mermaids singing, each to each.
125   I do not think that they will sing to me.

I have seen them riding seaward on the waves
Combing the white hair of the waves blown back
When the wind blows the water white and black.

We have lingered in the chambers of the sea
130   By sea-girls wreathed with seaweed red and brown
Till human voices wake us, and we drown.

T. S. Eliot (1888–1965)

QUESTIONS FOR DISCUSSION AND FURTHER STUDY

THE PASSIONATE SHEPHERD TO HIS LOVE

1. Who is the speaker of the poem, and who comprises the audience? Does the speaker intend what he says to be taken literally? If not, what does he in fact mean?
2. Basically the poem is written in iambic tetrameter, and the lines trip along at a rapid pace. Why do you suppose that Marlowe desired this effect in terms of what the poem says?
3. As an exercise, try to write a prose paraphrase of this poem in modern English, using the idiom common to your social life.

A VALEDICTION: FORBIDDING MOURNING

1. What two kinds of lovers are contrasted in the poem?
2. Discuss the imagery in the poem. What are the major images, and how do they operate to sustain the meaning of the poem?
3. Remember that here the poem's speaker is bidding goodbye to his lady. (In actual fact Donne wrote the poem for his wife as he was about to leave on a diplomatic mission.) How effective do you think the poem is in "forbidding mourning"? Is what the speaker says true?

TO THE VIRGINS, TO MAKE MUCH OF TIME

1. Know the definition of the term *carpe diem*, to be found in the glossary.
2. There are three images in this poem; all are commonly found in *carpe diem* poetry. Why do you suppose that this is so?
3. While this poem and the next one, Marvell's "To His Coy Mistress," have approximately the same message, they appeal to different audiences. Which poem do you consider more effective? Why?

TO HIS COY MISTRESS

1. In this poem the speaker attempts to convince his audience of something. There are three parts to the poem. Summarize the argument made in each part.
2. The Ganges is a large Indian river; the Humber, a rather insignificant English one. Why does Marvell mention them together here?
3. Identify the use of hyperbole in the poem. What part does it play in establishing the tone of the total poem?

THE GARDEN OF LOVE

1. What is the meter, rhyme scheme, and line length of this poem?
2. Blake symbolizes his attitude toward organized religion by his comment about priests. How would you describe this attitude?
3. In this twelve-line poem, seven of the lines begin with the word "and." Do you feel that this repetition contributes something to the poem?

JOHN ANDERSON, MY JO

1. What image does Burns use in the second stanza to describe one's progress through life?
2. Bearing in mind that "jo" means "sweetheart," who are the speaker and audience in this poem? At what stage in life are they?
3. Why is the description of death as sleeping "thegither at the foot" particularly appropriate for these two?

EPIPSYCHIDION

1. Roughly translated, "Epipsychidion" means "this soul out of my soul." How is the meaning of the poem related to this theme? Describe as well as you can Shelley's doctrine of love, as stated in this poem.
2. Is there any thematic progression in this long poem, or does Shelley circle around the same theme recurrently?
3. The poem has been described by one scholar as a plea for "spiritual bigamy." What internal evidence is there for such a description?

LA BELLE DAME SANS MERCI

1. What stanzaic form does Keats use? Is this stanzaic form particularly appropriate for this poem's setting and story?
2. How many speakers are there in this poem?
3. Do you feel the poem is more or less powerful because we do not know why the beautiful lady has no mercy?
4. Can a poem of enchantment and legend like this one have a theme? If so, what is it?

SONNETS FROM THE PORTUGUESE XLIII (HOW DO I LOVE THEE)

1. State the type, structure, and rhyme scheme of this sonnet.
2. Do you feel that the poem suffers from the introduction of God towards the end? Why or why not?
3. The entire poem is based upon a simple question-answer technique. Do you feel the answer is excessively repetitious?

MODERN LOVE: I (BY THIS HE KNEW SHE WEPT WITH WAKING EYES)

1. The setting of this poem is especially important. Who are the two
    people in the poem? What is their emotional relationship at the
    time of the poem? In terms of this, why is the bed referred to as a
    "marriage-tomb"?
2. State the type, structure, and rhyme scheme of this poem.
3. "The sword between" refers to a medieval legend in which an
    unsheathed sword separates an unwed man and woman while
    they are sharing the same bed. Why is it used here in terms of the
    couple's emotional state?

A SHROPSHIRE LAD XIII (WHEN I WAS ONE-AND-TWENTY)

1. Do you think the "wise man" is wise? Why or why not?
2. Do you feel that the speaker of the poem is wise to allow himself
    to become so disillusioned at so young an age?
3. How would you characterize the language used in this poem? Is it
    simple or complex, concrete or abstract, formal or informal?

THE LOVE SONG OF J. ALFRED PRUFROCK

1. Describe the narrator's character. How much self-knowledge does
    he have? Does he grow or develop in the poem or does he remain
    the same throughout? What irony, if any, do you find in the title of
    the poem?
2. Are we supposed to admire the women who can speak of Michel-
    angelo? Why or why not?
3. Lazarus was a beggar who, after a life of suffering, was rewarded
    by God. Why does Eliot mention his name here?
4. The poem contains numerous literary allusions, one of them to
    Marvell's "To His Coy Mistress." Can you find that allusion? How
    does Prufrock differ from the speaker of Marvell's poem?

NATURE AND MAN

The term *nature poetry* eludes easy definition. In the sense that all good poetry depends upon concrete observation of man's environment, all good poetry is nature poetry. But a more specific, if tentative, definition of nature poetry includes the notion that some scene or incident in nature intrudes itself upon the poet's attention, giving rise to appreciation of or meditation about some aspect of the human condition. Robert Frost had something like that in mind when he wrote that a poem is an experience which "begins in delight and ends in wisdom."

Poems which speak of the relationship between nature and man fall characteristically into two parts. In the first part of the poem, the lyric poet is impressed, moved, or inspired by some specific incident or phenomenon to be found in nature. It may be quite simple — the observation of woods during a softly falling snow, a bird flying into the distance, the song of a nightingale, or a thrush in mid-winter. In the second part the poet abstracts from the incident or phenomenon to meditate upon its meaning, implications, or symbolic value. Usually, there is involved either an awareness of the relationship between man and nature or a sense of mystery at the awe, beauty, or power which nature can inspire in man. One of these alternatives is exemplified in each of the twelve poems in this section.

The earliest poem on nature and man anthologized, Henry Vaughan's "Metrum 5," requires an understanding of *primitivism*, upon which it is based. In rhymed couplets Vaughan contrasts the holiness, peace, and tranquility of an earlier age with his own seventeenth century. He pictures man in an Eden-like existence, living on nature's plenty and free from the lust for gold or pearls. Civilization is seen as evil:

Vaughan believes the customs, practices, and institutions of society are responsible for man's degeneration into evil and decay. Man in his natural or primitive state, then, is good; man driven from nature, less so.

A different emphasis appears in Robert Burns' poem "To a Mouse." Here, in the dialect of the Scotch countryside, Burns, who was himself a farmer, tells of the way his plow uprooted the nest of a field-mouse. Burns establishes an identification between himself and the mouse. Both have problems, both suffer, for both, the best-laid schemes go amiss. In fact, Burns suggests that his situation is even worse than that of the homeless animal, who is not bothered by memory of the past or fear of the future.

William Wordsworth's "Tintern Abbey" treats the more complex idea that the effect on the viewer of the same scenes of nature changes with the viewer's increasing maturity. The author contrasts two visits to a ruined abbey on the river Wye, the first in 1793, the second (with his younger sister Dorothy) in 1798. In his earlier years Wordsworth had viewed nature as a thing in itself, to be enjoyed or feared without reference to external phenomena or ideas. Now, however, he looks upon nature as a source of somber reflection upon the plight of man. In a sense, the poem can be read as a hymn of praise and thanks to nature for the gifts she bestows upon those who love her.

The next poem was written by Samuel Taylor Coleridge, the close friend of William and Dorothy Wordsworth. In "The Nightingale" Coleridge argues that man too often has imposed his own emotions upon nature and by so doing has profaned her. Attacking the cliché that the song of the nightingale is sad, Coleridge asserts conversely that "In Nature there is nothing melancholy."

William Cullen Bryant's poem "To a Waterfowl," inspired by the sight of a lone bird flying toward the distant horizon, speaks of the purpose and providence of nature. Just as the waterfowl finds a home and companionship through the workings of nature, so also will man. The poem becomes a hymn to the necessity of trust in God and belief in the way He looks over us. In other words, to Bryant the poet who observes nature finds God.

Ralph Waldo Emerson's poem "The Snow-Storm" finds nature herself sufficient for admiration. The poem depends primarily upon a personification of the north wind; his architectural and artistic skills are praised as Emerson describes with admirable concreteness the way that snow changes the appearance of a New England farm.

Walt Whitman's poem "When I Heard the Learn'd Astronomer" contrasts an analytic approach to nature with an aesthetic one. Whitman, disgusted by the boring and unappreciative discussion of the stars given by the astronomer, leaves the lecture-room and goes outside to observe the clear night sky in awe and love. This brief free-verse poem eloquently testifies to the age-old conflict between the literal and the artistic temperament.

In alternating couplets Thomas Hardy finds in "The Darkling Thrush" a symbol of hope for mankind. The setting of the poem helps explain its meaning. The nineteenth century is ending; it is the dead of winter; all seems lifeless and hopeless. One bird sings alone in the leafless wilderness. Characteristically, Hardy sees in this incident a reason for endurance and hope.

"The Lake Isle of Innisfree" describes Yeats' youthful attempts to find happiness and peace by immersing himself in nature. The images in this poem are so provocative, and the details suggesting peaceful harmony so particular and concrete, that the poem becomes a moving record of the artist's persistent attempt to find a source of happiness in beautiful things.

Robert Frost's "Stopping by Woods on a Snowy Evening" deservedly remains one of the best-loved modern American poems. Frost deliberately keeps his language simple and conversational in a universal statement about life which commands our attention. The last stanza contrasts the loveliness of the woods with the obligations of the buggy-driver. The tension between these two realities has been interpreted in various ways, but, in any event, one feels the great force and reality of Frost's image-evoking power. Few poems evoke such tranquility and peace as this one does.

"Their Lonely Betters" by W. H. Auden also employs the phrase "promises to keep." Auden compares the songs and happiness of nature (symbolized by the robin and the flower) with man's language and desires. The poem conveys the idea that both man and nature sing — however mutely — of their happiness and sadness.

The last poem in this section shares some of the ideas of the first. Howard Nemerov's "A Day on the Big Branch," like Vaughan's lyric, contrasts the purity of nature with the degradations of civilized society. The nameless characters of Nemerov's poem drive into the wilderness in an almost ritualistic attempt to cleanse and purify themselves. Richly symbolic throughout, the poem ends with a strong statement of nature's power and endurance, here symbolized by the way the stream has bent, twisted, and "smashed practically back to nature" the several bridges which spanned its banks.

The nature poet usually uses some aspect of nature for his more general observations. The range of such meditation is extensive, as is clearly shown by these selections. Despite the gradual withdrawal of civilized man from his natural environment, there remains a special kind of intimacy between him and nature. These poems reflect something of the power and tenderness of that relationship.

METRUM 5

Happy that first white age! when we
Lived by the earth's mere charity,
No soft luxurious diet then
Had effeminated men,
5   No other meat, nor wine had any
Than the course mast, or simple honey,
And by the parents' care laid up
Cheap berries did the children sup.
No pompous wear was in those days
10   Of gummy silks, or scarlet bays,
Their beds were on some flowery brink
And clear spring-water was their drink.
The shady pine in the sun's heat
Was their cool and known retreat,
15   For then 'twas not cut down, but stood
The youth and glory of the wood.
The daring sailor with his slaves
Then had not cut the swelling waves,
Nor for desire of foreign store
20 —   Seen any but his native shore.
No stirring drum had scarr'd that age,
Nor the shrill trumpet's active rage,
No wounds by bitter hatred made
With warm blood soil'd the shining blade;
25   For how could hostile madness arm
An age of love to public harm?
When common justice none withstood,
Nor sought rewards for spilling blood.

O that at length our age would raise
30   Into the temper of those days!
But (worse than Aetna's fires!) debate
And avarice inflame our state.
Alas! who was it that first found
Gold hid of purpose under ground,
35   That sought our pearls, and div'd to find
Such precious perils for mankind!

Henry Vaughan (1622 – 1695)

TO A MOUSE

On turning up her nest with the plow, November, 1785

     Wee, sleekit, cowrin, tim'rous beastie,
     O, what a panic's in thy breastie!
     Thou need na start awa sae hasty
          Wi' bickering brattle!
5   I wad be laith to rin an' chase thee,
          Wi' murdering pattle!

     I'm truly sorry man's dominion
     Has broken Nature's social union,
     An' justifies that ill opinion
10   Which makes thee startle
     At me, thy poor, earth-born companion
         An' fellow-mortal!

     I doubt na, whyles, but thou may thieve;
     What then? poor beastie, thou maun live:
15   A daimen icker in a thrave
         'S a sma' request
     I'll get a blessin wi' the lave,
         An' never miss 't!

     Thy wee-bit housie, too, in ruin!
20   Its silly wa's the win's are strewin!
     An' naething, now, to big a new ane,
         O' foggage green!
     An' bleak December's win's ensuin,
         Baith snell an' keen!

25   Thou saw the fields laid bare an' waste,
     An' weary winter comin' fast,
     An' cozie here, beneath the blast,
         Thou thought to dwell,
     Till, crash! the cruel coulter passed
30   Out through thy cell.

That wee bit heap o' leaves an' stibble,
Has cost thee monie a weary nibble!
Now thou's turned out, for a' thy trouble,
          But house or hald,
35   To thole the winter's sleety dribble,
          An' cranreuch cauld!

But Mousie, thou art no thy lane,
In proving foresight may be vain:
The best-laid schemes o' mice an' men
40   Gang aft agley,
An' lea'e us naught but grief an' pain,
          For promised joy!

Still thou art blest, compared wi' me!
The present only toucheth thee:
45   But och! I backward cast my e'e,
          On prospects drear!
An' forward, though I canna see,
          I guess an' fear!

               Robert Burns   (1759–1796)

(Gloss: bickering brattle, hurried scamper; laith, loath; whyles, sometimes; daimen . . . thrave, an occasional ear of corn from twenty-four sheaves; lave, rest; wa's, walls; big, build; foggage, coarse grass; snell, sharp; stibble, stubble; but, without; hald, abode; thole, endure; cranreuch, hoar-frost; no thy lane, not alone; gang aft agley, go often awry.)

LINES COMPOSED A FEW MILES ABOVE TINTERN ABBEY, ON REVISITING THE BANKS OF THE WYE DURING A TOUR

Five years have past; five summers, with the length
Of five long winters! and again I hear
These waters, rolling from their mountain-springs
With a soft inland murmur.—Once again
5   Do I behold these steep and lofty cliffs,
That on a wild secluded scene impress
Thoughts of more deep seclusion; and connect
The landscape with the quiet of the sky.
The day is come when I again repose
10   Here, under this dark sycamore, and view
These plots of cottage-ground, these orchard-tufts,

Which at this season, with their unripe fruits,
Are clad in one green hue, and lose themselves
'Mid groves and copses. Once again I see
15 These hedge-rows, hardly hedge-rows, little lines
Of sportive wood run wild: these pastoral farms,
Green to the very door; and wreaths of smoke
Sent up, in silence, from among the trees!
With some uncertain notice, as might seem
20 Of vagrant dwellers in the houseless woods,
Or of some hermit's cave, where by his fire
The hermit sits alone.
                    These beauteous forms,
Through a long absence, have not been to me
As is a landscape to blind man's eye:
25 But oft, in lonely rooms, and 'mid the din
Of towns and cities, I have owed to them
In hours of weariness, sensations sweet,
Felt in the blood, and felt along the heart;
And passing even into my purer mind,
30 With tranquil restoration: —feelings too
Of unremembered pleasure: such, perhaps,
As have no slight or trivial influence
On that best portion of a good man's life,
His little, nameless, unremembered acts
35 Of kindness and of love. Nor less, I trust,
To them I may have owed another gift,
Of aspect more sublime; that blessed mood,
In which the burthen of the mystery,
In which the heavy and the weary weight
40 Of all this unintelligible world,
Is lightened; —that serene and blessed mood,
In which the affections gently lead us on, —
Until, the breath of this corporeal frame
And even the motion of our human blood
45 Almost suspended, we are laid asleep
In body, and become a living soul:
While with an eye made quiet by the power
Of harmony, and the deep power of joy,
We see into the life of things.
                              If this
50 Be but a vain belief, yet, oh! how oft—
In darkness and amid the many shapes
Of joyless daylight; when the fretful stir
Unprofitable, and the fever of the world,
Have hung upon the beatings of my heart—
55 How oft, in spirit, have I turned to thee,
O sylvan Wye! thou wanderer thro' the woods,
How often has my spirit turned to thee!

And now, with gleams of half-extinguished thought,
With many recognitions dim and faint,
60   And somewhat of a sad perplexity,
The picture of the mind revives again:
While here I stand, not only with the sense
Of present pleasure, but with pleasing thoughts
That in this moment there is life and food
65   For future years. And so I dare to hope,
Though changed, no doubt, from what I was when first
I came among these hills; when like a roe
I bounded o'er the mountains, by the sides
Of the deep rivers, and the lonely streams,
70   Wherever nature led: more like a man
Flying from something that he dreads, than one
Who sought the thing he loved. For nature then
(The coarser pleasures of my boyish days,
And their glad animal movements all gone by)
75   To me was all in all.—I cannot paint
What then I was. The sounding cataract
Haunted me like a passion: the tall rock,
The mountain, and the deep and gloomy wood,
Their colours and their forms, were then to me
80   An appetite; a feeling and a love,
That had no need of a remoter charm,
By thought supplied, nor any interest
Unborrowed from the eye.—That time is past,
And all its aching joys are now no more,
85   And all its dizzy raptures. Not for this
Faint I, nor mourn nor murmur; other gifts
Have followed; for such loss, I would believe,
Abundant recompense. For I have learned
To look on nature, not as in the hour
90   Of thoughtless youth; but hearing oftentimes
The still, sad music of humanity,
Nor harsh nor grating, though of ample power
To chasten and subdue. And I have felt
A presence that disturbs me with the joy
95   Of elevated thoughts; a sense sublime
Of something far more deeply interfused,
Whose dwelling is the light of setting suns,
And the round ocean and the living air,
And the blue sky, and in the mind of man:
100   A motion and a spirit, that impels
All thinking things, all objects of all thought,
And rolls through all things. Therefore am I still
A lover of the meadows and the woods,
And mountains; and of all that we behold
105   From this green earth; of all the mighty world
Of eye, and ear,—both what they half create,

And what perceive; well pleased to recognise
In nature and the language of the sense,
The anchor of my purest thoughts, the nurse,
110 The guide, the guardian of my heart, and soul
Of all my moral being.
                              Nor perchance,
If I were not thus taught, should I the more
Suffer my genial spirits to decay:
For thou art with me here upon the banks
115 Of this fair river; thou my dearest friend,
My dear, dear friend; and in thy voice I catch
The language of my former heart, and read
My former pleasures in the shooting lights
Of thy wild eyes. Oh! yet a little while
120 May I behold in thee what I was once,
My dear, dear sister! and this prayer I make,
Knowing that Nature never did betray
The heart that loved her; 'tis her privilege,
Through all the years of this our life, to lead
125 From joy to joy: for she can so inform
The mind that is within us, so impress
With quietness and beauty, and so feed
With lofty thoughts, that neither evil tongues,
Rash judgments, nor the sneers of selfish men,
130 Nor greetings where no kindness is, nor all
The dreary intercourse of daily life,
Shall e'er prevail against us, or disturb
Our cheerful faith, that all which we behold
Is full of blessings. Therefore let the moon
135 Shine on thee in thy solitary walk;
And let the misty mountain-winds be free
To blow against thee: and, in after years,
When these wild ecstasies shall be matured
Into a sober pleasure; when thy mind
140 Shall be a mansion for all lovely forms,
Thy memory be as a dwelling-place
For all sweet sounds and harmonies; oh! then,
If solitude, or fear, or pain, or grief,
Should be thy portion, with what healing thoughts
145 Of tender joy wilt thou remember me,
And these my exhortations! Nor, perchance—
If I should be where I no more can hear
Thy voice, nor catch from thy wild eyes these gleams
Of past existence—wilt thou then forget
150 That on the banks of this delightful stream
We stood together; and that I, so long
A worshipper of Nature, hither came
Unwearied in that service: rather say
With warmer love—oh! with far deeper zeal

155   Of holier love. Nor wilt thou then forget,
        That after many wanderings, many years
        Of absence, these steep woods and lofty cliffs,
        And this green pastoral landscape, were to me
        More dear, both for themselves and for thy sake!

                    William Wordsworth   (1770 – 1850)

THE NIGHTINGALE

A Conversation Poem, April, 1798

        No cloud, no relique of the sunken day
        Distinguishes the West, no long thin slip
        Of sullen light, no obscure trembling hues.
        Come, we will rest on this old mossy bridge!
5   You see the glimmer of the stream beneath,
        But hear no murmuring: it flows silently,
        O'er its soft bed of verdure. All is still,
        A balmy night! and though the stars be dim,
        Yet let us think upon the vernal showers
10   That gladden the green earth, and we shall find
        A pleasure in the dimness of the stars.
        And hark! the Nightingale begins its song,
        "Most musical, most melancholy" bird!
        A melancholy bird? Oh! idle thought!
15   In Nature there is nothing melancholy.
        But some night-wandering man whose heart was pierced
        With the remembrance of a grievous wrong,
        Or slow distemper, or neglected love,
        (And so, poor wretch! filled all things with himself,
20   And made all gentle sounds tell back the tale
        Of his own sorrow) he, and such as he,
        First named these notes a melancholy strain.
        And many a poet echoes the conceit;
        Poet who hath been building up the rhyme
25   When he had better far have stretched his limbs
        Beside a brook in mossy forest-dell,
        By sun or moon-light, to the influxes
        Of shapes and sounds and shifting elements
        Surrendering his whole spirit, of his song
30   And of his fame forgetful! so his fame
        Should share in Nature's immortality,
        A venerable thing! and so his song
        Should make all Nature lovelier, and itself
        Be loved like Nature! But 'twill not be so;

35   And youths and maidens most poetical,
     Who lose the deepening twilights of the spring
     In ball-rooms and hot theatres, they still
     Full of meek sympathy must heave their sighs
     O'er Philomela's pity-pleading strains.

40   My friend, and thou, our Sister! we have learnt
     A different lore: we may not thus profane
     Nature's sweet voices, always full of love
     And joyance! 'Tis the merry Nightingale
     That crowds, and hurries, and precipitates
45   With fast thick warble his delicious notes,
     As he were fearful that an April night
     Would be too short for him to utter forth
     His love-chant, and disburthen his full soul
     Of all its music!

                    And I know a grove
50   Of large extent, hard by a castle huge,
     Which the great lord inhabits not; and so
     This grove is wild with tangling underwood,
     And the trim walks are broken up, and grass,
     Thin grass and king-cups grow within the paths.
55   But never elsewhere in one place I knew
     So many nightingales; and far and near,
     In wood and thicket, over the wide grove,
     They answer and provoke each other's song,
     With skirmish and capricious passagings,
60   And murmurs musical and swift jug jug,
     And one low piping sound more sweet than all —
     Stirring the air with such a harmony,
     That should you close your eyes, you might almost
     Forget it was not day! On moonlight bushes,
65   Whose dewy leaflets are but half-disclosed,
     You may perchance behold them on the twigs,
     Their bright, bright eyes, their eyes both bright and full,
     Glistening, while many a glow-worm in the shade
     Lights up her love-torch.

                    A most gentle Maid,
70   Who dwelleth in her hospitable home
     Hard by the castle, and at latest eve
     (Even like a Lady vowed and dedicate
     To something more than Nature in the grove)
     Glides through the pathways; she knows all their notes,
75   What time the moon was lost behind a cloud,
     Hath heard a pause of silence; till the moon
     Emerging, hath awakened earth and sky
     With one sensation, and those wakeful birds

Have all burst forth in choral minstrelsy,
80   As if some sudden gale had swept at once
A hundred airy harps! And she hath watched
Many a nightingale perch giddily
On blossomy twig still swinging from the breeze,
And to that motion tune his wanton song
85   Like tipsy Joy that reels with tossing head.

Farewell, O Warbler! till to-morrow eve,
And you, my friends! farewell, a short farewell!
We have been loitering long and pleasantly,
And now for our dear homes. — That strain again!
90   Full fain it would delay me! My dear babe,
Who, capable of no articulate sound,
Mars all things with his imitative lisp,
How he would place his hand beside his ear,
His little hand, the small forefinger up,
95   And bid us listen! And I deem it wise
To make him Nature's play-mate. He knows well
The evening-star; and once, when he awoke
In most distressful mood (some inward pain
Had made up that strange thing, an infant's dream —)
100   I hurried with him to our orchard-plot,
And he beheld the moon, and, hushed at once,
Suspends his sobs, and laughs most silently,
While his fair eyes, that swam with undropped tears,
Did glitter in the yellow moon-beam! Well! —
105   It is a father's tale: But if that Heaven
Should give me life, his childhood shall grow up
Familiar with these songs, that with the night
He may associate joy. — Once more, farewell,
Sweet Nightingale! once more, my friends! farewell.

Samuel Taylor Coleridge   (1772 – 1834)

TO A WATERFOWL

Whither, midst falling dew,
While glow the heavens with the last steps of day,
Far, through their rosy depths, dost thou pursue
    Thy solitary way?

5   Vainly the fowler's eye
Might mark thy distant flight to do thee wrong,
As, darkly seen against the crimson sky,
    Thy figure floats along.

                    Seek'st thou the plashy brink
10   Of weedy lake, or marge of river wide,
              Or where the rocking billows rise and sink
                    On the chafed ocean-side?

                    There is a Power whose care
              Teaches thy way along that pathless coast —
15   The desert and illimitable air —
                    Lone wandering, but not lost.

                    All day thy wings have fanned,
              At that far height, the cold, thin atmosphere,
              Yet stoop not, weary, to the welcome land,
20   Though the dark night is near.

                    And soon that toil shall end;
              Soon shalt thou find a summer home, and rest,
              And scream among thy fellows; reeds shall bend,
                    Soon, o'er thy sheltered nest.

25   Thou'rt gone, the abyss of heaven
              Hath swallowed up thy form; yet, on my heart
              Deeply has sunk the lesson thou hast given,
                    And shall not soon depart.

                    He who, from zone to zone,
30   Guides through the boundless sky thy certain flight,
              In the long way that I must tread alone,
                    Will lead my steps aright.

                    William Cullen Bryant (1794 – 1878)

THE SNOW-STORM

              Announced by all the trumpets of the sky,
              Arrives the snow, and, driving o'er the fields,
              Seems nowhere to alight: the whited air
              Hides hills and woods, the river, and the heaven,
5   And veils the farm-house at the garden's end.
              The sled and traveller stopped, the courier's feet
              Delayed, all friends shut out, the housemates sit
              Around the radiant fireplace, enclosed
              In a tumultuous privacy of storm.

10   Come see the north wind's masonry.
              Out of an unseen quarry evermore

Furnished with tile, the fierce artificer
Curves his white bastions with projected roof
Round every windward stake, or tree, or door.
15   Speeding, the myriad-handed, his wild work
So fanciful, so savage, nought cares he
For number or proportion. Mockingly,
On coop or kennel he hangs Parian wreaths;
A swan-like form invests the hidden thorn;
20   Fills up the farmer's lane from wall to wall,
Maugre the farmer's sighs; and at the gate
A tapering turret overtops the work.
And when his hours are numbered, and the world
Is all his own, retiring, as he were not,
25   Leaves, when the sun appears, astonished Art
To mimic in slow structures, stone by stone,
Built in an age, the mad wind's night-work,
The frolic architecture of the snow.

Ralph Waldo Emerson   (1803 – 1882)

WHEN I HEARD THE LEARN'D ASTRONOMER

When I heard the learn'd astronomer,
When the proofs, the figures, were ranged in columns before
    me,
When I was shown the charts and diagrams, to add, divide, and
    measure them,
When I sitting heard the astronomer where he lectured with
    much applause in the lecture-room,
5   How soon unaccountable I became tired and sick,
Till rising and gliding out I wander'd off by myself,
In the mystical moist night-air, and from time to time,
Look'd up in perfect silence at the stars.

Walt Whitman   (1819 – 1892)

THE DARKLING THRUSH

I leant upon a coppice gate
    When Frost was spectre-gray,
And Winter's dregs made desolate
    The weakening eye of day.

5 The tangled bine-stems scored the sky
  Like strings of broken lyres,
 And all mankind that haunted nigh
  Had sought their household fires.

 The land's sharp features seemed to be
10 The Century's corpse outleant,
 His crypt the cloudy canopy,
  The wind his death-lament.
 The ancient pulse of germ and birth
  Was shrunken hard and dry,
15 And every spirit upon earth
  Seemed fervourless as I.

 At once a voice arose among
  The bleak twigs overhead
 In a full-hearted evensong
20 Of joy illimited;
 An aged thrush, frail, gaunt, and small,
  In blast-beruffled plume,
 Had chosen thus to fling his soul
  Upon the growing gloom.

25 So little cause for carolings
  Of such ecstatic sound
 Was written on terrestrial things
  Afar or nigh around,
 That I could think there trembled through
30 His happy good-night air
 Some blessed Hope, whereof he knew
  And I was unaware.

   Thomas Hardy (1840 – 1928)

THE LAKE ISLE OF INNISFREE

I will arise and go now, and go to Innisfree,
And a small cabin build there, of clay and wattles made:
Nine bean rows will I have there, a hive for the honey bee,
 And live alone in the bee-loud glade.

5 And I shall have some peace there, for peace comes dropping slow,
Dropping from the veils of the morning to where the cricket sings;
There midnight's all a glimmer, and noon a purple glow,
 And evening full of the linnet's wings.

10   I will arise and go now, for always night and day
I hear lake water lapping with low sounds by the shore;
While I stand on the roadway, or on the pavements gray,
    I hear it in the deep heart's core.

William Butler Yeats   (1865 – 1939)

STOPPING BY WOODS ON A SNOWY EVENING

Whose woods these are I think I know.
His house is in the village though;
He will not see me stopping here
To watch his woods fill up with snow.

5   My little horse must think it queer
To stop without a farmhouse near
Between the woods and frozen lake
The darkest evening of the year.

He gives his harness bells a shake
10   To ask if there is some mistake.
The only other sound's the sweep
Of easy wind and downy flake.

The woods are lovely, dark and deep,
But I have promises to keep,
15   And miles to go before I sleep,
And miles to go before I sleep.

Robert Frost   (1874 – 1963)

THEIR LONELY BETTERS

As I listened from a beach-chair in the shade
To all the noises that my garden made,
It seemed to me only proper that words
Should be withheld from vegetables and birds.

5   A robin with no Christian name ran through
The Robin-Anthem which was all it knew,
And rustling flowers for some third party waited
To say which pairs, if any, should get mated.

10   No one of them was capable of lying,
There was not one which knew that it was dying
Or could have with a rhythm or a rhyme
Assumed responsibility for time.

Let them leave language to their lonely betters
Who count some days and long for certain letters;
15   We, too, make noises when we laugh or weep,
Words are for those with promises to keep.

W. H. Auden   (1907 –   )

A DAY ON THE BIG BRANCH

Still half drunk, after a night at cards,
with the grey dawn taking us unaware
among our guilty kings and queens, we drove
far North in the morning, winners, losers,
5   to a stream in the high hills, to climb up to a place
one of us knew, with some vague view
of cutting losses or consolidating gains
by the old standard appeal to the wilderness,
the desert, the empty places of our exile,
10   bringing only the biblical bread and cheese
and cigarettes got from a grocer's on the way,
expecting to drink only the clear cold water
among the stones, and remember, or forget.
Though no one said anything about atonement,
15   there was still some purgatorial idea
in all those aching heads and ageing hearts
as we climbed the giant stair of the stream,
reaching the place around noon.

It was as promised, a wonder, with granite walls
20   enclosing ledges, long and flat, of limestone,
or, rolling, of lava; within the ledges
the water, fast and still, pouring its yellow light,
and green, over the tilted slabs of the floor,
blackened at shady corners, falling in a foam
25   of crystal to a calm where the waterlight
dappled the ledges as they leaned
against the sun; big blue dragonflies hovered
and darted and dipped a wing, hovered again
against the low wind moving over the stream,
30   and shook the flakes of light from their clear wings.

This surely was it, was what we had come for,
was nature, though it looked like art with its
grey fortress walls and laminated benches
as in the waiting room of some petrified station.

35   But we believed; and what it was we believed
made of the place a paradise
for ruined poker players, win or lose,
who stripped naked and bathed and dried out on the rocks
like gasping trout (the water they drank

40   making them drunk again), lit cigarettes and lay back
waiting for nature to say the last word
—as though the stones were Memnon stones,
which, caught in a certain light, would sing.

The silence (and even the noise of the waters

45   was silence) grew pregnant; that is the phrase,
grew pregnant; but nothing else did.
The mountain brought forth not a mouse, and the rocks,
unlike the ones you would expect to find
on the slopes of Purgatory or near Helicon,

50   mollified by muses and with a little give to 'em,
were modern American rocks, and hard as rocks.
Our easy bones groaned, our flesh baked
on one side and shuddered on the other; and each man
thought bitterly about primitive simplicity

55   and decadence, and how he had been ruined
by civilization and forced by circumstances
to drink and smoke and sit up all night
inspecting those perfectly arbitrary cards
until he was broken-winded as a trout on a rock

60   and had no use for the doctrines of Jean Jacques
Rousseau, and could no longer afford
a savagery whether noble or not; some
would never batter that battered copy of Walden
again.

      But all the same,

65   the water, the sunlight, and the wind
did something; even the dragonflies
did something to the minds full of telephone
numbers and flushes, to the flesh
sweating bourbon on one side and freezing on the other.

70   And the rocks, the old and tumbling boulders
which formed the giant stair of the stream,
induced (again) some purgatorial ideas
concerning humility, concerning patience
and enduring what had to be endured,

75   winning and losing and breaking even;
ideas of weathering in whatever weather,

being eroded, or broken, or ground down into pebbles
by the stream's necessitous and grave currents.
But to these ideas did any purgatory
80   respond? Only this one: that in a world
where even the Memnon stones were carved in soap
one might at any rate wash with the soap.

After a time we talked about the War,
about what we had done in the War, and how near
85   some of us had been to being drowned, and burned,
and shot, and how many people we knew
who had been drowned, or burned, or shot;
and would it have been better to have died
in the War, the peaceful old War, where we were young?
90   But the mineral peace, or paralysis, of those
great stones, the moving stillness of the waters,
entered our speech; the ribs and blood
of the earth, from which all fables grow,
established poetry and truth in us,
95   so that at last one said, "I shall play cards
until the day I die," and another said,
"in bourbon whisky are all the vitamins
and minerals needed to sustain man's life,"
and still another, "I shall live on smoke
100   until my spirit has been cured of flesh."

Climbing downstream again, on the way home
to the lives we had left empty for a day,
we noticed, as not before, how of three bridges
not one had held the stream, which in its floods
105   had twisted the girders, splintered the boards, hurled
boulder on boulder, and had broken into rubble,
smashed practically back to nature,
the massive masonry of span after span
with its indifferent rage; this was a sight
110   that sobered us considerably, and kept us quiet
both during the long drive home and after,
till it was time to deal the cards.

Howard Nemerov   (1920 –   )

QUESTIONS FOR DISCUSSION AND FURTHER STUDY

METRUM 5

1. Why were people happier in earlier times, according to Vaughan, than they are at the time he writes? Do you agree with his judgment? Why or why not?
2. The last line of the poem includes the phrase "precious perils"; can you state how a peril can be precious? How is the word *pearl* related to the phrase in question?
3. Mount Aetna is a volcanic mountain in southern Sicily. What relevance does this geographical site have in the poem, at least in terms of the context given it by Vaughan?

TO A MOUSE

1. Do you feel that the audience addressed in this poem – namely, a mouse – makes the poem ludicrous? How does Burns avoid the potentially silly situation which could exist when a man addresses a mouse?
2. Do you believe that Burns' judgment is correct when he says to the mouse that "Still thou art blest, compared wi' me!"?
3. This poem suggests a rather interesting theoretical question. What does a poet gain by using dialect? What does he lose?

LINES COMPOSED A FEW MILES ABOVE TINTERN ABBEY, ON REVISITING THE BANKS OF THE WYE DURING A TOUR

1. Name the speaker and audience in this poem. Why does the speaker of the poem wish for his audience something he no longer possesses himself?
2. What benefits does the speaker claim to have derived from nature?
3. Describe the "gift, / Of aspect more sublime." Does Wordsworth prefer his earlier or more mature contact with the natural surroundings of Tintern Abbey?

THE NIGHTINGALE

1. What special attributes, qualities, and power does nature have in this poem? How do you think Coleridge would define *nature*?
2. Discuss the setting of the poem. At what time of day does it occur?
3. As Coleridge speaks to Wordsworth and Wordsworth's sister Dorothy, he says "we have learnt / A different lore." What does he mean by this? What is the difference?

TO A WATERFOWL

1. What do the speaker in the poem and the waterfowl have in common?
2. Compare this poem with "The Nightingale." What are the chief differences in what is symbolized by the two birds?
3. Describe the setting of this poem. What concrete physical details does Bryant include to give his readers a sense of place?

THE SNOW-STORM

1. How is the north wind personified in this poem? What is the verse form used in this poem?
2. What images especially help to suggest a New England farm buried in the snow?
3. The word *Parian* refers to Paros, an island in the Aegean Sea, known for its beautiful marble which was used in Greek sculpture. Why does Emerson use the word here?

WHEN I HEARD THE LEARN'D ASTRONOMER

1. Would you say that this poem is anti-intellectual? Why or why not?
2. We have two attitudes toward nature expressed here. Discuss the personalities of the two men representing these attitudes. With whom would you agree? Or are they both right?
3. Have you ever had a similar experience of revulsion at the rational analysis of something that you viewed with awe or reverence?

THE DARKLING THRUSH

1. Why is the fact that Hardy wrote the poem during the winter and at the turn of the century relevant to the poem's theme?
2. As you discuss this theme, you might note that, although the poem appears generally bleak and pessimistic, it does contain some element of optimism. How significant do you consider the optimism to be?
3. What makes Hardy think that the thrush knows of some hope?

THE LAKE ISLE OF INNISFREE

1. What way of life is symbolized by the Isle of Innisfree? Why does Yeats wish to live alone there? In what other section of this anthology could this poem have been logically placed?
2. What do the last two lines of the second stanza mean? In literal terms, they seem not to make sense.

3. Discuss the various ways Yeats uses imagery to paint a picture of Innisfree.

STOPPING BY WOODS ON A SNOWY EVENING

1. The meaning of the poem emerges primarily from the last stanza. What is the theme of the poem, or does it have multiple meanings?
2. The language used by Frost is very simple. Is there a relationship between the simplicity of language and theme? What is it?
3. Manuscript evidence shows that Frost experienced his greatest difficulty with the last stanza. He tried several final lines before he decided to repeat the third line of the stanza. Do you consider the repetition effective? If so, why?

THEIR LONELY BETTERS

1. Who are the "lonely betters"?
2. How does Auden feel about language as such? Could this poem be read as a comment on the poetic vocation?
3. This poem, like Frost's "Stopping by Woods on a Snowy Evening" makes use of the phrase "promises to keep." Do you think the echo of Frost is intentional? Do the two poems share some common meaning?

A DAY ON THE BIG BRANCH

1. Does this poem remind you of any Hemingway short stories you may have read? If so, how?
2. The men go through a series of emotional stages as the poem progresses. Identify these stages. What causes each change?
3. Why does the sight of the three ruined bridges sober the men considerably?

PATRIOTISM

Few subjects have inspired so much poor poetry as *patriotism*. Partly, of course, this results from the fact that the subject often attracts poor poets. Yet even an otherwise excellent poet can experience difficulty dealing with patriotic themes. The lyric poet succeeds insofar as he is able to record a private emotion or a private experience in precise and sensitive language. He works best with personal subjects. Patriotism, however, tends to be a public or mass emotion, and the lyric poet cannot always reduce it to sufficiently personal terms to make good poetry. In other words, the public nature of the theme sometimes overwhelms the technique, and in poetry what is said relies significantly on how it is said.

Here, in fact, is a good opportunity to discuss this relationship between theme and technique. A beginning student of poetry often makes the mistake of thinking that a poem is "good" if it expresses some idea with which he agrees. For example, a typical reader might think a poem praising the American way of life is "good," and one praising communism is "bad," simply because of what the poems state. This is a rather narrow-minded way to read poetry; the student of poetry must look into the merits of the poem's language before he decides to like a poem simply because he agrees with the emotion it expresses. In fact the student should welcome the opportunity to read a poem which opposes his own ideas on any given subject. When the student comes across such a poem, he should view the situation as a chance to broaden his mind, to enlarge his ideas, and perhaps even to change his life. Reading only poetry – or anything else – which reinforces one's own convictions is the surest way to close one's mind and to become intellectually dead.

Moving to the specific poems on patriotism in this section, we again find wide variety. The selection taken from Shakespeare's *Richard II* pays poetic tribute to England in language of splendid distinction. Note especially that the country being praised is not identified until the very end of the passage, after the glowing phrases have first been presented to the reader. This climactic or periodic structure is very effective, since the emotional pitch of the selection is then at its highest point. Note also that England is praised primarily in terms of her insularity. Her beauty in large part rests upon the fact that she is separated from the rest of Europe. It is almost as if physical, geographical contact with some other country would contaminate England. This insular, parochial attitude is commonly found in patriotic poems.

England's geographical separation from the European continent again plays a major part in Samuel Taylor Coleridge's "Fears in Solitude." The sub-title of this poem reads "Written in April 1798, During the Alarm of an Invasion," and the poem is concerned with the projected French invasion of England which, of course, never occurred. Unlike Shakespeare, however, Coleridge contrasts England's physical beauty with her "pollutions from the brimming cup of wealth." England is praised as a "Mother Isle," but Coleridge combines such praise with attacks on the evils present in his society. This qualified love of his country, which Coleridge expresses as a hymn to God, is somehow much more convincing and effective than it would have been had the poet simply praised his country and been blind to her faults.

"Concord Hymn" is Emerson's less critical tribute to the first dead of the Revolutionary War. The poem was first sung in 1837, at the completion of a monument honoring those who fell at Concord. The poem expresses in simple terms the hope that the bravery and patriotism of those first American war heroes will not be forgotten by succeeding generations.

"Love Thou Thy Land with Love Far-Brought" is an expression of patriotism by Alfred Tennyson, then poet laureate of England. Tennyson urges a love of country which views past, present, and future as a unified progression of history and tradition. His position, fundamentally that of the English conservative Edmund Burke, is that knowledge must be balanced with reverence; change, balanced with prudence. The extremes of haste and delay must be avoided, and change should take place peacefully. The argument for middle-of-the-road patriotism has perhaps never been better expressed in a lyric poem.

In his poem "Old Ironsides," Oliver Wendell Holmes sees the historic ship as a symbol of his own love of country. The simple but appealing poem suggests that it would be more dignified for the grand old vessel to be sunk at sea than to suffer being dismantled. This emotional lyric served an important part in the battle to save the ship from the wrecker's crowbar and to preserve it as a historical source of patriotic pride.

Walt Whitman's poem "For You O Democracy" departs from some others in this section in that it stresses the unity mankind can achieve in a democratic system. The words *indissoluble, magnetic, comrades, companionship,* and *inseparable* hammer home the idea of unity with great force in this free-verse poem, and Whitman even ends the poem by stating that he sees his poetic vocation as a means of working for this unity.

The next two poems in this section were written, respectively, about the fiftieth and sixtieth anniversaries of Queen Victoria's reign, a period during which the British Empire was reaching its greatest height. Both sound the note of discordant patriotism. Housman's lyric suggests with subtle irony (and, indeed, mild blasphemy) that while God may have saved the queen, He was assisted considerably by the young men of England who gave their lives on the far-flung battlefields of the empire.

Written in the form of a hymn to God, Rudyard Kipling's "Recessional 1897" actually cautions his countrymen against their chauvinistic pride in the power of the British Empire. It too will pass away. Coming as it did at a time of national celebration, Kipling's somber poem shocked many of his fellow Englishmen, including the queen herself.

"Easter, 1916" takes still another view of the relationship between oneself and one's country. Yeats, perhaps the greatest British poet of this century, writes here of the Irish rebellion against English rule which occurred at Easter, 1916. The sentence "A terrible beauty is born" underlines Yeats' ambivalent feelings about the Irish uprising. This sympathy with the cause and his understanding of the very real persecutions suffered by the Irish is undoubted, yet he is appalled by the horror of war, and he senses that the Irish will be defeated.

Rupert Brooke's "The Soldier" was written in 1914, just one year before the author died while in the service of his country. The sonnet records a soldier's rich love for his country and the willingness to face death without fear. Its first sentence has been often quoted as a sort of patriotic aphorism.

Robinson Jeffers' "Shine, Perishing Republic" protests America's growth into a vulgar, conforming empire. Jeffers concerns himself particularly with the increasing urbanization of America and recommends to his readers that they flee from the crowd. Love of man should be practiced moderately, notes Jeffers, for such love can be a "trap that catches noblest spirits"; indeed, it is responsible for the death of Christ.

The last poem in this section launches an acid attack upon uncritical, cliché-ridden patriotism. The speaker of E. E. Cummings' "next to of course god" is a flag-waving orator, and his speech consists of mere fragments of patriotic songs, meaningless oratorical flourishes, and snippets of the worst kind of thoughtless chauvinism. In essence, the poem parodies the sort of windbag patriotism that we hear too often.

The range of poems about patriotism is not extensive. Poets who write about love of country are generally of one of two minds – they praise their country or, trying to improve what they find wrong, they censure it. Yet, though the range may be narrow, the emotional involvement with which both poets and readers approach this subject is usually strong and forceful.

from RICHARD II

Act II, Scene I (John of Gaunt)

> This royal throne of kings, this sceptred isle,
> This earth of majesty, this seat of Mars,
> This other Eden, demi-paradise,
> This fortress built by Nature for herself
> 5 Against infection and the hand of war,
> This happy breed of men, this little world,
> This precious stone set in the silver sea,
> Which serves it in the office of a wall
> Or as a moat defensive to a house
> 10 Against the envy of less happier lands,
> This blessed plot, this earth, this realm, this England . . .

William Shakespeare (1564 – 1616)

FEARS IN SOLITUDE

Written in April 1798, during the alarm of an invasion

> A green and silent spot, amid the hills,
> A small and silent dell! O'er stiller place
> No singing sky-lark ever poised himself.
> The hills are heathy, save that swelling slope,
> 5 Which hath a gay and gorgeous covering on,
> All golden with the never-bloomless furze,
> Which now blooms most profusely: but the dell,
> Bathed by the mist, is fresh and delicate
> As vernal corn-field, or the unripe flax,
> 10 When, through its half-transparent stalks, at eve,
> The level sunshine glimmers with green light.
> Oh! 'tis a quiet spirit-healing nook!
> Which all, methinks, would love; but chiefly he,
> The humble man, who, in his youthful years,
> 15 Knew just so much of folly, as had made
> His early manhood more securely wise!
> Here he might lie on fern or withered heath,
> While from the singing lark (that sings unseen
> The minstrelsy that solitude loves best),
> 20 And from the sun, and from the breezy air,
> Sweet influences trembled o'er his frame;

And he, with many feelings, many thoughts,
Made up a meditative joy, and found
Religious meanings in the forms of Nature!
25   And so, his senses gradually wrapt
In a half sleep, he dreams of better worlds,
And dreaming hears thee still, O singing lark,
That singest like an angel in the clouds!

My God! it is a melancholy thing
30   For such a man, who would full fain preserve
His soul in calmness, yet perforce must feel
For all his human brethren — O my God!
It weighs upon the heart, that he must think
What uproar and what strife may now be stirring
35   This way or that way o'er these silent hills —
Invasion, and the thunder and the shout,
And all the crash of onset; fear and rage,
And undetermined conflict — even now,
Even now, perchance, and in his native isle:
40   Carnage and groans beneath this blessed sun!
We have offended, Oh! my countrymen!
We have offended very grievously,
And been most tyrannous. From east to west
A groan of accusation pierces Heaven!
45   The wretched plead against us; multitudes
Countless and vehement, the sons of God,
Our brethren! Like a cloud that travels on,
Steamed up from Cairo's swamps of pestilence,
Even so, my countrymen! have we gone forth
50   And borne to distant tribes slavery and pangs,
And, deadlier far, our vices, whose deep taint
With slow perdition murders the whole man,
His body and his soul! Meanwhile, at home,
All individual dignity and power
55   Engulfed in Courts, Committees, Institutions,
Associations and Societies,
A vain, speech-mouthing, speech-reporting Guild,
One Benefit-Club for mutual flattery,
We have drunk up, demure as at a grace,
60   Pollutions from the brimming cup of wealth;
Contemptuous of all honourable rule,
Yet bartering freedom and the poor man's life
For gold, as at a market! The sweet words
Of Christian promise, words that even yet
65   Might stem destruction, were they wisely preached,
Are muttered o'er by men, whose tones proclaim
How flat and wearisome they feel their trade:
Rank scoffers some, but most too indolent

To deem them falsehoods or to know their truth.
70   Oh! blasphemous! the Book of Life is made
A superstitious instrument, on which
We gabble o'er the oaths we mean to break;
For all must swear—all and in every place,
College and wharf, council and justice-court;
75   All, all must swear, the briber and the bribed,
Merchant and lawyer, senator and priest,
The rich, the poor, the old man and the young;
All, all make up one scheme of perjury,
That faith doth reel; the very name of God
80   Sounds like a juggler's charm; and, bold with joy,
Forth from his dark and lonely hiding-place,
(Portentous sight!) the owlet Atheism,
Sailing on obscene wings athwart the noon,
Drops his blue-fringéd lids, and holds them close,
85   And hooting at the glorious sun in Heaven,
Cries out, "Where is it?"

                              Thankless too for peace,
(Peace long preserved by fleets and perilous seas)
Secure from actual warfare, we have loved
To swell the war-whoop, passionate for war!
90   Alas! for ages ignorant of all
Its ghastlier workings, (famine or blue plague,
Battle, or siege, or flight through wintry snows.)
We, this whole people, have been clamorous
For war and bloodshed; animating sports,
95   The which we pay for as a thing to talk of,
Spectators and not combatants! No guess
Anticipative of a wrong unfelt,
No speculation on contingency,
However dim and vague, too vague and dim
100   To yield a justifying cause; and forth,
(Stuffed out with big preamble, holy names,
And adjurations of the God in Heaven,)
We send our mandates for the certain death
Of thousands and ten thousands! Boys and girls,
105   And women, that would groan to see a child
Pull off an insect's leg, all read of war,
The best amusement for our morning meal!
The poor wretch, who has learnt his only prayers
From curses, who knows scarcely words enough
110   To ask a blessing from his Heavenly Father,
Becomes a fluent phraseman, absolute
And technical in victories and defeats,
And all our dainty terms for fratricide;
Terms which we trundle smoothly o'er our tongues
115   Like mere abstractions, empty sounds to which

We join no feeling and attach no form!
As if the soldier died without a wound;
As if the fibres of this godlike frame
Were gored without a pang; as if the wretch,
120 Who fell in battle, doing bloody deeds,
Passed off to Heaven, translated and not killed;
As though he had no wife to pine for him,
No God to judge him! Therefore, evil days
Are coming on us, O my countrymen!
125 And what if all-avenging Providence,
Strong and retributive, should make us know
The meaning of our words, force us to feel
The desolation and the agony
Of our fierce doings?

                Spare us yet awhile,
130 Father and God! O! spare us yet awhile!
Oh! let not English women drag their flight
Fainting beneath the burthen of their babes,
Of the sweet infants, that but yesterday
Laughed at the breast! Sons, brothers, husbands, all
135 Who ever gazed with fondness on the forms
Which grew up with you round the same fire-side,
And all who ever heard the sabbath-bells
Without the infidel's scorn, make yourselves pure!
Stand forth! be men! repel an impious foe,
140 Impious and false, a light yet cruel race,
Who laugh away all virtue, mingling mirth
With deeds of murder; and still promising
Freedom, themselves too sensual to be free,
Poison life's amities, and cheat the heart
145 Of faith and quiet hope, and all that soothes,
And all that lifts the spirit! Stand we forth;
Render them back upon the insulted ocean,
And let them toss as idly on its waves
As the vile sea-weed, which some mountain-blast
150 Swept from our shores! And oh! may we return
Not with a drunken triumph, but with fear,
Repenting of the wrongs with which we stung
So fierce a foe to frenzy!

                I have told,
O Britons! O my brethren! I have told
155 Most bitter truth, but without bitterness.
Nor deem my zeal or factious or mistimed;
For never can true courage dwell with them,
Who, playing tricks with conscience, dare not look
At their own vices. We have been too long
160 Dupes of a deep delusion! Some, belike,

Groaning with restless enmity, expect
All change from change of constituted power;
As if a Government had been a robe,
On which our vice and wretchedness were tagged
165   Like fancy-points and fringes, with the robe
Pulled off at pleasure. Fondly these attach
A radical causation to a few
Poor drudges of chastising Providence,
Who borrow all their hues and qualities
170   From our own folly and rank wickedness,
Which gave them birth and nursed them. Others, meanwhile,
Dote with a mad idolatry; and all
Who will not fall before their images,
And yield them worship, they are enemies
175   Even of their country!

Such have I been deemed. —
But, O dear Britain! O my Mother Isle!
Needs must thou prove a name most dear and holy
To me, a son, a brother, and a friend,
A husband, and a father! who revere
180   All bonds of natural love, and find them all
Within the limits of thy rocky shores.
O native Britain! O my Mother Isle!
How shouldst thou prove aught else but dear and holy
To me, who from thy lakes and mountain-hills,
185   Thy clouds, thy quiet dales, thy rocks and seas,
Have drunk in all my intellectual life,
All sweet sensations, all ennobling thoughts,
All adoration of the God in nature,
All lovely and all honourable things,
190   Whatever makes this mortal spirit feel
The joy and greatness of its future being?
There lives nor form nor feeling in my soul
Unborrowed from my country! O divine
And beauteous island! thou hast been my sole
195   And most magnificent temple, in the which
I walk with awe, and sing my stately songs,
Loving the God that made me! —

May my fears,
My filial fears, be vain! and may the vaunts
And menace of the vengeful enemy
200   Pass like the gust, that roared and died away
In the distant tree: which heard, and only heard
In this low dell, bowed not the delicate grass.

But now the gentle dew-fall sends abroad
The fruit-like perfume of the golden furze:

205   The light has left the summit of the hill,
            Though still a sunny gleam lies beautiful,
            Aslant the ivied beacon. Now farewell,
            Farewell, awhile, O soft and silent spot!
            On the green sheep-track, up the heathy hill,
210   Homeward I wind my way; and lo! recalled
            From bodings that have well-nigh wearied me,
            I find myself upon the brow, and pause
            Startled! And after lonely sojourning
            In such a quiet and surrounded nook,
215   This burst of prospect, here the shadowy main,
            Dim-tinted, there the mighty majesty
            Of that huge amphitheatre of rich
            And elmy fields, seems like society—
            Conversing with the mind, and giving it
220   A livelier impulse and a dance of thought!
            And now, belovéd Stowey! I behold
            Thy church-tower, and, methinks, the four huge elms
            Clustering, which mark the mansion of my friend;
            And close behind them, hidden from my view,
225   Is my own lowly cottage, where my babe
            And my babe's mother dwell in peace! With light
            And quickened footsteps thitherward I tend,
            Remembering thee, O green and silent dell!
            And grateful, that by nature's quietness
230   And solitary musings, all my heart
            Is softened, and made worthy to indulge
            Love, and the thoughts that yearn for human kind.

Samuel Taylor Coleridge   (1772 – 1834)

CONCORD HYMN

Sung at the Completion of the Battle Monument, July 4, 1837

      By the rude bridge that arched the flood,
         Their flag to April's breeze unfurled,
      Here once the embattled farmers stood
         And fired the shot heard round the world.

5   The foe long since in silence slept;
         Alike the conqueror silent sleeps;
      And Time the ruined bridge has swept
         Down the dark stream which seaward creeps.

On this green bank, by this soft stream,
10   We set to-day a votive stone;
That memory may their deed redeem,
     When, like our sires, our sons are gone.

Spirit, that made those heroes dare
     To die, and leave their children free,
15   Bid Time and Nature gently spare
     The shaft we raise to them and thee.

Ralph Waldo Emerson   (1803 – 1882)

LOVE THOU THY LAND WITH LOVE FAR-BROUGHT

Love thou thy land, with love far-brought
     From out the storied Past, and used
     Within the Present, but transfused
Thro' future time by power of thought.

5   True love turn'd round on fixed poles,
     Love, that endures not sordid ends,
     For English natures, freemen, friends,
Thy brothers and immortal souls.

But pamper not a hasty time,
10   Nor feed with crude imaginings
     The herd, wild hearts and feeble wings
That every sophister can lime.

Deliver not the tasks of might
     To weakness, neither hide the ray
15   From those, not blind, who wait for day,
Tho' sitting girt with doubtful light.

Make knowledge circle with the winds;
     But let her herald, Reverence, fly
     Before her to whatever sky
20   Bear seed of men and growth of minds.

Watch what main-currents draw the years:
     Cut Prejudice against the grain:
     But gentle words are always gain:
Regard the weakness of thy peers:

25   Nor toil for title, place, or touch
        Of pension, neither count on praise:
        It grows to guerdon after-days:
    Nor deal in watch-words overmuch:

    Not clinging to some ancient saw;
30   Not master'd by some modern term;
        Not swift nor slow to change, but firm:
    And in its season bring the law;

    That from Discussion's lip may fall
        With Life, that, working strongly, binds—
35   Set in all lights by many minds,
    To close the interests of all.

    For Nature also, cold and warm,
        And moist and dry, devising long,
        Thro' many agents making strong,
40   Matures the individual form.

    Meet is it changes should control
        Our being, lest we rust in ease.
        We all are changed by still degrees,
    All but the basis of the soul.

45   So let the change which comes be free
        To ingroove itself with that which flies,
        And work, a joint of state, that plies
    Its office, moved with sympathy.

    A saying, hard to shape in act;
50   For all the past of Time reveals
        A bridal dawn of thunder-peals,
    Wherever Thought hath wedded Fact.

    Ev'n now we hear with inward strife
        A motion toiling in the gloom—
55   The Spirit of the years to come
    Yearning to mix himself with Life.

    A slow-develop'd strength awaits
        Completion in a painful school;
        Phantoms of other forms of rule,
60   New Majesties of mighty States—

    The warders of the growing hour,
        But vague in vapour, hard to mark;
        And round them sea and air are dark
    With great contrivances of Power.

65   Of many changes, aptly join'd,
            Is bodied forth the second whole.
            Regard gradation, lest the soul
        Of Discord race the rising wind;

        A wind to puff your idol-fires,
70   And heap their ashes on the head;
            To shame the boast so often made,
        That we are wiser than our sires.

        Oh yet, if Nature's evil star
            Drive men in manhood, as in youth,
75   To follow flying steps of Truth
        Across the brazen bridge of war —

        If New and Old, disastrous feud,
            Must ever shock, like armed foes,
            And this be true, till Time shall close,
80   That Principles are rain'd in blood;

        Not yet the wise of heart would cease
            To hold his hope thro' shame and guilt,
            But with his hand against the hilt,
        Would pace the troubled land, like Peace;

85   Not less, tho' dogs of Faction bay,
            Would serve his kind in deed and word,
            Certain, if knowledge bring the sword,
        That knowledge takes the sword away —

        Would love the gleams of good that broke
90   From either side, nor veil his eyes:
            And if some dreadful need should rise
        Would strike, and firmly, and one stroke:

        To-morrow yet would reap to-day,
            As we bear blossom of the dead;
95   Earn well the thrifty months, nor wed
        Raw Haste, half-sister to Delay.

                Alfred, Lord Tennyson   (1809 – 1892)

OLD IRONSIDES

        Ay, tear her tattered ensign down!
            Long has it waved on high,

And many an eye has danced to see
 That banner in the sky;
5 Beneath it rung the battle shout,
 And burst the cannon's roar; —
The meteor of the ocean air
 Shall sweep the clouds no more.

Her deck, once red with heroes' blood,
10 Where knelt the vanquished foe,
When winds were hurrying o'er the flood,
 And waves were white below,
No more shall feel the victor's tread,
 Or know the conquered knee; —
15 The harpies of the shore shall pluck
 The eagle of the sea!

Oh, better that her shattered hulk
 Should sink beneath the wave;
Her thunders shook the mighty deep,
20 And there should be her grave;
Nail to the mast her holy flag,
 Set every threadbare sail,
And give her to the god of storms,
 The lightning and the gale!

 Oliver Wendell Holmes *(1809 – 1894)*

FOR YOU O DEMOCRACY

Come, I will make the continent indissoluble,
I will make the most splendid race the sun ever shone upon,
I will make divine magnetic lands,
 With the love of comrades,
5 With the life-long love of comrades.

I will plant companionship thick as trees along all the rivers of
 America, and along the shores of the great lakes, and all over the
  prairies,
I will make inseparable cities with their arms about each other's necks,
 By the love of comrades,
  By the manly love of comrades.

10 For you these from me, O Democracy, to serve you ma femme!
For you, for you I am trilling these songs.

 Walt Whitman *(1819 – 1892)*

A SHROPSHIRE LAD I (From Clee to Heaven the beacon burns)

From Clee to Heaven the beacon burns,
    The shires have seen it plain,
From north and south the sign returns
    And beacons burn again.

5   Look left, look right, the hills are bright,
    The dales are light between,
Because 'tis fifty years to-night
    That God has saved the Queen.

Now, when the flame they watch not towers
10   About the soil they trod,
Lads, we'll remember friends of ours
    Who shared the work with God.

To skies that knit their heartstrings, right,
    To fields that bred them brave,
15   The Saviours come not home to-night
    Themselves they could not save.

It dawns in Asia, tombstones show
    And Shropshire names are read;
And the Nile spills his overflow
20   Beside the Severn's dead.

We pledge in peace by farm and town
    The Queen they served in war,
And fire the beacons up and down
    The land they perished for.

25   'God save the Queen' we living sing,
    From height to height 'tis heard;
And with the rest your voices ring,
    Lads of the Fifty-third.

Oh, God will save her, fear you not:
30   Be you the men you've been,
Get you the sons your fathers got,
    And God will save the Queen.

A. E. Housman   (1859 – 1936)

RECESSIONAL

1897

God of our fathers, known of old,
    Lord of our far-flung battle-line,
Beneath whose awful Hand we hold
    Dominion over palm and pine—
5   Lord God of Hosts, be with us yet,
Lest we forget—lest we forget!

The tumult and the shouting dies;
    The Captains and the Kings depart:
Still stands Thine ancient sacrifice,
10   An humble and a contrite heart.
Lord God of Hosts, be with us yet,
Lest we forget—lest we forget!

Far-called, our navies melt away;
    On dune and headland sinks the fire:
15 Lo, all our pomp of yesterday
    Is one with Nineveh and Tyre!
Judge of the Nations, spare us yet,
Lest we forget—lest we forget!

If, drunk with sight of power, we loose
20   Wild tongues that have not Thee in awe,
Such boastings as the Gentiles use,
    Or lesser breeds without the Law—
Lord God of Hosts, be with us yet,
Lest we forget—lest we forget!

25 For heathen heart that puts her trust
    In reeking tube and iron shard,
All valiant dust that builds on dust,
    And guarding, calls not Thee to guard,
For frantic boast and foolish word—
30 Thy mercy on Thy People, Lord!

Rudyard Kipling   (1865 – 1936)

EASTER, 1916

I have met them at close of day
Coming with vivid faces
From counter or desk among grey
Eighteenth-century houses.
5   I have passed with a nod of the head
Or polite meaningless words,
Or have lingered awhile and said
Polite meaningless words,
And thought before I had done
10   Of a mocking tale or a gibe
To please a companion
Around the fire at the club,
Being certain that they and I
But lived where motley is worn:
15   All changed, changed utterly:
A terrible beauty is born.

That woman's days were spent
In ignorant good-will,
Her nights in argument
20   Until her voice grew shrill.
What voice more sweet than hers
When, young and beautiful,
She rode to harriers?
This man had kept a school
25   And rode our wingèd horse;
This other his helper and friend
Was coming into his force;
He might have won fame in the end,
So sensitive his nature seemed,
30   So daring and sweet his thought.
This other man I had dreamed
A drunken, vainglorious lout.
He had done most bitter wrong
To some who are near my heart,
35   Yet I number him in the song;
He, too, has resigned his part
In the casual comedy;
He, too, has been changed in his turn,
Transformed utterly:
40   A terrible beauty is born.

Hearts with one purpose alone
Through summer and winter seem
Enchanted to a stone
To trouble the living stream.

45   The horse that comes from the road,
     The rider, the birds that range
     From cloud to tumbling cloud,
     Minute by minute they change;
     A shadow of cloud on the stream
50   Changes minute by minute;
     A horse-hoof slides on the brim,
     And a horse plashes within it;
     The long-legged moor-hens dive,
     And hens to moor-cocks call;
55   Minute by minute they live:
     The stone's in the midst of all.

     Too long a sacrifice
     Can make a stone of the heart.
     O when may it suffice?
60   That is Heaven's part, our part
     To murmur name upon name,
     As a mother names her child
     When sleep at last has come
     On limbs that had run wild.
65   What is it but nightfall?
     No, no, not night but death;
     Was it needless death after all?
     For England may keep faith
     For all that is done and said.
70   We know their dream; enough
     To know they dreamed and are dead;
     And what if excess of love
     Bewildered them till they died?
     I write it out in a verse—
75   MacDonagh and MacBride
     And Connolly and Pearse
     Now and in time to be,
     Wherever green is worn,
     Are changed, changed utterly:
80   A terrible beauty is born.

          William Butler Yeats   (1865 – 1939)

THE SOLDIER

     If I should die, think only this of me:
          That there's some corner of a foreign field
     That is for ever England. There shall be

In that rich earth a richer dust concealed;
5   A dust whom England bore, shaped, made aware,
Gave, once, her flowers to love, her ways to roam,
A body of England's, breathing English air,
Washed by the rivers, blest by suns of home.

And think, this heart, all evil shed away,
10   A pulse in the eternal mind, no less
Gives somewhere back the thoughts by England given;
Her sights and sounds; dreams happy as her day;
And laughter, learnt of friends; and gentleness,
In hearts at peace, under an English heaven.

Rupert Brooke   (1887 – 1915)

SHINE, PERISHING REPUBLIC

While this America settles in the mould of its vulgarity,
heavily thickening to empire,
And protest, only a bubble in the molten mass, pops
and sighs out, and the mass hardens,

5   I sadly smiling remember that the flower fades to make
fruit, the fruit rots to make earth.
Out of the mother; and through the spring exultances,
ripeness and decadence; and home to the mother.

You making haste haste on decay: not blameworthy;
10   life is good, be it stubbornly long or suddenly
A mortal splendor: Meteors are not needed less than
mountains: shine, perishing republic.

But for my children, I would have them keep their
distance from the thickening center; corruption
15   Never has been compulsory, when the cities lie at the
monster's feet there are left the mountains.

And boys, be in nothing so moderate as in love of man,
a clever servant, insufferable master.
There is the trap that catches noblest spirits, that
20   caught — they say — God, when he walked on earth.

Robinson Jeffers   (1887 – 1962)

NEXT TO OF COURSE GOD

"next to of course god america i
love you land of the pilgrims' and so forth oh
say can you see by the dawn's early my
country 'tis of centuries come and go
5   and are no more what of it we should worry
in every language even deafanddumb
thy sons acclaim your glorious name by gorry
by jingo by gee by gosh by gum
why talk of beauty what could be more beaut-
10   iful than these heroic happy dead
who rushed like lions to the roaring slaughter
they did not stop to think they died instead
then shall the voice of liberty be mute?"

He spoke. And drank rapidly a glass of water

E. E. Cummings   (1894 – 1962)

QUESTIONS FOR DISCUSSION AND FURTHER STUDY

FROM RICHARD II, *ACT II, SCENE I, (JOHN OF GAUNT)*

1. Discuss Shakespeare's use of metaphor to describe Gaunt's feelings for England.
2. What is the verse form employed by Shakespeare in this passage?

FEARS IN SOLITUDE

1. There are several audiences addressed in this poem; name them. Why does Coleridge shift from one audience to another? How effective is this shift?
2. Describe the setting Coleridge creates in the poem, particularly toward the beginning.
3. This poem was written in 1798, when Coleridge feared England might be invaded by the French. Do you think that the poem is now a historical curiosity or does it still have relevance? In other words, can the poem be read as any man's love for his country at any time or place?

CONCORD HYMN

1. Since this hymn is considered both a piece of poetry and a piece of music, the student has here an excellent opportunity to examine the relationship between two art forms. The student should, if possible, listen to a recording of this hymn and compare the different effects which occur when the same creation is rendered through two art forms.
2. In what verse form is this poem written?
3. What role does memory play in this poem?
4. Do you think the imagery in this poem is concrete and effective, or do you feel it is trite and commonplace? Why?

LOVE THOU THY LAND WITH LOVE FAR-BROUGHT

1. What is the rhyme scheme used in this poem? (The student may wish to note that a similar rhyme scheme appears in the "In Memoriam" selection.) What particular sound effects are created by this rhyme scheme?
2. How would you characterize the political philosophy expressed in the poem? Does this philosophy have relevance for you today?
3. Tennyson's reliance upon personification is obvious throughout the poem. How effective is it?

OLD IRONSIDES

1. Discuss Holmes' use of alliteration in this poem.
2. Who comprises the audience addressed in this poem?
3. What role did this particular ship play in American naval history?

FOR YOU O DEMOCRACY

1. Discuss Whitman's use of the word "comrades" in this poem. How is his repetition of the word related to the poem's theme?
2. Describe the two rather unusual images Whitman uses in the second stanza. Do you find them bizarre, or do you feel they help to sustain Whitman's theme? Why or why not?
3. Do you feel that Whitman's optimism about America's future has indeed been justified by subsequent history? Defend your answer.

A SHROPSHIRE LAD I (FROM CLEE TO HEAVEN THE BEACON BURNS)

1. Compare this poem to "Concord Hymn," "Love Thou Thy Land with Love Far-Brought," and "Recessional." What similarities and differences do you observe? Is there any consistent strain to be observed?
2. What stanzaic form does Housman employ in this poem? Identify the refrain which appears in the poem. How does the refrain help to unify the poem?
3. Housman mentions two rivers, the Nile and the Severn. The Severn is a sleepy little stream flowing through Shropshire. Why does Housman link the two as he does here?

RECESSIONAL

1. Identify the refrain used in the poem, and discuss its relationship to the rest of the poem. How is it that the refrain is trite and yet produces such a striking effect?
2. Compare this poem to "next to of course god." What points of comparison can you find? What do you think accounts for the shift in attitudes revealed in the two poems?
3. Nineveh, now buried beneath desert sands, was the ancient capital of Assyria; Tyre, now an insignificant seaport, was one of the greatest cities of Phoenicia. What warning is implicit in the allusion to these once glorious cities? Knowing what you do of England's past and present position as a world power, would you say that the warning had relevance?

EASTER, 1916

1. What does the line "A terrible beauty is born" mean?
2. This poem is about the unsuccessful Irish rebellion against English rule which occurred at Easter in 1916. What is Yeats' attitude toward this rebellion?
3. What images does Yeats use to convey his impressions of the various kinds of people who participated in the rebellion?

THE SOLDIER

1. Is this poem a sonnet? Why or why not?
2. This poem is one of the most moving of all patriotic poems. What makes it so? In answering this question the student might wish to consider the quiet tone and understated manner of the poem's language.

SHINE, PERISHING REPUBLIC

1. Why does Jeffers think that the republic is "perishing"?
2. What is Jeffers' attitude toward the city as opposed to the country? Why is rural life to be preferred over that of the city?
3. What is the meaning of the last stanza? How can it be that man caught God when He walked on earth?

NEXT TO OF COURSE GOD

1. Who is the speaker in this poem? What kind of situation is taking place in this poem? On what day of the year might the situation occur?
2. Does the speaker mean what he says? Does he really love God more than his country? You can answer these questions more easily if you first characterize the tone of the language in this poem.
3. Why is there so little punctuation in the poem? What effect does this absence of punctuation create?

POETRY AND LITERATURE

When poets write of literature, their attitudes range all the way from intense love of their art to sad regret and even anger at the demands that poetry makes of all who study it. The poems in this section clearly reflect both these extremes, as well as a number of intermediate attitudes.

The most formal poem in this section is also the earliest, Thomas Gray's "The Progress of Poesy: A Pindaric Ode." Pindaric odes originated in imitation of certain movements and speeches used by the chorus in Greek drama. Normally, these include three stanzas: the strophe, antistrophe, and epode. Gray's ode observes all the usual conventions, even to an opening invocation, and in heightened, rather artificial language Gray celebrates the beauties of verse.

"Nuns Fret Not" involves a discussion of form also. Wordsworth develops a series of images in this sonnet to suggest, paradoxically, that he finds freedom within the rather narrow boundaries of the fourteen-line "prison."

"Kubla Khan," on the other hand, reflects an entirely different attitude toward poetry. Coleridge admits himself that the poem is a curiosity, the result of a "dream-vision" caused by both drugs and drink. The dream world created for us here is undeniably attractive and real, and the poem closes with Coleridge's regret that he cannot build a poetic equivalent of the pleasure-dome. Especially entrancing are the incantatory lines of tetrameter, as they weave an enchanting, spell-binding mood for us.

"On First Looking into Chapman's Homer," a sonnet in the Italian form, expresses Keats' joy at discovering the blank verse translation of Homer's epics. (The common translation during Keats's life would have been Pope's, which is in heroic couplets and which would not have appealed to Keats.) The two images which sustain the poem are those in which Keats compares himself to the discoverer of a planet or of the Pacific Ocean. In light of the poem's enthusiasm and loveliness, it seems almost beside the point to note that, of course, Balboa, and not Cortez, discovered the Pacific Ocean.

"I Broke the Spell That Held Me Long," a brief three-stanza poem written mainly in tetrameter, puts beautifully the relationship between nature and poetry. Bryant, displeased at the rigor, discipline, and sacrifice involved in writing poetry, states that he is pleased finally to break the writing habit. But when he looks about him and sees in nature all that inspires poetry, he realizes that as long as he lives he must write.

Alfred Tennyson's "The Poet" stresses not so much the beauties of poetry, but the sense of mission a writer ought to have. In a series of quatrains Tennyson points out, in the words of the cliché, that, indeed, the pen is mightier than the sword. In other words, like Sidney, Shelley, Tolstoy, and Eliot, Tennyson pays homage to the power of poetry to teach morality. Throughout history writers have noted the power of literature to instruct and improve, often even more effectively than formal religion.

A sense of morality also accounts for Matthew Arnold's praise of Goethe, Byron, and Wordsworth in "Memorial Verses," written in 1850, the year of Wordsworth's death. Basically in blank verse, the poem reminds us that each of the three men praised gave us some special gift: Goethe, a "sage mind"; Byron, "force"; Wordsworth, "healing power." Wordsworth is honored most. Arnold suggests that time may replace Goethe and Byron, but Wordsworth can never be replaced.

Dante Gabriel Rossetti's "The Sonnet" is another example of the Italian sonnet. Certainly the poem compares easily to Wordsworth's "Nuns Fret Not"; like the Wordsworth poem, "The Sonnet" praises in succinct and figurative terms the beauties of this particular poetic form.

Yeats' brief poem "A Coat" distinguishes itself from the other lyrics in this section in that it declares a change in the poet's style and subject matter. The early Yeats, romantically attracted to subjects drawn from Ireland's mythology, declares in the little poem that he will henceforth turn to greater realism in matter and manner.

Marianne Moore's "Poetry" amounts almost to a discussion between a reader and a writer of verse. The terse opening statement tends to disarm the reader, telling him frankly that the poet, too, can dislike poetry and admitting to him—not without some irony—that "there are things that are important beyond all this fiddle." Yet, she continues, if we seek the genuine in poetry, if we seek "imaginary gardens with real toads in them," if in short we demand that the raw and genuine materials of life constitute the substance of poetry, then poetry becomes important and we become interested in it.

Archibald MacLeish carries the defense of poetry still further in his "Ars Poetica," a title borrowed from Horace. The art of poetry consists,

MacLeish argues, in the willingness to accept the individual poem as a self-sufficient entity, complete in itself, and with its own reason for being. "Ars Poetica" consists almost entirely of a catalog of similes, things poetry should be like. And all of them are things that simply exist and have value without the need for explanation or meaning. The last two lines of the lyric ("A poem should not mean / But be.") have often been quoted by modern critics who believe that a poem creates its own logic and its own existence, and should therefore be judged only in terms of that inner logic and life.

There remains, finally, A. J. M. Smith's lyric "To Hold in a Poem." Smith uses five quatrains of alternating rhyme pattern to suggest in very concrete terms how poetry works. Smith wants his poems to rely upon crisp, sharp, fresh imagery which appeals to the senses. Like MacLeish's poem, this one relies upon the sustained use of simile to communicate its impression.

It should be no surprise that poets have often attempted to define and defend poetry as an important human endeavor. Many of the most significant analyses, however, were written in prose: for example, Sidney's *Apology for Poetry*, Wordsworth's "Preface" to the *Lyrical Ballads*, Shelley's *A Defense of Poetry*, and several of T. S. Eliot's essays. Yet the short lyric poems in this section, because of their personal approach, present us with a variety of attitudes from which an individual craftsman viewed his art form.

THE PROGRESS OF POESY

I. 1

Awake, Æolian lyre, awake,
And give to rapture all thy trembling strings.
   From Helicon's harmonious springs
A thousand rills their mazy progress take:
5   The laughing flowers, that round them blow,
     Drink life and fragrance as they flow.
Now the rich stream of music winds along
    Deep, majestic, smooth, and strong,
Thro' verdant vales, and Ceres' golden reign:
10   Now rolling down the steep amain,
     Headlong, impetuous, see it pour:
The rocks, and nodding groves rebellow to the roar.

I. 2

O! sovereign of the willing soul,
Parent of sweet and solemn-breathing airs,
15   Enchanting shell! the sullen Cares,
And frantic Passions hear thy soft controul.
    On Thracia's hills the Lord of War
    Has curb'd the fury of his car,
And drop'd his thirsty lance at thy command.
20   Perching on the sceptred hand
Of Jove, thy magic lulls the feather'd king
    With ruffled plumes, and flagging wing:
    Quench'd in dark clouds of slumber lie
    The terror of his beak, and light'nings of his eye.

I. 3

25   Thee the voice, the dance, obey,
    Temper'd to thy warbled lay.
    O'er Idalia's velvet-green
    The rosy-crowned Loves are seen
      On Cytherea's day
30   With antic Sports, and blue-eyed Pleasures,
    Frisking light in frolic measures;
    Now pursuing, now retreating,
     Now in circling troops they meet:
    To brisk notes in cadence beating
35   Glance their many-twinkling feet.
Slow melting strains their Queen's approach declare:
    Where'er she turns the Graces homage pay.
With arms sublime, that float upon the air,
    In gliding state she wins her easy way:
40   O'er her warm cheek, and rising bosom, move
    The bloom of young Desire, and purple light of Love.

II. 1

    Man's feeble race what ills await,
Labour, and Penury, the racks of Pain,
    Disease, and Sorrow's weeping train,
45   And Death, sad refuge from the storms of Fate!
        The fond complaint, my song, disprove,
        And justify the laws of Jove.
    Say, has he giv'n in vain the heav'nly Muse?
        Night, and all her sickly dews,
50   Her spectres wan, and birds of boding cry,
        He gives to range the dreary sky:
        Till down the eastern cliffs afar
        Hyperion's march they spy, and glitt'ring shafts of war.

II. 2

    In climes beyond the solar road,
55   Where shaggy forms o'er ice-built mountains roam,
        The Muse has broke the twilight-gloom
To chear the shiv'ring native's dull abode.
        And oft, beneath the od'rous shade
        Of Chili's boundless forests laid,
60   She deigns to hear the savage youth repeat
        In loose numbers wildly sweet
Their feather-cinctur'd chiefs, and dusky loves.
        Her track, where'er the goddess roves,
        Glory pursue, and generous Shame,
65   Th' unconquerable Mind, and Freedom's holy flame.

II. 3

    Woods, that wave o'er Delphi's steep,
    Isles, that crown th' Aegean deep,
    Fields, that cool Ilissus laves,
    Or when Maeander's amber waves
70   In lingering lab'rinths creep,
    How do your tuneful echoes languish,
    Mute, but to the voice of Anguish?
    Where each old poetic mountain
        Inspiration breath'd around:
75   Ev'ry shade and hallow'd fountain
        Murmur'd deep a solemn sound:
Till the sad Nine in Greece's evil hour
    Left their Parnassus for the Latian plains.
Alike they scorn the pomp of tyrant-Power,
80   And coward Vice, that revels in her chains.
When Latium had her lofty spirit lost,
    They sought, O Albion! next thy sea-encircled coast.

III. 1

Far from the sun and summer-gale,
In thy green lap was Nature's darling laid,
85   What time, where lucid Avon stray'd,
To him the mighty Mother did unveil
        Her aweful face: the dauntless child
        Stretch'd forth his little arms, and smiled.
"This pencil take," she said, "whose colours clear
90   Richly paint the vernal year:
Thine too these golden keys, immortal boy!
        This can unlock the gates of Joy;
        Of Horror that, and thrilling Fears,
        Or ope the sacred source of sympathetic tears."

III. 2

95   Nor second he, that rode sublime
Upon the seraph-wings of Extasy,
        The secrets of th' Abyss to spy.
He pass'd the flaming bounds of Place and Time:
        The living throne, the saphire-blaze,
100   Where angels tremble, while they gaze,
He saw; but blasted with excess of light,
        Clos'd his eyes in endless night.
Behold, where Dryden's less presumptuous car,
        Wide o'er the fields of Glory bear
105   Two coursers of ethereal race,
        With necks in thunder cloath'd, and long-resounding pace.

III. 3

Hark, his hands the lyre explore!
Bright-eyed Fancy, hovering o'er,
Scatters from her pictur'd urn
110   Thoughts that breathe, and words that burn.
        But ah! 'tis heard no more—
O lyre divine, what daring spirit
Wakes thee now? Though he inherit
Nor the pride, nor ample pinion,
115   That the Theban Eagle bear
Sailing, with supreme dominion
        Thro' the azure deep of air:
Yet oft before his infant eyes would run
        Such forms, as glitter in the Muse's ray
120   With orient hues, unborrow'd of the sun:
        Yet shall he mount, and keep his distant way
Beyond the limits of a vulgar fate,
        Beneath the good how far—but far above the great.

                                        Thomas Gray   (1716–1771)

NUNS FRET NOT

Nuns fret not at their convent's narrow room;
And hermits are contented with their cells;
And students with their pensive citadels;
Maids at the wheel, the weaver at his loom,
5   Sit blithe and happy; bees that soar for bloom,
High as the highest Peak of Furness-fells,
Will murmur by the hour in foxglove bells:
In truth the prison, into which we doom
Ourselves, no prison is: and hence for me,
10   In sundry moods, 'twas pastime to be bound
Within the Sonnet's scanty plot of ground;
Pleased if some Souls (for such there needs must be)
Who have felt the weight of too much liberty,
Should find brief solace there, as I have found.

William Wordsworth   (1770 – 1850)

KUBLA KHAN

In Xanadu did Kubla Khan
  A stately pleasure-dome decree:
Where Alph, the sacred river, ran
Through caverns measureless to man
5   Down to a sunless sea.
So twice five miles of fertile ground
With walls and towers were girdled round:
And here were gardens bright with sinuous rills,
Where blossomed many an incense-bearing tree,
10   And here were forests ancient as the hills,
Enfolding sunny spots of greenery.

But oh! that deep romantic chasm which slanted
Down the green hill athwart a cedarn cover!
A savage place! as holy and enchanted
15   As e'er beneath a waning moon was haunted
By woman wailing for her demon-lover!
And from this chasm, with ceaseless turmoil seething,
As if this earth in fast thick pants were breathing,
A mighty fountain momently was forced,
20   Amid whose swift half-intermitted burst
Huge fragments vaulted like rebounding hail,
Or chaffy grain beneath the thresher's flail:
And 'mid these dancing rocks at once and ever

It flung up momently the sacred river.
25   Five miles meandering with a mazy motion
Through wood and dale the sacred river ran,
Then reached the caverns measureless to man,
And sank in tumult to a lifeless ocean:
And 'mid this tumult Kubla heard from far
30   Ancestral voices prophesying war!

    The shadow of the dome of pleasure
    Floated midway on the waves;
    Where was heard the mingled measure
    From the fountain and the caves.
35   It was a miracle of rare device,
A sunny pleasure-dome with caves of ice!
    A damsel with a dulcimer
    In a vision once I saw:
    It was an Abyssinian maid,
40   And on her dulcimer she played,
    Singing of Mount Abora.
    Could I revive within me
    Her symphony and song,
    To such a deep delight 'twould win me,
45   That with music loud and long,
I would build that dome in air,
That sunny dome! those caves of ice!
And all who heard should see them there,
And all should cry, Beware! Beware!
50   His flashing eyes, his floating hair!
Weave a circle round him thrice,
And close your eyes with holy dread,
For he on honey-dew hath fed,
And drunk the milk of Paradise.

    Samuel Taylor Coleridge (1772 – 1834)

ON FIRST LOOKING INTO CHAPMAN'S HOMER

Much have I travell'd in the realms of gold,
   And many goodly states and kingdoms seen;
   Round many western islands have I been
Which bards in fealty to Apollo hold.
5   Oft of one wide expanse had I been told
   That deep-brow'd Homer ruled as his demesne;
   Yet did I never breathe its pure serene
Till I heard Chapman speak out loud and bold:
Then felt I like some watcher of the skies

10   When a new planet swims into his ken;
Or like stout Cortez when with eagle eyes
   He star'd at the Pacific—and all his men
Look'd at each other with a wild surmise—
   Silent, upon a peak in Darien.

              John Keats   (1795–1821)

I BROKE THE SPELL THAT HELD ME LONG

I broke the spell that held me long,
The dear, dear witchery of song.
I said, the poet's idle lore
Shall waste my prime of years no more,
5   For Poetry, though heavenly born,
Consorts with poverty and scorn.

I broke the spell—nor deemed its power
Could fetter me another hour.
Ah, thoughtless! how could I forget
10   Its causes were around me yet?
For wheresoe'er I looked, the while,
Was Nature's everlasting smile.

Still came and lingered on my sight
Of flowers and streams the bloom and light,
15   And glory of the stars and sun;
And these and poetry are one.
They, ere the world had held me long,
Recalled me to the love of song.

        William Cullen Bryant   (1795–1878)

THE POET

The poet in a golden clime was born,
   With golden stars above;
Dower'd with the hate of hate, the scorn of scorn,
   The love of love.

5   He saw thro' life and death, thro' good and ill,
   He saw thro' his own soul.
The marvel of the everlasting will,
   An open scroll,

Before him lay; with echoing feet he threaded
10   The secretest walks of fame:
The viewless arrows of his thoughts were headed
    And wing'd with flame,

Like Indian reeds blown from his silver tongue,
   And of so fierce a flight,
15 From Calpe unto Caucasus they sung,
    Filling with light

And vagrant melodies the winds which bore
   Them earthward till they lit;
Then, like the arrow-seeds of the field flower,
20   The fruitful wit

Cleaving took root, and springing forth anew
   Where'er they fell, behold,
Like to the mother plant in semblance, grew
    A flower all gold,

25 And bravely furnish'd all abroad to fling
   The winged shafts of truth,
To throng with stately blooms the breathing spring
    Of Hope and Youth.

So many minds did gird their orbs with beams,
30   Tho' one did fling the fire;
Heaven flow'd upon the soul in many dreams
    Of high desire.

Thus truth was multiplied on truth, the world
   Like one great garden show'd,
35 And thro' the wreaths of floating dark upcurl'd,
    Rare sunrise flow'd.

And Freedom rear'd in that august sunrise
   Her beautiful bold brow,
When rites and forms before his burning eyes
40   Melted like snow.

There was no blood upon her maiden robes
   Sunn'd by those orient skies;
But round about the circles of the globes
    Of her keen eyes

45 And in her raiment's hem was traced in flame
   Wisdom, a name to shake
All evil dreams of power—a sacred name.
    And when she spake,

Her words did gather thunder as they ran,
50   And as the lightning to the thunder
Which follows it, riving the spirit of man,
              Making earth wonder,

So was their meaning to her words. No sword
      Of wrath her right arm whirl'd,
55   But one poor poet's scroll, and with *his* word
          She shook the world.

              Alfred, Lord Tennyson   *(1809 – 1892)*

MEMORIAL VERSES

April, 1850

Goethe in Weimar sleeps, and Greece,
Long since, saw Byron's struggle cease.
But one such death remain'd to come;
The last poetic voice is dumb —
5   We stand to-day by Wordsworth's tomb.

When Byron's eyes were shut in death,
We bow'd our head and held our breath.
He taught us little; but our soul
Had *felt* him like the thunder's roll.
10   With shivering heart the strife we saw
Of passion with eternal law;
And yet with reverential awe
We watch'd the fount of fiery life
Which served for that Titanic strife.

15   When Goethe's death was told, we said:
Sunk, then, is Europe's sagest head.
Physician of the iron age,
Goethe has done his pilgrimage.
He took the suffering human race,
20   He read each wound, each weakness clear;
And struck his finger on the place,
And said: *Thou ailest here, and here!*
He look'd on Europe's dying hour
Of fitful dream and feverish power;
25   His eye plunged down the weltering strife,
The turmoil of expiring life —
He said: *The end is everywhere,*
Art still has truth, take refuge there!

And he was happy, if to know
30   Causes of things, and far below
His feet to see the lurid flow
Of terror, and insane distress,
And headlong fate, be happiness.

And Wordsworth!—Ah, pale ghosts, rejoice!
35   For never has such soothing voice
Been to your shadowy world convey'd,
Since erst, at morn, some wandering shade
Heard the clear song of Orpheus come
Through Hades, and the mournful gloom.
40   Wordsworth has gone from us—and ye,
Ah, may ye feel his voice as we!
He too upon a wintry clime
Had fallen—on this iron time
Of doubts, disputes, distractions, fears.
45   He found us when the age had bound
Our souls in its benumbing round;
He spoke, and loosed our heart in tears.
He laid us as we lay at birth
On the cool flowery lap of earth,
50   Smiles broke from us and we had ease;
The hills were round us, and the breeze
Went o'er the sun-lit fields again;
Our foreheads felt the wind and rain.
Our youth return'd; for there was shed
55   On spirits that had long been dead,
Spirits dried up and closely furl'd,
The freshness of the early world.

Ah! since dark days still bring to light
Man's prudence and man's fiery might,
60   Time may restore us in his course
Goethe's sage mind and Byron's force;
But where will Europe's latter hour
Again find Wordsworth's healing power?
Others will teach us how to dare,
65   And against fear our breast to steel;
Others will strengthen us to bear—
But who, ah! who, will make us feel?
The cloud of mortal destiny,
Others will front it fearlessly—
70   But who, like him, will put it by?

Keep fresh the grass upon his grave
O Rotha, with thy living wave!
Sing him thy best! for few or none
Hears thy voice right, now he is gone.

Matthew Arnold   (1822 – 1888)

THE SONNET

A Sonnet is a moment's monument, —
  Memorial from the Soul's eternity
  To one dead deathless hour. Look that it be,
Whether for lustral rite or dire portent,
5 Of its own arduous fullness reverent:
  Carve it in ivory or in ebony,
  As Day or Night may rule; and let Time see
Its flowering crest impearled and orient.

A Sonnet is a coin: its face reveals
10 The soul, — its converse, to what Power 'tis due: —
Whether for tribute to the august appeals
  Of Life, or dower in Love's high retinue,
It serve; or, 'mid the dark wharf's cavernous breath,
In Charon's palm it pay the toll to Death.

Dante Gabriel Rossetti   *(1828 – 1882)*

A COAT

I made my song a coat
Covered with embroideries
Out of old mythologies
From heel to throat;
5 But the fools caught it,
Wore it in the world's eyes
As though they'd wrought it.
Song, let them take it,
For there's more enterprise
10 In walking naked.

William Butler Yeats   *(1865 – 1939)*

POETRY

I, too, dislike it: there are things that are important beyond all this
    fiddle.
  Reading it, however, with a perfect contempt for it, one discovers in
  it after all, a place for the genuine.
    Hands that can grasp, eyes
5   that can dilate, hair that can rise
      if it must, these things are important not because a

high-sounding interpretation can be put upon them but because they
    are
useful. When they become so derivative as to become unintelligible,
the same thing may be said for all of us, that we
10   do not admire what
    we cannot understand: the bat
        holding on upside down or in quest of something to

eat, elephants pushing, a wild horse taking a roll, a tireless wolf under
    a tree, the immovable critic twitching his skin like a horse that feels
    a flea, the base-
15   ball fan, the statistician —
    nor is it valid
        to discriminate against "business documents and

school-books"; all these phenomena are important. One must make a
    distinction
however: when dragged into prominence by half poets, the result is
    not poetry,
20   nor till the poets among us can be
    "literalists of
    the imagination" — above
        insolence and triviality and can present

for inspection, "imaginary gardens with real toads in them" shall we
    have
25   it. In the meantime, if you demand on the one hand,
    the raw material of poetry in
        all its rawness and
    that which is on the other hand
        genuine, you are interested in poetry.

Marianne Moore   (1887 –   )

ARS POETICA

A poem should be palpable and mute
As a globed fruit,

Dumb
As old medallions to the thumb,

5   Silent as the sleeve-worn stone
Of casement ledges where the moss has grown —

A poem should be wordless
As the flight of birds.

.   .   .   .   .   .

A poem should be motionless in time
10   As the moon climbs,

Leaving, as the moon releases
Twig by twig the night-entangled trees,

Leaving, as the moon behind the winter leaves,
Memory by memory the mind—

15   A poem should be motionless in time
As the moon climbs.

.   .   .   .   .   .

A poem should be equal to:
Not true.

For all the history of grief
20   An empty doorway and a maple leaf.

For love
The leaning grasses and two lights above the sea—

A poem should not mean
But be.

Archibald MacLeish   (1892 –   )

TO HOLD IN A POEM

I would take words
As crisp and as white
As our snow; as our birds
Swift and sure in their flight;

5   As clear and as cold
As our ice; as strong as a jack pine;
As young as a trillium, and old
As Laurentia's long undulant line;

Sweet-smelling and bright
10   As new rain; as hard
And as smooth and as white
As a brook pebble cold and unmarred;

To hold in a poem of words
Like water in colorless glass
15   The spirit of mountains like birds,
Of forests as pointed as grass;

To hold in a verse as austere
As the spirit of prairie and river,
Lonely, unbuyable, dear,
20   The North, as a deed, and forever.

A. J. M. Smith   (1902 –   )

QUESTIONS FOR DISCUSSION AND FURTHER STUDY

THE PROGRESS OF POESY

1. Identify the following terms by using a dictionary or other reference work: Æolian, Helicon, Ceres, Jove, Thracia, Cytherea, Hyperion, Chili, Delphi, Ægean, Mæander, Parnassus, Latian, Latium, Albion, Avon, and Theban.
2. John Dryden (d. 1700) was the greatest writer of the period in English literature known as the Restoration (1600-1700). Why is his car "less presumptuous"?
3. This poem is a Pindaric ode. Look up the term *ode* in the glossary and be able to tell how this poem exemplifies this type of poetry.

NUNS FRET NOT

1. Why does Wordsworth choose nuns to exemplify the discipline the sonnet imposes on a poet?
2. What is the theme of this poem? Do you think the theme is as important as the theme of a poem dealing, for example, with social consciousness?
3. Why is the solace Wordsworth finds "brief"?

KUBLA KHAN

1. The poem divides itself roughly into three parts or verse paragraphs. Can you paraphrase in prose the meaning or effect of each? Which is more prominent, meaning or effect?
2. Because Coleridge himself believed that poetry was an intellectual activity, he published this poem only as a curiosity, not for its poetic merit. (Recall that he claims to have been under the influence of both drink and medication when he conceived the poem.) Do you agree with Coleridge's estimate of his own work? Why or why not?
3. Who or what is symbolized by the "damsel with a dulcimer"?

ON FIRST LOOKING INTO CHAPMAN'S HOMER

1. Keats wrote this poem immediately after a friend had brought him a copy of Homer's *Iliad* as translated by the Elizabethan poet and dramatist George Chapman. The sonnet records Keats' enthusiasm at "discovering" Homer for the first time (he could not read Greek). In what way does Keats communicate the sense of awe that accompanied this new reading experience?

2.   Discuss the imagery in this poem. Keats compares himself to two people in the poem. Who are they?

3.   Other translations of Homer were available to Keats, particularly the famous rendering by Alexander Pope. Does the sonnet suggest that he had ever seen other translations? Explain your answer.

I BROKE THE SPELL THAT HELD ME LONG

1.   Describe the poet's developing attitude toward his craft as the poem progresses.

2.   What recalls the poet "to the love of song"?

3.   Do you agree that poetry "Consorts with poverty and scorn"? Explain.

THE POET

1.   Describe the stanzaic form used by Tennyson in this poem.

2.   Shelley writes that poets are "the unacknowledged legislators of the world." Does Tennyson agree with this view?

3.   Why does Tennyson relate poetry to freedom? What is the substance of this relationship?

MEMORIAL VERSES

1.   What images does Arnold employ in this poem? Are these images appropriate in terms of his theme?

2.   Why does Arnold regard Wordsworth so highly? What qualities does he admire in Wordsworth? Does Arnold regard Wordsworth primarily as a poet or as a moralist?

3.   Lines twenty-nine through thirty-three are actually a very close translation of a passage in Virgil's *Georgics*, and Arnold intended that his readers would recognize the passage. This fact, along with other allusions in the poem, suggests that Arnold was addressing what sort of reader?

THE SONNET

1.   Compare this poem to "Nuns Fret Not." Which poem do you like better? Why?

2.   Rossetti uses two metaphors in the poem: he compares the sonnet to a monument, and he compares it to a coin. Do you feel both comparisons are appropriate, and do you feel that the two work well together in the same poem?

3.   According to Greek mythology, Charon pilots the boat which takes

the dead across the river surrounding the land of afterlife. Often the Greeks observed the custom of placing a coin under a dead person's tongue to pay for the ferry. How does this fact affect the poem's meaning?

A COAT

1. This poem declares a change in the author's style and subject matter. What does he mean when he equates his previous poetry with "a coat"? What is meant later by "going naked"?
2. Would you expect a poem like "An Irish Airman Foresees His Death" to have been written before or after this poem? Why?
3. Who or what is the audience addressed by Yeats in this poem?

POETRY

1. Does Miss Moore really dislike poetry? How can you determine her attitude on this subject?
2. What do you think of Miss Moore's test to determine whether or not "you are interested in poetry"?
3. Discuss the imagery used in this poem. Is it effective? Why or why not?

ARS POETICA

1. The stanzaic form used by MacLeish in this poem is a brief and varied couplet. Why does this form sustain MacLeish's comments about the nature of poetry?
2. The poem depends primarily on what figure of speech?
3. The title of the poem is borrowed from Horace and can be directly translated as "the art of poetry." What is MacLeish's concept of the poetic art? What indeed does he mean when he argues that a poem should not be "true" and should not "mean"?

TO HOLD IN A POEM

1. What is the meaning of the poem's title?
2. Like "Ars Poetica," this poem leans heavily on one figure of speech. What is the type of figure involved, and which of the two poems makes more effective use of it? Why?
3. The Laurentian Mountains stretch between Hudson Bay and the St. Lawrence River, and they provide an appropriate allusion for A. J. M. Smith, who is a Canadian poet. Are the other images similarly appropriate? Explain.

SOCIAL CONSCIOUSNESS

In his lengthy essay *A Defense of Poetry*, Percy Bysshe Shelley contends that "Poets are the unacknowledged legislators of the world." His basic argument is that the poet should place before his readers such gloriously idealistic pictures of the world as would inspire them to achieve a new order. Of course, while this is not the only aim of poetry, it is an important one.

Poets are often sensitive to social and political injustice, and often they try to rectify those things they consider wrong. Sometimes they deal with a particular social problem, movement, or injustice. At other times they deal more generally with social ills in an attempt to inculcate a more widespread sense of brotherhood, compassion, or love among all mankind.

John Milton's "On the Late Massacre in Piedmont" is the earliest of these poems linked to a specific event. While some of the poems in this section cry out for economic or industrial reform, this well-known sonnet tells of a Protestant sect (the Waldenses) whose people lived in the Piedmont in northern Italy. Their freedom of worship was abruptly terminated in 1655, and the entire community was massacred by the troops of the Catholic Duke of Savoy. In strong and Biblical language Milton asks the Lord to remember and avenge the massacre.

Shelley's "Song to the Men of England" deals not with a specific incident, but instead with the problems of unequal distribution of wealth. Written in tetrameter quatrains, the militant poem first asks a series of rhetorical questions designed to illustrate the abuses of England's nineteenth-century industrial system, then exhorts the workers to a militant course of action against the injustice of the system. It is significant that this poem was reprinted countless times in the radical publications of the nineteenth and early twentieth centuries.

Like Shelley, Thomas Hood was a Romantic poet greatly concerned with social conditions in England. His "The Song of the Shirt" denounces specifically the exploitation of female labor. As in Mrs. Browning's "The Cry of the Children," the meter and rhythm of this poem are somewhat jogging and, perhaps, inappropriate. However, the reader should remember that the speaker in the poem is a seamstress herself, and not an accomplished poetess. In any event, the repetition of the phrase "Work-work-work!" certainly conveys the brutalizing monotony connected with unskilled manual labor.

Elizabeth Barrett Browning's "The Cry of the Children" continues the attack on nineteenth-century industrial capitalism. In a poem using an alternating rhyme scheme, Mrs. Browning attacks the cruel and barbarous employment of children in mines and factories. Mrs. Browning wrote the poem in a frenzy after reading a report on child labor. Especially noteworthy is the poem's statement that the pitiful, cruel, hopeless lives of the children have made them lose their faith in a loving, providential God.

"The Day Is Coming" by William Morris states in effective satirical terms its author's view of the society of the future. A leader in the socialist movement, Morris envisions a society without private ownership, a society in which the worker will enjoy the full benefit of his labor. And in a way not unlike the pleas of American Negroes in our country today, the poem asks for action *now*. The powerfully accented octosyllabic couplets are well selected for the audience Morris tried to reach—the common worker. This poem, like Shelley's "Song to the Men of England" was often reprinted in socialist newspapers and magazines.

The most recent poem related to a specific historical event is Howard Nemerov's "Boom." The poem begins by reprinting an Associated Press story about President Eisenhower's pastor. The tone of the poem is consistently ironic, and the work really attacks the comfortable, self-satisfied, prosperous morality that equates abundance with virtue. Particularly, Nemerov effectively exposes a certain kind of distinctively American parochialism.

Turning to the poems on social consciousness which are not so closely related to any specific issue, we note that the oldest is William Blake's "Auguries of Innocence." The poem strings together a series of aphorisms in jogging tetrameter couplets. The most biting, incisive lines in the poem are those which speak of the horror, hypocrisy, or cruelty with which freedom, love, and individuality are restricted, and certainly the first four lines of the poem deserve the fame they have earned.

Blake's poem suggests a corrupt society with too many restrictions placed upon man's freedom. At almost the same time Wordsworth wrote "London, 1802," which also attacks the general decay of English freedoms. This Italian sonnet makes use of the poetic device *apostrophe* to suggest that England, now "a fen / Of stagnant waters," has need again for the powerful pen of John Milton, who in both his prose and poetry had attacked social and political injustice.

"Much Madness Is Divinest Sense," by the American poetess Emily Dickinson, deals with one of the problems especially prevalent in a democratic society, the tyranny of the majority. In simple but eloquent terms the poem describes the evil of mob psychology. He who departs from the herd puts himself in danger, and the stark reality of the last sentence in the poem remains undeniable:

> Demur, — you're straightway dangerous,
> And handled with a chain.

"The Man with the Hoe" interests us especially because it is one of those works of art inspired by another kind of art — in this case, painting. Edwin Markham wrote his poem after seeing a painting by Jean François Millet (1814-1874) which depicts a man bent and bowed by the hard and unrewarding labor of a lifetime. The poem tells of a man degraded and dehumanized by menial, arduous labor. Again, a series of rhetorical questions is used in this blank-verse poem to show mankind cheapened and cheated by the effects of hard, unremitting labor. Many poems, incidentally, tend to idealize rural life, but this poem is of special interest in its harshly realistic delineation of life close to the soil.

"I Am the People, the Mob" states in free verse Sandburg's belief that when the common people cease to forget who robbed them last year, "The mob — the crowd — the mass — will arrive then." The sense of universal brotherhood in the poem strikes us as sincere and strong. This poem, like the one preceding it, contains an implied threat to the established order; both strongly suggest a violent social upheaval in the future.

The last poem in this section is "The Unknown Citizen," by W. H. Auden. Indirectly, the work tells the life story of an anonymous, modern-day Everyman. The poem relies upon its consistent irony to attack the values of our highly organized, highly centralized, highly planned society. Here is a man whose entire life conformed perfectly with statistical expectation and the desires of social engineers; indeed, he has lost his identity as a free individual.

Poems of social consciousness, then, may reveal the writer's concern with a particular social issue, or they may deal more universally with elements not closely related to a specific law, custom, or injustice. One thing remains certain: the sincerity of any poet in this section cannot be questioned, and the evident sincerity to be found in these poems lends strength and vigor to the poetic language of any lyric dealing with social consciousness.

ON THE LATE MASSACRE IN PIEDMONT

Avenge, O Lord, thy slaughtered saints, whose bones
  Lie scattered on the Alpine mountains cold;
  Even them who kept thy truth so pure of old
  When all our fathers worshipped stocks and stones,
5 Forget not; in thy book record their groans
  Who were thy sheep and in their ancient fold
  Slain by the bloody Piedmontese that rolled
  Mother with infant down the rocks. Their moans
The vales redoubled to the hills, and they
10   To heaven. Their martyred blood and ashes sow
  O'er all the Italian fields where still doth sway
The triple tyrant: that from these may grow
  A hundredfold, who having learned thy way
  Early may fly the Babylonian woe.

John Milton   (1608 – 1674)

AUGURIES OF INNOCENCE

To see a World in a Grain of Sand
And a Heaven in a Wild Flower,
Hold Infinity in the palm of your hand
And Eternity in an hour.

5   A Robin Red breast in a Cage
Puts all Heaven in a Rage.
A dove house fill'd with doves & Pigeons
Shudders Hell thro' all its regions.
A dog starv'd at his Master's Gate
10   Predicts the ruin of the State.
A Horse misus'd upon the Road
Calls to Heaven for Human blood.
Each outcry of the hunted Hare
A fibre from the Brain does tear.
15   A Skylark wounded in the wing,
A Cherubim does cease to sing.
The Game Cock clip'd & arm'd for fight
Does the Rising Sun affright.
Every Wolf's & Lion's howl
20   Raises from Hell a Human Soul.
The wild deer, wand'ring here & there,
Keeps the Human Soul from Care.
The Lamb misus'd breeds Public strife

And yet forgives the Butcher's Knife.
25   The Bat that flits at close of Eve
Has left the Brain that won't Believe.
The Owl that calls upon the Night
Speaks the Unbeliever's fright.
He who shall hurt the little Wren
30   Shall never be belov'd by Men.
He who the Ox to wrath has mov'd
Shall never be by Woman lov'd.
The wanton Boy that kills the Fly
Shall feel the Spider's enmity.
35   He who torments the Chafer's sprite
Weaves a Bower in endless Night.
The Catterpiller on the Leaf
Repeats to thee thy Mother's grief.
Kill not the Moth nor Butterfly,
40   For the Last Judgment draweth nigh.
He who shall train the Horse to War
Shall never pass the Polar Bar.
The Beggar's Dog & Widow's Cat,
Feed them & thou wilt grow fat.
45   The Gnat that sings his Summer's song
Poison gets from Slander's tongue.
The poison of the Snake & Newt
Is the sweat of Envy's Foot.
The Poison of the Honey Bee
50   Is the Artist's Jealousy.
The Prince's Robes & Beggar's Rags
Are Toadstools on the Miser's Bags.
A truth that's told with bad intent
Beats all the Lies you can invent.
55   It is right it should be so;
Man was made for Joy & Woe;
And when this we rightly know
Thro' the World we safely go,
Joy & Woe are woven fine,
60   A Clothing for the Soul divine;
Under every grief & pine
Runs a joy with silken twine.
The Babe is more than swadling Bands;
Throughout all these Human Lands
65   Tools were made, & Born were hands,
Every Farmer Understands.
Every Tear from Every Eye
Becomes a Babe in Eternity;
This is caught by Females bright
70   And return'd to its own delight.
The Bleat, the Bark, Bellow & Roar
Are Waves that Beat on Heaven's Shore.
The Babe that weeps the Rod beneath

Writes Revenge in realms of death.
75   The Beggar's Rags, fluttering in Air,
Does to Rags the Heavens tear.
The Soldier, arm'd with Sword & Gun,
Palsied strikes the Summer's Sun.
The poor Man's Farthing is worth more
80   Than all the Gold on Afric's Shore.
One Mite wrung from the Labrer's hands
Shall buy & sell the Miser's Lands:
Or, if protected from on high,
Does that whole Nation sell & buy.
85   He who mocks the Infant's Faith
Shall be mock'd in Age & Death.
He who shall teach the Child to Doubt
The rotting Grave shall ne'er get out.
He who respects the Infant's faith
90   Triumphs over Hell & Death.
The Child's Toys & the Old Man's Reasons
Are the Fruits of the Two seasons.
The Questioner, who sits so sly,
Shall never know how to Reply.
95   He who replies to words of Doubt
Doth put the Light of Knowledge out.
The Strongest Poison ever known
Came from Caesar's Laurel Crown.
Nought can deform the Human Race
100   Like to the Armour's iron brace.
When Gold & Gems adorn the Plow
To peaceful Arts shall Envy Bow.
A Riddle or the Cricket's Cry
Is to Doubt a fit Reply.
105   The Emmet's Inch & Eagle's Mile
Make Lame Philosophy to smile.
He who Doubts from what he sees
Will ne'er Believe, do what you Please.
If the Sun & Moon should doubt,
110   They'd immediately Go out.
To be in a Passion you Good may do,
But no Good if a Passion is in you.
The Whore & Gambler, by the State
Licenc'd, build that Nation's Fate.
115   The Harlot's cry from Street to Street
Shall weave Old England's winding Sheet.
The Winner's Shout, the Loser's Curse,
Dance before dead England's Hearse.
Every Night & every Morn
120   Some to Misery are Born.
Every Morn & every Night
Some are Born to sweet delight.

Some are Born to sweet delight,
Some are Born to Endless Night.
125 We are led to Believe a Lie
When we see not Thro' the Eye
Which was Born in a Night to perish in a Night
When the Soul Slept in Beams of Light.
God Appears & God is Light
130 To those poor Souls who dwell in Night,
But does a Human Form Display
To those who Dwell in Realms of day.

William Blake   (1757 – 1827)

LONDON, 1802

Milton! thou should'st be living at this hour:
England hath need of thee: she is a fen
Of stagnant waters: altar, sword, and pen,
Fireside, the heroic wealth of hall and bower,
5 Have forfeited their ancient English dower
Of inward happiness. We are selfish men;
Oh! raise us up, return to us again;
And give us manners, virtue, freedom, power.
Thy soul was like a Star, and dwelt apart;
10 Thou hadst a voice whose sound was like the sea:
Pure as the naked heavens, majestic, free,
So didst thou travel on life's common way,
In cheerful godliness; and yet thy heart
The lowliest duties on herself did lay.

William Wordsworth   (1770 – 1850)

SONG TO THE MEN OF ENGLAND

Men of England, wherefore plough
For the lords who lay ye low?
Wherefore weave with toil and care
The rich robes your tyrants wear?

5 Wherefore feed, and clothe, and save,
From the cradle to the grave,
Those ungrateful drones who would
Drain your sweat — nay, drink your blood?

Wherefore, Bees of England, forge
10   Many a weapon, chain, and scourge,
That these stingless drones may spoil
The forced produce of your toil?

Have ye leisure, comfort, calm,
Shelter, food, love's gentle balm?
15   Or what is it ye buy so dear
With your pain and with your fear?

The seed ye sow, another reaps;
The wealth ye find, another keeps;
The robes ye weave, another wears;
20   The arms ye forge, another bears.

Sow seed, — but let no tyrant reap;
Find wealth, — let no impostor heap;
Weave robes, — let not the idle wear;
Forge arms, — in your defence to bear.

25   Shrink to your cellars, holes, and cells;
In halls ye deck another dwells.
Why shake the chains ye wrought? Ye see
The steel ye tempered glance on ye.

With plough and spade, and hoe and loom,
30   Trace your grave, and build your tomb,
And weave your winding-sheet, till fair
England be your sepulchre.

Percy Bysshe Shelley   (1792 – 1822)

SONG OF THE SHIRT

With fingers weary and worn,
  With eyelids heavy and red,
A Woman sat, in unwomanly rags,
  Plying her needle and thread —
5   Stitch! stitch! stitch!
In poverty, hunger, and dirt,
    And still with a voice of dolorous pitch
She sang the 'Song of the Shirt!'

'Work! work! work!
10   While the cock is crowing aloof!

And work — work — work,
   Till the stars shine through the roof!
It's O! to be a slave
   Along with the barbarous Turk,
15   Where woman has never a soul to save,
   If this is Christian work!

'Work — work — work
   Till the brain begins to swim;
Work — work — work
20   Till the eyes are heavy and dim!
Seam, and gusset, and band,
   Band, and gusset, and seam,
Till over the buttons I fall asleep,
   And sew them on in a dream!

25 'O! Men with Sisters dear!
   O! Men with Mothers and Wives,
It is not linen you're wearing out,
   But human creatures' lives
Stitch — stitch — stitch,
30   In poverty, hunger, and dirt,
Sewing at once, with a double thread,
   A Shroud as well as a Shirt.

'But why do I talk of Death?
   That Phantom of grisly bone,
35 I hardly fear his terrible shape,
   It seems so like my own —
   It seems so like my own,
   Because of the fasts I keep,
Oh! God! that bread should be so dear,
40   And flesh and blood so cheap!

Work — work — work!
   My labour never flags;
And what are its wages? A bed of straw,
   A crust of bread — and rags.
45 That shatter'd roof, — and this naked floor —
   A table — a broken chair —
And a wall so blank, my shadow I thank
   For sometimes falling there!

'Work — work — work!
50   From weary chime to chime,
Work — work — work —
   As prisoners work for crime!
Band, and gusset, and seam,
   Seam, and gusset, and band,

55 Till the heart is sick, and the brain benumb'd,
  As well as the weary hand.

 'Work — work — work,
  In the dull December light,
 And work — work — work,
60 When the weather is warm and bright —
 While underneath the eaves
  The brooding swallows cling,
 As if to show me their sunny backs
  And twit me with the spring.

65 'Oh! but to breathe the breath
  Of the cowslip and primrose sweet —
 With the sky above my head,
  And the grass beneath my feet,
 For only one short hour
70 To feel as I used to feel,
 Before I knew the woes of want
  And the walk that costs a meal!

 'Oh but for one short hour!
  A respite however brief!
75 No blessed leisure for love or hope,
  But only time for grief!
 A little weeping would ease my heart,
  But in their briny bed
 My tears must stop, for every drop
80 Hinders needle and thread!'

 Seam, and gusset, and band,
  Band, and gusset, and seam,
 Work, work, work,
  Like the Engine that works by Steam!
85 A mere machine of iron and wood
  That toils for Mammon's sake —
 Without a brain to ponder and craze,
  Or a heart to feel — and break!

 With fingers weary and worn,
90 With eyelids heavy and red,
 A Woman sat in unwomanly rags,
  Plying her needle and thread —
   Stitch! stitch! stitch!
 In poverty, hunger, and dirt,
95 And still with a voice of dolorous pitch,
  Would that its tone could reach the Rich! —
  She sang this 'Song of the Shirt!'

   Thomas Hood (1799 – 1845)

THE CRY OF THE CHILDREN

I

Do ye hear the children weeping, O my brothers,
    Ere the sorrow comes with years?
They are leaning their young heads against their mothers,
    And *that* cannot stop their tears.
5   The young lambs are bleating in the meadows,
    The young birds are chirping in the nest,
The young fawns are playing with the shadows,
    The young flowers are blowing toward the west—
But the young, young children, O my brothers,
10   They are weeping bitterly!
They are weeping in the playtime of the others,
    In the country of the free.

II

Do you question the young children in the sorrow
    Why their tears are falling so?
15   The old man may weep for his to-morrow
    Which is lost in Long Ago;
The old tree is leafless in the forest,
    The old year is ending in the frost,
The old wound, if stricken, is the sorest,
20   The old hope is hardest to be lost:
But the young, young children, O my brothers,
    Do you ask them why they stand
Weeping before the bosoms of their mothers,
    In our happy Fatherland?

III

25   They look up with their pale and sunken faces,
    And their looks are sad to see,
For the man's hoary anguish draws and presses
    Down the cheeks of infancy.
'Your old earth,' they say, 'is very dreary;
30   Our young feet,' they say, 'are very weak!
Few paces have we taken, yet are weary—
    Our grave-rest is very far to seek.
Ask the aged why they weep, and not the children;
    For the outside earth is cold;
35   And we young ones stand without, in our bewildering,
    And the graves are for the old.'

IV

'True,' say the children, 'it may happen
    That we die before our time;
Little Alice died last year—her grave is shapen
40   Like a snowball, in the rime.
We looked into the pit prepared to take her:
    Was no room for any work in the close clay!
From the sleep wherein she lieth none will wake her,
    Crying, "Get up, little Alice! it is day."
45 If you listen by that grave, in sun and shower,
    With your ear down, little Alice never cries;
Could we see her face, be sure we should not know her,
    For the smile has time for growing in her eyes:
And merry go her moments, lulled and stilled in
50   The shroud by the kirk-chime.
It is good when it happens,' say the children,
    'That we die before our time.'

V

Alas, alas, the children! they are seeking
    Death in life, as best to have;
55 They are binding up their hearts away from breaking,
    With a cerement from the grave.
Go out, children, from the mine and from the city,
    Sing out, children, as the little thrushes do;
Pluck your handfuls of the meadow-cowslips pretty,
60   Laugh aloud, to feel your fingers let them through!
But they answer, 'Are your cowslips of the meadows
    Like our weeds anear the mine?
Leave us quiet in the dark of the coal-shadows,
    From your pleasures fair and fine!

VI

65 'For oh,' say the children, 'we are weary,
    And we cannot run or leap;
If we cared for any meadows, it were merely
    To drop down in them and sleep.
Our knees tremble sorely in the stooping,
70   We fall upon our faces, trying to go;
And, underneath our heavy eyelids drooping
    The reddest flower would look as pale as snow.
For, all day, we drag our burden tiring
    Through the coal-dark, underground;
75 Or, all day, we drive the wheels of iron
    In the factories, round and round.

VII

'For all day the wheels are droning, turning, —
     Their wind comes in our faces, —
Till our hearts turn, — our heads with pulses burning,
80   And the walls turn in their places:
Turns the sky in the high window, blank and reeling
     Turns the long light that drops adown the wall,
Turn the black flies that crawl along the ceiling:
     All are turning, all the day, and we with all.
85 And all day the iron wheels are droning,
     And sometimes we could pray,
"O ye wheels" (breaking out in a mad moaning),
     "Stop! be silent for to-day!"

VIII

Aye! be silent! Let them hear each other breathing
90   For a moment, mouth to mouth!
Let them touch each other's hands, in a fresh wreathing
     Of their tender human youth!
Let them feel that this cold metallic motion
     Is not all the life God fashions or reveals:
95 Let them prove their living souls against the notion
     That they live in you, or under you, O wheels!
Still, all day, the iron wheels go onward,
     Grinding life down from its mark;
And the children's souls, which God is calling sunward,
100   Spin on blindly in the dark.

IX

Now tell the poor young children, O my brothers,
     To look up to Him and pray;
So the blessèd One who blesseth all the others,
     Will bless them another day.
105 They answer, 'Who is God that He should hear us,
     While the rushing of the iron wheels is stirred?
When we sob aloud, the human creatures near us
     Pass by, hearing not, or answer not a word.
And we hear not (for the wheels in their resounding)
110   Strangers speaking at the door:
Is it likely God, with angels singing round Him,
     Hears our weeping any more?

X

'Two words, indeed, of praying we remember,
     And at midnight's hour of harm,

115   "Our Father," looking upward in the chamber,
        We say softly for a charm.
  We know no other words, except "Our Father,"
        And we think that, in some pause of angels' song,
  God may pluck them with the silence sweet to gather,
120   And hold both within His right hand which is strong.
  "Our Father!" If He heard us, He would surely
        (For they call Him good and mild)
  Answer, smiling down the steep world very purely,
        "Come and rest with me, my child."

    XI

125   'But no!' say the children, weeping faster,
        'He is speechless as a stone;
  And they tell us, of His image is the master
        Who commands us to work on.
  Go to!' say the children,—'up in Heaven,
130   Dark, wheel-like, turning clouds are all we find.
  Do not mock us; grief has made us unbelieving—
        We look up for God, but tears have made us blind.'
  Do you hear the children weeping and disproving,
        O my brothers, what ye preach?
135   For God's possible is taught by His world's loving,
        And the children doubt of each.

    XII

  And well may the children weep before you!
        They are weary ere they run;
  They have never seen the sunshine, nor the glory
140   Which is brighter than the sun.
  They know the grief of man, without its wisdom;
      They sink in man's despair, without its calm;
  Are slaves, without the liberty in Christdom,
      Are martyrs, by the pang without the palm,—
145   Are worn as if with age, yet unretrievingly
        The harvest of its memories cannot reap,—
  Are orphans of the earthly love and heavenly.
        Let them weep! let them weep!

    XIII

  They look up with their pale and sunken faces,
150   And their look is dread to see,
  For they mind you of their angels in high places,
        With eyes turned on Deity.
  'How long,' they say, 'how long, O cruel nation,
      Will you stand, to move the world, on a child's heart,—

155   Stifle down with a mailed heel its palpitation,
           And tread onward to your throne amid the mart?
       Our blood splashes upward, O gold-heaper,
           And your purple shows your path!
       But the child's sob in the silence curses deeper
160   Than the strong man in his wrath.'

Elizabeth Barrett Browning   (1806 – 1861)

MUCH MADNESS IS DIVINEST SENSE

Much madness is divinest sense
To a discerning eye;
Much sense the starkest madness.
'Tis the majority
5   In this, as all, prevails.
Assent, and you are sane;
Demur, — you're straightway dangerous,
And handled with a chain.

Emily Dickinson   (1830 – 1886)

THE DAY IS COMING

Come hither, lads, and hearken, for a tale there is to tell,
Of the wonderful days a-coming, when all shall be better than well.

And the tale shall be told of a country, a land in the midst of the sea,
And folk shall call it England in the days that are going to be.

5   There more than one in a thousand in the days that are yet to come,
Shall have some hope of the morrow, some joy of the ancient home.

For then, laugh not, but listen to this strange tale of mine,
All folk that are in England shall be better lodged than swine.

Then a man shall work and bethink him, and rejoice in the deeds of
      his hand,
10   Nor yet come home in the even too faint and weary to stand.

Men in that time a-coming shall work and have no fear
For to-morrow's lack of earning and the hunger-wolf anear.

I tell you this for a wonder, that no man then shall be glad
Of his fellow's fall and mishap to snatch at the work he had.

15   For that which the worker winneth shall then be his indeed,
Nor shall half be reaped for nothing by him that sowed no seed.

O strange new wonderful justice! But for whom shall we gather the
      gain? ⁄
For ourselves and for each of our fellows, and no hand shall labour in
      vain.

Then all Mine and all Thine shall be Ours, and no more shall any man
      crave
20   For riches that serve for nothing but to fetter a friend for a slave.

And what wealth then shall be left us when none shall gather gold
To buy his friend in the market, and pinch and pine the sold?

Nay, what save the lovely city, and the little house on the hill,
And the wastes and the woodland beauty, and the happy fields we till;

25   And the homes of ancient stories, the tombs of the mighty dead;
And the wise men seeking out marvels, and the poet's teeming head;

And the painter's hand of wonder; and the marvelous fiddle-bow,
And the banded choirs of music: all those that do and know.

For all these shall be ours and all men's, nor shall any lack a share
30   Of the toil and the gain of living in the days when the world grows fair.

Ah! such are the days that shall be! But what are the deeds of to-day,
In the days of the years we dwell in, that wear our lives away?

Why, then, and for what are we waiting? There are three words to
      speak;
We *will it*, and what is the foeman but the dream-strong wakened and
      weak?

35   O why and for what are we waiting? while our brothers droop and die,
And on every wind of the heavens a wasted life goes by.

How long shall they reproach us where crowd on crowd they dwell,
Poor ghosts of the wicked city, the gold-crushed hungry hell?

Through squalid life they laboured, in sordid grief they died,
40   Those sons of a mighty mother, those props of England's pride.

They are gone; there is none can undo it, nor save our souls from the
      curse;
But many a million cometh, and shall they be better or worse?

It is we must answer and hasten, and open wide the door
For the rich man's hurrying terror, and the slow-foot hope of the poor.

Yea, the voiceless wrath of the wretched, and their unlearned
45   discontent.
We must give it voice and wisdom till the waiting-tide be spent.

Come, then, since all things call us, the living and the dead,
And o'er the weltering tangle a glimmering light is shed.

Come, then, let us cast off fooling, and put by ease and rest,
50 For the Cause alone is worthy till the good days bring the best.

Come, join in the only battle wherein no man can fail,
Where whoso fadeth and dieth, yet his deed shall still prevail.

Ah! come, cast off all fooling, for this, at least, we know:
That the Dawn and the Day is coming, and forth the Banners go.

William Morris   (1834 – 1896)

THE MAN WITH THE HOE

God made man in His own image
In the image of God He made him. — GENESIS

Bowed by the weight of centuries he leans
Upon his hoe and gazes on the ground,
The emptiness of ages in his face,
And on his back the burden of the world.
5 Who made him dead to rapture and despair,
A thing that grieves not and that never hopes,
Stolid and stunned, a brother to the ox?
Who loosened and let down this brutal jaw?
Whose was the hand that slanted back this brow?
10 Whose breath blew out the light within this brain?

Is this the Thing the Lord God made and gave
To have dominion over sea and land;
To trace the stars and search the heavens for power;
To feel the passion of Eternity?
15 Is this the dream He dreamed who shaped the suns
And markt their ways upon the ancient deep?
Down all the caverns of Hell to their last gulf
There is no shape more terrible than this —

More tongued with censure of the world's blind greed —
20   More filled with signs and portents for the soul —
More packt with danger to the universe.

What gulfs between him and the seraphim!
Slave of the wheel of labor, what to him
Are Plato and the swing of Pleiades?
25   What the long reaches of the peaks of song,
The rife of dawn, the reddening of the rose?
Through this dread shape the suffering ages look;
Time's tragedy is in that aching stoop;
Through this dread shape humanity betrayed,
30   Plundered, profaned and disinherited,
Cries protest to the Powers that made the world,
A protest that is also prophecy.

O masters, lords and rulers in all lands,
Is this the handiwork you give to God,
35   This monstrous thing distorted and soul-quencht?
How will you ever straighten up this shape;
Touch it again with immortality;
Give back the upward looking and the light;
Rebuild in it the music and the dream;
40   Make right the immemorial infamies,
Perfidious wrongs, immedicable woes?

O masters, lords and rulers in all lands,
How will the future reckon with this Man?
How answer his brute question in that hour
45   When whirlwinds of rebellion shake all shores?
How will it be with kingdoms and with kings —
With those who shaped him to the thing he is —
When this dumb Terror shall rise to judge the world,
After the silence of the centuries?

Edwin Markham   (1852 – 1940)

I AM THE PEOPLE, THE MOB

I am the people — the mob — the crowd — the mass.
Do you know that all the great work of the world is done through me?
I am the workingman, the inventor, the maker of the world's food and
    clothes.
5   I am the audience that witnesses history. The Napoleons come from
    me and the Lincolns. They die. And then I send forth more Napo-
    leons and Lincolns.

I am the seed ground. I am a prairie that will stand for much plowing.
Terrible storms pass over me. I forget. The best of me is sucked out
10   and wasted. I forget. Everything but Death comes to me and
makes me work and give up what I have. And I forget.
Sometimes I growl, shake myself and spatter a few red drops for history
to remember. Then—I forget.
When I, the People, learn to remember, when I, the People, use the
15   lessons of yesterday and no longer forget who robbed me last
year, who played me for a fool—then there will be no speaker in
all the world say the name: "The People," with any fleck of a sneer
in his voice or any far-off smile of derision.
The mob—the crowd—the mass—will arrive then.

Carl Sandburg   (1878—1967)

THE UNKNOWN CITIZEN

(To JS/07/M/378
This Marble Monument
Is Erected by the State)

He was found by the Bureau of Statistics to be
One against whom there was no official complaint,
And all the reports of his conduct agree
That, in the modern sense of an old-fashioned word, he was a saint,
5   For in everything he did he served the Greater Community.
Except for the War till the day he retired
He worked in a factory and never got fired,
But satisfied his employers, Fudge Motors Inc.
Yet he wasn't a scab or odd in his views,
10   For his Union reports that he paid his dues,
(Our report on his Union shows it was sound)
And our Social Psychology workers found
That he was popular with his mates and liked a drink.
The Press are convinced that he bought a paper every day
15   And that his reactions to advertisements were normal in every way.
Policies taken out in his name prove that he was fully insured,
And his Health-card shows he was once in hospital but left it cured.
Both Producers Research and High-Grade Living declare
He was fully sensible to the advantages of the Installment Plan
20   And had everything necessary to the Modern Man,
A phonograph, a radio, a car and a frigidaire.
Our researchers into Public Opinion are content
That he held the proper opinions for the time of year;

When there was peace, he was for peace; when there was war, he went.
25   He was married and added five children to the population,
Which our Eugenist says was the right number for a parent of his gen-
        eration,
And our teachers report that he never interfered with their education.
Was he free? Was he happy? The question is absurd:
Had anything been wrong, we should certainly have heard.

W. H. Auden   (1907 –   )

BOOM!

Sees Boom in Religion, Too

Atlantic City, June 23, 1957 (AP). — President Eisenhower's pastor said tonight
that Americans are living in a period of "unprecedented religious activity"
caused partially by paid vacations, the eight-hour day and modern conveniences.

    "These fruits of material progress," said the Rev. Edward L. R. Elson of the
National Presbyterian Church, Washington, "have provided the leisure, the
energy, and the means for a level of human and spiritual values never before
reached."

Here at the Vespasian-Carlton, it's just one
religious activity after another; the sky
is constantly being crossed by cruciform
airplanes, in which nobody disbelieves
5   for a second, and the tide, the tide
of spiritual progress and prosperity
miraculously keeps rising, to a level
never before attained. The churches are full,
the beaches are full, and the filling-stations
10   are full, God's great ocean is full
of paid vacationers praying an eight-hour day
to the human and spiritual values, the fruits,
the leisure, the energy, and the means, Lord,
the means for the level, the unprecedented level,
15   and the modern conveniences, which also are full.
Never before, O Lord, have the prayers and praises
from belfry and phonebooth, from ballpark and barbecue
the sacrifices, so endlessly ascended.

It was not thus when Job in Palestine
20   sat in the dust and cried, cried bitterly;
when Damien kissed the lepers on their wounds
it was not thus; it was not thus
when Francis worked a fourteen-hour day
strictly for the birds; when Dante took
25   a week's vacation without pay and it rained
part of the time, O Lord, it was not thus.
But now the gears mesh and the tires burn
and the ice chatters in the shaker and the priest
in the pulpit, and Thy Name, O Lord,
30   is kept before the public, while the fruits
ripen and religion booms and the level rises
and every modern convenience runneth over,
that it may never be with us as it hath been
with Athens and Karnak and Nagasaki,
35   nor Thy sun for one instant refrain from shining
on the rainbow Buick by the breezeway
or the Chris Craft with the uplift life raft;
that we may continue to be the just folks we are,
plain people with ordinary superliners and
40   disposable diaperliners, people of the stop'n'shop
'n'pray as you go, of hotel, motel, boatel,
the humble pilgrims of no deposit no return
and please adjust thy clothing, who will give to Thee,
if Thee will keep us going, our annual
45   Miss Universe, for Thy Name's Sake, Amen.

Howard Nemerov (1920 –   )

QUESTIONS FOR DISCUSSION AND FURTHER STUDY

ON THE LATE MASSACRE IN PIEDMONT

1. In this Italian sonnet the mood of the verbs used by Milton is rather uncommon. What is the mood, and why is knowing this important in terms of the poem's meaning and forcefulness?
2. Who is the "triple tyrant" of line twelve?
3. Since this is a poem lamenting religious persecution, how appropriate is the Biblical phrase "Babylonian woe"? What does this phrase mean?

AUGURIES OF INNOCENCE

1. How would you describe the tone of the language used in this poem?
2. Do you agree with Blake in the observations he makes? Do you feel that he is literally correct? What social and religious attitudes underlie Blake's statements?
3. The poem is actually a collection of aphorisms, perhaps never intended to be printed as a single, unified work. Each couplet or quatrain provides the subject upon which a short essay could be written. Select one and, as directed by your instructor, prepare an explanation of or an elaboration upon its meaning.

LONDON, 1802

1. It has been often suggested that this poem lacks imagery. Do you agree with this judgment? Why or why not?
2. What qualities in Milton's personality particularly appeal to Wordsworth? Do you agree that Milton deserves to stand as a symbol of moral righteousness?
3. Does Wordsworth use the caesura and the run-on line to bring a more conversational tone to his poem? How effective are these devices?

SONG TO THE MEN OF ENGLAND

1. Much of Shelley's poem depends on the interrogative mood. In fact he asks a series of questions in a direct, forceful manner. Do you feel that this technique brings the audience closer to the poem and to its meaning?
2. How would you characterize the social philosophy expressed in

the poem? Does it reflect communistic or capitalistic traits? How just is Shelley's estimate of social conditions?

3. This poem was written at a time when working conditions in England were severe. For example, the working day for a laborer might easily be twelve or fourteen hours long. Shelley, although often deeply in debt, was himself a wealthy aristocrat. Do you feel that these facts alter the meaning and validity of the poem?

SONG OF THE SHIRT

1. After the first stanza of this poem, the point of view changes. After the change, who becomes the speaker of the poem? How successfully is the speaker characterized?
2. Describe the meter, rhyme scheme, and line length of this poem. Do you feel that the rather static, erratic quality of the poem is justified in terms of its theme and speaker?
3. How is repetition employed in this poem? Is the device used effectively?

THE CRY OF THE CHILDREN

1. How does this poem compare to "The Song of the Shirt"? Which of the two poems do you prefer? Why?
2. How effectively are the children portrayed in this poem?
3. What role does God play in this poem? Is he characterized fairly or does Elizabeth Barrett Browning find in Him a kind of scapegoat or whipping boy for the world's problems?

MUCH MADNESS IS DIVINEST SENSE

1. Emily Dickinson uses punctuation very effectively in this poem. Discuss this use of punctuation; how does she employ it to manipulate pace and rhythm?
2. One scholar has written that this poem identifies "the critical problem in a democratic society." Can you explain what he might have meant?
3. Can you identify any opinions which were once thought to be wildly nonconformist, but have since been embraced by the majority? What limits, if any, should a society place upon dissenting opinion?

THE DAY IS COMING

1. This poem was originally published in a socialist newspaper read primarily by English workingmen. How successfully did Morris use language appropriate to his audience?

2.   What specifically are some of the "wrongs" that Morris identifies? Has twentieth-century society attempted to rectify them? How?

3.   Do you consider this a revolutionary poem? Explain your answer.

THE MAN WITH THE HOE

1.   How is the quotation which introduces the poem related to the theme of the poem itself?

2.   Plato and the Pleiades are mentioned in the poem. Plato, of course, is one of the greatest classic philosophers. The Pleiades are, in Greek mythology, the seven daughters of Atlas and Pleione; they were placed by Zeus among the stars. Why does Markham refer to them in this poem?

3.   The poem poses a threat of things to come when "this dumb Terror shall rise to judge the world." Does Markham seem to share Morris' optimism about the future?

I AM THE PEOPLE, THE MOB

1.   Is this poem related to "The Song of the Shirt" or "The Cry of the Children"? How?

2.   This poem is written in free verse. Do you think that this verse form is appropriate for this particular poem? Why?

3.   State what you consider to be the poem's theme. Does the theme imply any threat to the established order of society? If so, how?

THE UNKNOWN CITIZEN

1.   Auden capitalizes a great many words and phrases that we would not ordinarily expect to be capitalized. What is his purpose in doing so? What particular effect does he achieve?

2.   Does Auden intend his readers to agree with the last line of the poem: "Had anything been wrong, we should certainly have heard"?

3.   Could you compare this poem to the novels *1984* or *Brave New World*? How? What complaint does Auden have against modern society? Do you share his feelings?

BOOM!

1.   Do you agree with the pastor mentioned in the Associated Press news story? Do you think Nemerov agrees with him? Why or why not?

2.   Can you identify Job, Damien, St. Francis, and Dante, all of whom are named in one sentence? For what purpose are they

mentioned here? Similarly, why does Nemerov allude to "Athens and Karnak and Nagasaki"?

3.   Do you see any similarities between this poem and Auden's "The Unknown Citizen"? Explain your answer.

WAR

Unfortunately, the waging of war seems to be a permanent part of human nature. Since man seems to fight his own kind so naturally, so inevitably, and so often, poems dealing with war are numerous. As one might expect, poets who write of war express various views and attitudes about it. Some poets sing of the glories of war; others express bitter antiwar statements. Many write of the death and suffering associated with war; others may write ironically and even ludicrously of the folly of war.

The earliest poem about war included in this text is "To Lucasta. Going to the Wars" by Richard Lovelace, a seventeenth-century courtier. In these simple quatrains Lovelace explains to his mistress Lucasta (who evidently prefers not to be left alone) that he would not be worthy of her love if he did not observe the military obligations owed by an honorable man. The poem, while universal in theme, evokes an intensely personal feeling; here is *one* soldier saying farewell to *one* lover, and, although the scene is commonplace, we feel the intensity of one couple experiencing an unwanted separation.

"The Battle of Blenheim," by Robert Southey, while dealing with a specific historical event, retains a similar personal note. In Bavaria, Blenheim was the scene of a battle in 1704 where the English, Dutch, and Austrians (under the leadership of the Duke of Marlborough and Prince Eugene of Austria) defeated the French in a bloody battle. Southey sets his poem at a point in time long after the battle. A grandfather comments to his grandchildren on the number of skulls to be found at the former battlefield. Like Lovelace, Southey uses a simple stanza to relate in unrelieved irony the false statement that Blenheim "was a famous victory." Strong in its antiwar sentiment, the poem finally states that war is totally purposeless, for Kaspar cannot answer the question put by little Peterkin about the famous victory: "But what good came of it at last?"

A poem entirely different in tone from Southey's is Tennyson's "The Charge of the Light Brigade." The galloping rhythm of the poem suggests emphatically the mounted troops urging their horses into the enemy's murderous fire. Again, the language and stanzaic form of the poem are simple, as Tennyson unabashedly testifies to the bravery and heroism of the gallant six hundred. Tennyson writes here, incidentally, of the Crimean War, fought between England and Russia. Because of confused orders, evidently, a brigade of British troops rode into the Russian fortified artillery; three fourths of the cavalry were killed. Incidentally, Tennyson is reputed to have written the poem immediately after reading a newspaper account of the disastrous battle.

Like Tennyson's poem, "Shiloh: A Requiem (April, 1862)," by Herman Melville, reflects upon a specific battle. In one nineteen-line stanza, Melville makes the point that soldiers from opposing armies may be foes while alive, but they are all friends in death: "(What like a bullet can undeceive!)" The poem opens and closes with a wonderful image that appeals both to our visual and kinesthetic senses, that of the swallows skimming low over the fields at Shiloh.

Another poem inspired by the American Civil War is Walt Whitman's "Vigil Strange I Kept on the Field One Night." During that conflict Whitman served as a volunteer male nurse, and the poem tells in free verse of his vigil with a dying young soldier whom he eventually buries.

Antiwar feeling appears with bitter intensity and irony in Thomas Hardy's "The Man He Killed." The poem speaks of the paradoxical fact that most opposing soldiers have much in common and might even be friends if they met under different circumstances. They would likely buy each other drinks if they chanced across each other in a bar somewhere; here, on the battlefield, however, they must attempt to take each other's lives. Hardy concerns himself in these simple stanzas with the meaningless way that war disrupts man's universal brotherhood and the one-ness of life.

The same thought appears again in William Butler Yeats' poem "An Irish Airman Foresees His Death." These alternating couplets tell us of a World War I aviator who has no quarrel with his enemy and who experiences a premonition of his own death.

The title of Stephen Crane's poem "War Is Kind" suggests the restrained irony which colors and dominates the poem. Crane actually commands a lover, a child, and a mother not to mourn for their beloved dead; the fact that Crane does not tell us why war is kind prompts us to a realization of the irony in his argument.

A more lengthy antiwar poem is Amy Lowell's "Patterns." The poem's meaning depends on its main symbol, the dress made from brocade. The young lady in the poem has just received news of her fiancé's death. Until this news came, she had been anticipating free, happy, uninhibited love (note the symbol of the flower petal). Now she will remain, as it were, imprisoned in the confining stiffness of brocade, because "The man who should loose me is dead."

"Buttons" also depends primarily on the symbolism reflected in the title. The first two stanzas of this free-verse poem simply describe a typical war map with markers on it to indicate the battle positions of opposing forces. The last stanza speaks of the dying agonies of ten thousand young men. The reader then feels forcefully and dramatically the contrast between the horrifying reality of war and the unreal and indifferent way it appears at a distance.

Alan Seeger's poem "I Have a Rendezvous with Death" in some ways resembles the poem by Yeats about the Irish airman. Both poems are about the First World War; again a young soldier foresees his death, again he feels a sense of fate, of inevitability about it. Especially poignant is the paradox which permeates the poem. Spring is the season for love, the season for a rendezvous with a lover—not with death. The final stanza of the poem states the paradox in explicit terms, and the final promise of a rendezvous is cast in the language of one betrothed to death.

Like the two poems just discussed, "Arms and the Boy" was also inspired by World War I. Here, Wilfred Owen gives the qualities of vicious, predatory beasts to the weapons of war. In contrast, human beings have no claws, talons, or antlers; they are helpless in war. Especially effective is the way Owen pictures the bayonet "famishing for flesh" and the bullets longing "to nuzzle in the hearts of lads."

This section contains poems on war which range over a two-hundred-year period. Several different wars have inspired them, but the experience of war is so constant and similar at all times and in all places that the human emotions and attitudes aroused by any one war tend to be true of all of them.

TO LUCASTA, GOING TO THE WARS

Tell me not, sweet, I am unkind,
  That from the nunnery
Of thy chaste breast and quiet mind,
  To war and arms I fly.

5   True, a new mistress now I chase:
  The first foe in the field;
And with a stronger faith embrace
  A sword, a horse, a shield.

Yet this inconstancy is such
10   As you, too, shall adore;
I could not love thee, dear, so much,
  Loved I not honor more.

Richard Lovelace   (1618 – 1658)

THE BATTLE OF BLENHEIM

It was a summer's evening,
  Old Kaspar's work was done,
And he before his cottage door
  Was sitting in the sun.
5   And by him sported on the green
His little grandchild Wilhelmine.

She saw her brother Peterkin
  Roll something large and round,
Which he beside the rivulet,
10   In playing there had found;
He came to ask what he had found,
That was so large and smooth and round.

Old Kaspar took it from the boy,
  Who stood expectant by;
15   And then the old man shook his head,
  And, with a natural sigh,
"'Tis some poor fellow's skull," said he,
"Who fell in the great victory.

"I find them in the garden,
    For there's many here about;
And often, when I go to plow,
    The plowshare turns them out!
For many thousand men," said he,
"Were slain in that great victory."

"Now tell us what 'twas all about,"
    Young Peterkin he cries;
And little Wilhelmine looks up
    With wonder-waiting eyes;
"Now tell us all about the war,
And what they fought each other for."

"It was the English," Kaspar cried,
    "Who put the French to rout;
But what they fought each other for,
    I could not well make out;
But everybody said," quoth he,
"That 'twas a famous victory.

"My father lived at Blenheim then,
    Yon little stream hard by;
They burnt his dwelling to the ground,
    And he was forced to fly;
So with his wife and child he fled,
Nor had he where to rest his head.

"With fire and sword the country round
    Was wasted far and wide,
And many a childing mother then,
    And new-born baby, died;
But things like that, you know, must be
At every famous victory.

"They say it was a shocking sight
    After the field was won;
For many thousand bodies here
    Lay rotting in the sun:
But things like that, you know, must be
After a famous victory.

"Great praise the Duke of Marlborough won,
    And our good Prince Eugene."
"Why, 'twas a very wicked thing!"
    Said little Wilhelmine.
"Nay . . . nay . . . my little girl," quoth he;
"It was a famous victory.

"And everybody praised the Duke,
  Who this great fight did win."
"But what good came of it at last?"
  Quoth little Peterkin.
65 "Why, that I cannot tell," said he;
"But 'twas a famous victory."

Robert Southey   *(1774 – 1843)*

THE CHARGE OF THE LIGHT BRIGADE

I

Half a league, half a league,
Half a league onward,
All in the valley of Death
  Rode the six hundred.
5 "Forward the Light Brigade!
Charge for the guns!" he said.
Into the valley of Death
  Rode the six hundred.

II

"Forward, the Light Brigade!"
10 Was there a man dismay'd?
Not tho' the soldier knew
  Some one had blunder'd.
Theirs not to make reply,
Theirs not to reason why,
15 Theirs but to do and die.
Into the valley of Death
  Rode the six hundred.

III

Cannon to right of them,
Cannon to left of them,
20 Cannon in front of them
  Volley'd and thunder'd;

Storm'd at with shot and shell,
Boldly they rode and well,
Into the jaws of Death,
25   Into the mouth of hell
Rode the six hundred.

IV

Flash'd all their sabres bare,
Flash'd as they turn'd in air
Sabring the gunners there,
30   Charging an army, while
All the world wonder'd.
Plunged in the battery-smoke
Right thro' the line they broke;
Cossack and Russian
35   Reel'd from the sabre-stroke
Shatter'd and sunder'd.
Then they rode back, but not,
Not the six hundred.

V

Cannon to right of them,
40   Cannon to left of them,
Cannon behind them
Volley'd and thunder'd;
Storm'd at with shot and shell,
While horse and hero fell,
45   They that had fought so well
Came thro' the jaws of Death,
Back from the mouth of hell,
All that was left of them,
Left of six hundred.

VI

50   When can their glory fade?
O the wild charge they made!
All the world wonder'd.
Honor the charge they made!
Honor the Light Brigade,
55   Noble six hundred!

Alfred, Lord Tennyson (1809 – 1892)

SHILOH

A Requiem (April, 1862)

Skimming lightly, wheeling still,
   The swallows fly low
Over the field in clouded days,
   The forest-field of Shiloh —
5   Over the field where April rain
Solaced the parched one stretched in pain
Through the pause of night
That followed the Sunday fight
   Around the church of Shiloh —
10   The church so lone, the log-built one,
That echoed to many a parting groan
     And natural prayer
   Of dying foemen mingled there —
Foemen at morn, but friends at eve —
15   Fame or country least their care:
(What like a bullet can undeceive!)
   But now they lie low,
While over them the swallows skim,
   And all is hushed at Shiloh.

              Herman Melville   (1819 – 1891)

VIGIL STRANGE I KEPT ON THE FIELD ONE NIGHT

Vigil strange I kept on the field one night;
When you my son and my comrade dropt at my side that day,
One look I but gave which your dear eyes return'd with a look I shall
     never forget,
One touch of your hand to mine O boy, reach'd up as you lay on the
5   ground,
Then onward I sped in the battle, the even-contested battle,
Till late in the night reliev'd to the place at last again I made my way,
Found you in death so cold dear comrade, found your body son of
     responding kisses, (never again on earth responding,)
Bared your face in the starlight, curious the scene, cool blew the
     moderate night-wind,
Long there and then in vigil I stood, dimly around me the battlefield
10   spreading,
Vigil wondrous and vigil sweet there in the fragrant silent night,
But not a tear fell, not even a long-drawn sigh, long, long I gazed,

Then on the earth partially reclining sat by your side leaning my chin
 in my hands,
Passing sweet hours, immortal and mystic hours with you dearest com-
 rade — not a tear, not a word,
Vigil of silence, love and death, vigil for you my son and my soldier,
As onward silently stars aloft, eastward new ones upward stole,
Vigil final for you brave boy, (I could not save you, swift was your
 death,
I faithfully loved you and cared for you living, I think we shall surely
 meet again,)
Till at latest lingering of the night, indeed just as the dawn appear'd,
My comrade I wrapt in his blanket, envelop'd well his form,
Folded the blanket well, tucking it carefully over head and carefully
 under feet,
And there and then and bathed by the rising sun, my son in his grave,
 in his rude-dug grave I deposited,
Ending my vigil strange with that, vigil of night and battle-field dim,
Vigil for boy of responding kisses, (never again on earth
 responding,)
Vigil for comrade swiftly slain, vigil I never forget, how as day
 brighten'd,
I rose from the chill ground and folded my soldier well in his blanket,
And buried him where he fell.

          Walt Whitman (1819 – 1892)

THE MAN HE KILLED

  Had he and I but met
  By some old ancient inn,
We should have sat us down to wet
  Right many a nipperkin!

  But ranged as infantry,
  And staring face to face,
I shot at him as he at me,
  And killed him in his place.

  I shot him dead because —
  Because he was my foe,
Just so: my foe of course he was;
  That's clear enough: although

  He thought he'd 'list, perhaps
  Off-hand-like — just as I —
Was out of work — had sold his traps —
  No other reason why.

Yes; quaint and curious war is!
You shoot a fellow down
You'd treat if met where any bar is,
20   Or help to half-a-crown.

Thomas Hardy   (1840–1928)

AN IRISH AIRMAN FORESEES HIS DEATH

I know that I shall meet my fate
Somewhere among the clouds above;
Those that I fight I do not hate,
Those that I guard I do not love;
5   My country is Kiltartan Cross,
My countrymen Kiltartan's poor,
No likely end could bring them loss
Or leave them happier than before.
Nor law, nor duty bade me fight,
10   Nor public men, nor cheering crowds,
A lonely impulse of delight
Drove to this tumult in the clouds;
I balanced all, brought all to mind,
The years to come seemed waste of breath,
15   A waste of breath the years behind
In balance with this life, this death.

William Butler Yeats   (1865–1939)

WAR IS KIND

Do not weep, maiden, for war is kind.
Because your lover threw wild hands toward the sky
And the affrighted steed ran on alone,
Do not weep.
5   War is kind.

Hoarse, booming drums of the regiment,
Little souls who thirst for fight,
These men were born to drill and die.
The unexplained glory flies above them,
10   Great is the battle-god, great, and his kingdom—
A field where a thousand corpses lie.

Do not weep, babe, for war is kind.
Because your father tumbled in the yellow trenches,
Raged at his breast, gulped and died,
15 Do not weep.
War is kind.

Swift blazing flag of the regiment,
Eagle with crest of red and gold,
These men were born to drill and die.
20 Point for them the virtue of slaughter,
Make plain to them the excellence of killing
And a field where a thousand corpses lie.

Mother whose heart hung humble as a button
25 On the bright splendid shroud of your son,
Do not weep.
War is kind.

Stephen Crane   (1871 – 1900)

PATTERNS

I walk down the garden-paths,
      And all the daffodils
Are blowing, and the bright blue squills.
I walk down the patterned garden-paths
5   In my stiff, brocaded gown.
With my powdered hair and jewelled fan,
I too am a rare
Pattern. As I wander down
The garden-paths.
10 My dress is richly figured,
And the train
Makes a pink and silver stain
On the gravel, and the thrift
Of the borders.
15 Just a plate of current fashion,
Tripping by in high-heeled, ribboned shoes.
Not a softness anywhere about me,
Only whale-bone and brocade.
And I sink on a seat in the shade
20 Of a lime-tree. For my passion
Wars against the stiff brocade.
The daffodils and squills
Flutter in the breeze
As they please.

25   And I weep;
        For the lime-tree is in blossom
        And one small flower has dropped upon my bosom.

        And the plashing of waterdrops
        In the marble fountain
30   Comes down the garden-paths.
        The dripping never stops.
        Underneath my stiffened gown
        Is the softness of a woman bathing in a marble basin,
        A basin in the midst of hedges grown
35   So thick, she cannot see her lover hiding.
        But she guesses he is near,
        And the sliding of the water
        Seems the stroking of a dear
        Hand upon her.
40   What is Summer in a fine brocaded gown!
        I should like to see it lying in a heap upon the ground.
        All the pink and silver crumpled upon the ground.

        I would be the pink and silver as I ran along the paths,
        And he would stumble after,
45   Bewildered by my laughter.
        I should see the sun flashing from his sword-hilt and the buckles on his shoes
        I would choose
        To lead him in a maze along the patterned paths,
        A bright and laughing maze for my heavy-booted lover,
50   Till he caught me in the shade,
        And the buttons of his waistcoat bruised my body as he clasped me
        Aching, melting, unafraid.
        With the shadows of the leaves and the sundrops,
        And the plopping of the waterdrops,
55   All about us in the open afternoon —
        I am very like to swoon
        With the weight of this brocade,
        For the sun sifts through the shade.

        Underneath the fallen blossom
60   In my bosom,
        Is a letter I have hid.
        It was brought to me this morning by a rider from the Duke,
        "Madam, we regret to inform you that Lord Hartwell
        Died in action Thursday se'nnight."
65   As I read it in the white, morning sunlight,

The letters squirmed like snakes.
"Any answer, Madam?" said my footman.
"No," I told him.
70 "See that the messenger takes some refreshment.
No, no answer."
And I walked into the garden,
Up and down the patterned paths,
In my stiff, correct brocade.
The blue and yellow flowers stood up proudly in the sun,
75 Each one.
I stood upright too,
Held rigid to the pattern
By the stiffness of my gown.
Up and down I walked,
80 Up and down.
In a month he would have been my husband.
In a month, here, underneath this lime,
We would have broke the pattern;
He for me, and I for him,
85 He as Colonel, I as Lady,
On this shady seat.
He had a whim
That sunlight carried blessing.
And I answered, "It shall be as you have said."
90 Now he is dead.

In Summer and in Winter I shall walk
Up and down
The patterned garden-paths
In my stiff brocaded gown.
95 The squills and daffodils
Will give place to pillared roses, and to asters, and to snow.
I shall go
Up and down,
In my gown.
100 Gorgeously arrayed,
Boned and stayed.
And the softness of my body will be guarded from embrace
By each button, hook and lace.
For the man who should loose me is dead,
105 Fighting with the Duke in Flanders,
In a pattern called a war.
Christ! What are patterns for?

Amy Lowell   (1874 – 1925)

BUTTONS

I have been watching the war map slammed up for advertising in front
  of the newspaper office.
Buttons — red and yellow buttons — blue and black buttons — are shoved
  back and forth across the map.

A laughing young man, sunny with freckles,
Climbs a ladder, yells a joke to somebody in the crowd,
5 And then fixes a yellow button one inch west
And follows the yellow button with a black button one inch west.

(Ten thousand men and boys twist on their bodies in a red soak along
  a river edge,
Gasping of wounds, calling for water, some rattling death in their
  throats.)
Who would guess what it cost to move two buttons one inch on the
  war map here in front of the newspaper office where the freckle-faced
  young man is laughing to us?

Carl Sandburg   (1878 – 1967)

I HAVE A RENDEZVOUS WITH DEATH

I have a rendezvous with Death
At some disputed barricade,
When Spring comes back with rustling shade
And apple-blossoms fill the air —
5 I have a rendezvous with Death
When Spring brings back blue days and fair.

It may be he shall take my hand
And lead me into his dark land
And close my eyes and quench my breath —
10 It may be I shall pass him still.
I have a rendezvous with Death
On some scarred slope of battered hill,
When Spring comes round again this year
And the first meadow-flowers appear.

15 God knows 'twere better to be deep
Pillowed in silk and scented down,
Where Love throbs out in blissful sleep,

Pulse nigh to pulse, and breath to breath,
Where hushed awakenings are dear . . .
20   But I've a rendezvous with Death
At midnight in some flaming town,
When Spring trips north again this year,
And I to my pledged word am true,
I shall not fail that rendezvous.

Alan Seeger   (1888 – 1916)

ARMS AND THE BOY

Let the boy try along this bayonet-blade
How cold steel is, and keen with hunger of blood;
Blue with all malice, like a madman's flash;
And thinly drawn with famishing for flesh.

5   Lend him to stroke these blind, blunt bullet-heads
Which long to nuzzle in the hearts of lads,
Or give him cartridges of fine zinc teeth,
Sharp with the sharpness of grief and death.

For his teeth seem for laughing round an apple.
10   There lurk no claws behind his fingers supple;
And God will grow no talons at his heels,
Nor antlers through the thickness of his curls.

Wilfred Owen   (1893 – 1918)

QUESTIONS FOR DISCUSSION AND FURTHER STUDY

TO LUCASTA, GOING TO THE WAR

1. How does Lovelace combine sexual and religious imagery to flatter the lady addressed in the poem?
2. In a sense this poem is about war; in another sense, it is about something altogether different. Discuss Lovelace's multiple intentions in writing this poem. Perhaps a larger question can also be discussed in terms of this poem; *i.e.*, how is it that poetry can serve two or even more themes at the same time?

THE BATTLE OF BLENHEIM

1. Who is the speaker in this poem? Who is the audience? Why are the answers to these questions necessary in order to understand the poem's theme?
2. Discuss the last stanza of the poem. The statement made by old Kaspar ("Why, that I cannot tell") reveals Southey's attitude toward the Duke of Marlborough (a famous eighteenth-century general) and toward war itself. What is this attitude?
3. The most striking concrete aspect of the poem is the skull young Peterkin finds beside the stream. Why is this image so effective as a commentary on war and even on human existence?

THE CHARGE OF THE LIGHT BRIGADE

1. Describe the meter, rhyme scheme, and line length of this poem. Why is the jogging quality of the poem particularly appropriate in terms of the actual situation described here?
2. Tennyson changes the poetic form of his lyric in the last stanza. What was his probable reason for doing so? Is the change effective?
3. The war described here is the Crimean War, which was fought in the middle of the nineteenth century. Do you feel that, because horses and sabres are involved, the comment on war is dated? Does the poem still hold universality and relevance?

SHILOH

1. Shiloh was the scene of a terribly bloody battle of the American Civil War. Since the combatants in this war were all Americans, why is Melville's use of the word "foemen" especially effective and ironic?

2. The poem begins and ends with the image of the swallows "skimming lightly" over the battlefield. This seems to be a strange way to introduce a poem about those who fell in battle. Why does Melville use this device, and how successful is it?

3. What is the significance of the phrase "Foemen at morn, but friends at eve"?

VIGIL STRANGE I KEPT ON THE FIELD ONE NIGHT

1. Discuss Whitman's repetition of the word "vigil." Normally the word carries a religious connotation. Of what importance is that fact in terms of this particular poem?

2. What does Whitman mean when he says "I think we shall surely meet again"?

3. Why does Whitman refer to his vigil as being "strange"? Given the circumstances of the poem's situation, what makes the vigil "strange"?

THE MAN HE KILLED

1. The rhymes in the poem are deliberately uneven (ancient inn, nipperkin; because, he was; perhaps, his traps; war is, bar is). Given the kind of person the speaker of the poem is, why are these uneven rhymes justified and even effective?

2. The middle stanza of the poem purports to give clear reasons for the speaker's killing his foe. Is that stanza consistent with the irony which provides a basis for the entire poem? Explain your answer.

3. How close in theme is this poem to "The Battle of Blenheim"?

AN IRISH AIRMAN FORESEES HIS DEATH

1. The first four lines of the poem provide a kind of summary for the rest, which is explanatory. Do you feel that the Irish airman's attitude is morally justifiable?

2. Discuss Yeats' use of repetition in this poem. What words are repeated and why?

3. Yeats had World War I in mind when he wrote this poem. Of what particular importance is the fact that the speaker is an Irish rather than an English airman? Does the poem have relevance today?

WAR IS KIND

1. Who are the three people addressed in this poem? Why is the audience described in the poem so important to its meaning?

2.   Explain exactly what Crane means when he says "War is kind."
3.   Look up the definition of *irony* to be found in this anthology's glossary. Why is that definition central to the meaning of Crane's poem?

PATTERNS

1.   This poem depends on a contrast. What is this contrast and how does Amy Lowell manipulate it?
2.   The lady who functions as the speaker of the poem mentions the "letter" relatively late in the lyric. Do you feel that this is effective or not? Why?
3.   Discuss Miss Lowell's use of imagery in this poem. Why does she concentrate so much upon images and words which appeal to the sense of touch?

BUTTONS

1.   The title of this poem arrests our attention. Why? Do you feel that Sandburg's choice of title is a good one?
2.   Why does Sandburg take care to mention that the young man arranging the war map is "laughing"?
3.   Can you contrast the people at the newspaper office with the "ten thousand men and boys" who have died in battle? How? Does Sandburg wish to suggest this contrast?

I HAVE A RENDEZVOUS WITH DEATH

1.   Why is the word "rendezvous" effectively used in the title? Do you think it is common for people to describe their deaths this way?
2.   Why does Seeger note that his meeting with Death will come in Spring? How do we usually think of the Spring?
3.   The contrast between the first and second halves of the last stanza is striking. Is the contrast consistent with the rest of the poem?

ARMS AND THE BOY

1.   What verbal mood predominates in this poem — indicative, imperative, or interrogative? Why is this relevant?
2.   Discuss Owen's use of alliteration in this poem. What effect does it impart to the poem?
3.   Is the narrator of the poem to be taken literally, or does his tone convey some ironic meaning?

GLOSSARY OF LITERARY TERMS

Accent

Two accent marks are commonly used for poetic scansion (see METRICAL FOOT, p. 328). The *acute* accent (´) marks syllables with primary stress; the *breve* accent (˘) marks unstressed syllables:

> Hăd wé bŭt wórld ĕnoúgh, ănd tíme,
> This cóynĕss, ládў, wére nŏ críme.

Alexandrine

An iambic hexameter line which often appears within or at the end of an iambic pentameter poem to achieve variety or a sense of finality. A long line, the *Alexandrine* tends to be slow and heavy moving. The last line of Dryden's "To the Memory of Mr. Oldham" illustrates its use:

> Thy brows with ivy, and with laurels bound,
> But fate and gloomy night encompass thee around.

Alliteration

Repetition of the same initial sound in words or stressed syllables which are close together. Once a chief structural device in Old and Middle English poetry, *alliteration* is now used either to ornament or to achieve a particular effect. In the following lines Coleridge alliterates the breathy *b* and *f* sounds to suggest the brisk breeze and rapid movement of the ancient mariner's ship:

> The fair breeze blew, the white foam flew,
> The furrow followed free.

Allusion

A reference to a well-known person or event, usually from history, literature, or religion. An *allusion* allows the reader—provided that he recognizes the person or event alluded to—an additional dimension of understanding. The following lines from Robinson's "Mr. Flood's Party" rely for their full meaning upon the reader's knowledge of the medieval romance *The Song of Roland*.

> Alone, as if enduring to the end
> A valiant armor of scarred hopes outworn,
> He stood there in the middle of the road
> Like Roland's ghost winding a silent horn.

Ambiguity

The term *ambiguity* has developed a favorable as well as an unfavorable meaning. When he uses the word, the literary critic most
often employs the favorable meaning to refer to a verbal nuance
allowing multiple reactions or interpretations of a passage of literary text. For example, when Wordsworth in his "Ode: Intimations
of Immortality" talks of "The Youth, who daily farther from the
east / Must travel," he allows a multiple interpretation of the passage: (1) traveling east to west represents the passage of time and,
hence, the process of growing older; (2) the east represents spiri-
tuality and the seat of the godhead, hence, moving from it involves
a loss of sanctity. Both interpretations are compatible with the total context of the poem.

Anapest

A metrical foot consisting of two unstressed syllables followed by
a stressed syllable (see METRICAL FOOT, p. 328).

Antithesis

A figure of speech in which two or more strikingly different ideas
are expressed in balanced rhetorical units. The balance may consist of paired words, phrases, clauses, or even entire sentences.
The effect of a successful antithesis is surprise. Pope used *antithesis* when he wrote that a woman's screams of anguish occur
equally "When husbands and when lap-dogs breathe their last."
When husbands and *when lap-dogs* are balanced structurally, yet
there is a significant contrast between them.

Apostrophe

A figure of speech in which an object or a person not present is
addressed by the speaker or the author. John Donne employs *apostrophe* in his "The Sun Rising":

> Busy old fool, unruly Sun,
> Why dost thou thus,
> Through windows, and through curtains call on us?

Assonance

The repetition of identical or similar vowel sounds. An example of
assonance occurs in Poe's "The Raven" with the repetition of *o*
sounds:

> Once upon a midnight dreary, while I pondered, weak and weary,
> Over many a quaint and curious volume of forgotten lore. . .

Bathos

A comic quality in a literary work resulting from pathos or sentiment which is so overdone as to become laughable, or from a sudden shift from something serious to something trivial. Uninten-

tional *bathos*, of course, is an unfavorable quality in a poem. Sometimes, however, the poet achieves an intended comic effect by juxtaposing the serious with the trivial, as does Byron in his description of Don Juan's military education:

> He learned the arts of riding, fencing, gunnery,
> And how to scale a fortress — or a nunnery.

Blank Verse

Unrhymed iambic pentameter lines (see METRICAL FEET, p. 328). In English and American poetry *blank verse* has been primarily used in narrative, dramatic, and philosophic poetry; only rarely is it employed in lyric poems.

Caesura

A pause or break within a line of poetry, usually marked with punctuation. In classical verse the *caesura* occurred at or near the middle of the line. Yet many poets try to achieve rhythmic diversity by varying its position, as in the following selection:

> No cloud, // no relique of the sunken day
> Distinguishes the West, // no long thin slip
> Of sullen light, // no obscure trembling hues.
> Come, // we will rest on this old mossy bridge.

Carpe diem

A phrase from the Latin of Horace meaning "seize the day." The *carpe diem* theme is particularly prominent in lyric poetry: live life fully today; tomorrow may never come. In Herrick's "To the Virgins, to Make Much of Time" or in Marvell's "To His Coy Mistress" the poet urges his lady to immediate love, reminding her that all beautiful things fade and that the grave ultimately awaits us all.

Closed Couplet

See COUPLET.

Conceit

A figure of speech frequently employed by the metaphysical poets of the seventeenth century. A *conceit* is an ingenious, sometimes seemingly farfetched, analogy which shocks the imagination to perceive likenesses in objects and/or ideas that are commonly not associated with each other. John Donne uses a conceit in "A Valediction: Forbidding Mourning" when he describes the separation of the souls of two lovers in terms of a pair of compasses:

> If they be two, they are two so
> As stiff twin compasses are two;
> Thy soul, the fixed foot, makes no show

To move, but doth, if th' other do.

And though it in the center sit,
Yet when the other far doth roam,
It leans, and harkens after it,
And grows erect, as that comes home.

Couplet

Two successive rhyming lines of poetry. A *couplet* may be an entire poem (then often called a *distich*); more frequently, however, couplets are used as a verse pattern for a longer poem. Couplets may be written in lines of various length and meter, yet the iambic pentameter couplet has been the most popular in English and American poetry. The iambic pentameter couplet is called a *closed* or *heroic couplet* when it contains a complete grammatical unit, in which case the second line is likely to end with a mark of terminal punctuation (a period, question mark, exclamation point, semicolon, or colon). The following lines from Pope's "Elegy: To the Memory of an Unfortunate Lady" illustrate the use of closed couplets:

But thou, false guardian of a charge too good,
Thou, mean deserter of thy brother's blood!
See on these ruby lips the trembling breath,
These cheeks now fading at the blast of death:
Cold is that breast which warmed the world before,
And those love-darting eyes must roll no more.

An *open* couplet, on the other hand, makes use of enjambment to avoid the repetitive rhythm of the closed couplet. The following passage from Keats' "Sleep and Poetry" is comprised of open couplets which comment upon the use of closed couplets in eighteenth-century poetry:

Yes, a schism
Nurtured by foppery and barbarism,
Made great Appollo blush for this his land.
Men were thought wise who could not understand
His glories: with a puling infant's force
They sway'd about upon a rocking horse,
And thought it Pegasus. Ah dismal soul'd!
The winds of heaven blew, the ocean roll'd
Its gathering waves—ye felt it not. The blue
Bared its eternal bosom, and the dew
Of summer nights collected still to make
The morning precious: beauty was awake!
Why were ye not awake?

Dactyl

A metrical foot consisting of an accented syllable followed by two unaccented syllables (see **METRICAL FOOT**, p. 328).

Didacticism

The instructional purpose in a literary work. Though the term *di-dacticism* is often used in an unfavorable context, it would be difficult to find a literary work which does not, though often indirectly, serve to instruct mankind on some aspect of life. Few lyric poems are overtly didactic in the manner, for example, of Dylan Thomas' "Do Not Go Gentle into that Good Night" or John Donne's "A Valediction: Forbidding Mourning." In most, the didacticism is subtly imbedded in the action of the poem. Didactic elements need not degrade a poem if they are subordinated to artistic considerations and if they avoid striking the reader as a mere catalog of self-righteous moral platitudes.

Dimeter

A poetic line consisting of two metrical feet (see METRICAL FOOT, p. 328).

Dramatic Monologue

A form of lyric poem which involves the speaker in a dramatic situation but records only his words. The other characters in a *dramatic monologue* participate only insofar as the words of the main speaker reveal their action or conversation. In this respect reading a dramatic monologue resembles listening to a person who is having a telephone conversation. The form was brought to perfection by Robert Browning, whose major work in it attempted a fourfold revelation: character analysis of the speaker, who is usually caught in a moment of crisis or decision; character analysis of the person or persons spoken to; analysis of the person or thing spoken about; a picture of the historical period in which the poem is set.

Elegy

In the literature of classical Greece and Rome an *elegy* was a meditative poem written in a particular couplet form. As used by literary critics today, however, the term refers only to a poem dealing with the subject of death. An elegy may commemorate the death of an individual (e.g., W. H. Auden's "In Memory of W. B. Yeats" or Walt Whitman's "When Lilacs Last in the Dooryard Bloom'd," which mourns Lincoln's death), or it may commemorate the general fact of death as it applies to a particular group of men or even all mankind (e.g., Allen Tate's "Ode to the Confederate Dead" and Thomas Gray's "Elegy Written in a Country Churchyard"). The *pastoral elegy*, represented in this collection by Milton's "Lycidas," Shelley's "Adonais," and Arnold's "Thyrsis," is a specific type of personal elegy in which the dead person is presented as a shepherd being mourned by his fellows. Such elegies are characterized by dignified, serious language and by the observance of set pastoral conventions. Regardless of its type —personal, general, pastoral, or otherwise—a great elegy usually

326 LYRIC POEMS ON TWELVE THEMES

reaches beyond grief for a specific individual, or even for mankind
in general, and finds in the fact of death some reason for resignation, acceptance, and ultimate joy.

Enjambment

The practice of continuing one line of poetry to the next without a
grammatical break at the end of the line. The use of *enjambment*
helps to reduce the singsong quality which may result if each line
ends with a strong punctuation break; it is a common feature in
blank verse, though it can occur in other poetic forms as well. The
following lines from Frost's "Birches" illustrate its use and effect:

> He learned all there was
> To learn about not launching out too soon
> And so not carrying the tree away
> Clear to the ground. He always kept his poise
> To the top branches, climbing carefully
> With the same pains you use to fill a cup
> Up to the brim, and even above the brim.

Free Verse

A form of verse which departs from the conventional patterns of
uniform meter and rhyme and seeks its metrical effect instead
from the cadences and rhythms of natural speech. *Free verse* allows the poet an almost limitless variety of possible effects, many
of which are achieved through the repetition of key words and
phrases (often in successive stanzas) and the use of alliteration
and other devices. To be skillfully written, free verse requires a
talent just as acutely developed as that for the composition of
conventional poetry. No short selection can properly illustrate the
form, yet the several Walt Whitman poems in this anthology provide excellent examples of free verse.

Genre

A category or type of literary composition. The word *genre* is most
commonly applied to broadly defined literary types, such as tragedy, comedy, short story, novel, epic, lyric. Sometimes, however, it
is used in talking about such subtypes as the mystery novel, ode,
or sonnet.

Heptameter

A poetic line consisting of seven metrical feet (see METRICAL
FOOT, p. 328).

Heroic Couplet

See COUPLET, p. 324.

Hexameter

A poetic line consisting of six metrical feet (see METRICAL FOOT,
p. 328).

Hyperbole

A figure of speech employing extravagant exaggeration. *Hyperbole* is the basis of much folk humor, but often it is used for a serious effect, as in Alexander Pope's line from "Elegy: to the Memory of an Unfortunate Lady": "Cold is that breast which warmed the world before."

Iamb

A metrical foot consisting of an unaccented syllable followed by an accented syllable (see METRICAL FOOT, p. 328).

Image

A literary device which yields a sense impression. An *image* is produced by figurative language and functions to enrich the presentation of a subject often by reference to several or all of the five senses. By its very nature, poetry relies upon images to convey its particular kind of meaning and tone. One notices, for example, the images of darkness which abound in the last part of Arnold's "Dover Beach" or the persistent images of new life and growth in Whitman's "There Was a Child Went Forth."

Irony

A figure of speech in which the literal meaning is exactly opposed to the intended meaning. This kind of *irony* is exemplified in E. E. Cummings' "next to of course god" or Stephen Crane's "War Is Kind." In a broader sense, however, irony refers to that quality of a literary work best defined as the inability of the characters (or speaker or poet) to understand and foresee the tragic consequences or incongruity of their actions. Thus Amy Lowell's "Patterns" demonstrates a sort of pervading irony: the speaker participates in a world of patterns, social and otherwise, which have denied her the thing she wanted most in life, a consummated love.

Lyric

Though the word was originally used by the Greeks to signify a song sung to the accompaniment of a lyre by a single member of the chorus, the term *lyric* has subsequently broadened in its application. As a literary term, lyric refers to any poem which records the emotions and personal meditations of a single author dealing with an essentially non-narrative subject. Most lyrics are relatively short, and the emphasis in a lyrical poem is upon the individual author's imaginative response to an isolated incident or idea. The sight of birch trees bending left and right, for example, inspired Frost's "Birches." The somber atmosphere of a village graveyard provided the impetus for Gray's "Elegy Written in a Country Churchyard."
Both the subject matter and the form of the lyric are so varied as to make definitions most difficult. This anthology demonstrates the great diversity of form within the twelve themes presented.

Indeed, any subject capable of imaginative personal treatment can provide the point of departure for a lyric poem. Lyric poems may be written within recognized forms such as the ode, sonnet, elegy; they may also employ various stanzaic and metrical patterns, including free verse.

Metaphor

A figure of speech in which one thing is implicitly compared with another. A *metaphor* claims that one thing *is* something else, as when Wordsworth writes, "Our birth is but a sleep and a forgetting." A simile (see p. 331), in contrast, claims that one thing is *like* something else. The term *metaphor*, as well as its derivatives *metaphorical* and *metaphorically*, are sometimes used in a more general sense to refer to all figurative language.

Metonymy

A figure of speech in which the name of a thing closely associated with an object or person is substituted for that person or object. When Whitman refers to a *coffin* as though it were the dead Lincoln, he employs *metonymy*.

Metrical Foot

A unit of rhythm which recurs regularly within a line of poetry. The various *metrical feet* most commonly employed in the English language are identified by the following specific combinations of accented and unaccented syllables.

ANAPEST	two unaccented syllables followed by an accented syllable (uň·děr·stánd).
DACTYL	an accented followed by two unaccented syllables (súb·sĭ·dў).
IAMB	an unaccented followed by an accented syllable (ře·tréat).
SPONDEE	two successive accented syllables (chíld·líke).
TROCHEE	an accented followed by an unaccented syllable (ríd·ěr).

Octave

A term employed to refer either to a complete poem consisting of eight lines or to an eight-line stanza or division within a longer poem (see also SONNET, p. 331).

Ode

A type of lyric poem, sometimes lengthy, dealing in a dignified and exalted style with a serious subject. The word comes from the Greek for "song," and the form was originally used as a choral interlude in dramatic productions. Such an interlude had a regular structure: the *strophe*, during which the choral group moved toward one side of the stage; the *antistrophe*, during which it moved away on the other side; and the *epode*, during which the group stood in the center position. The strophe and antistrophe had similar metric patterns; the epode differed. *Odes* following this regular pattern are called *Pindaric*, for the Greek poet Pindar. The Pindaric ode has been used infrequently in English and American poetry, though Thomas Gray's "Progress of Poesy" is an example of it in this anthology. In place of the Pindaric ode, English literature has developed two separate ode forms. The first, the *homostrophic ode* (e.g., Shelley's "Ode to the West Wind" and Keats' "Ode on Melancholy") contains a series of stanzas, identical in length and generally similar in both rhyme and meter. The second type is called the *irregular ode* (e.g., Coleridge's "Dejection: An Ode" and Wordsworth's "Ode: Intimations of Immortality"). Each stanza, often called a strophe, is developed independently according to the emotional and artistic needs of the subject; neither the length nor rhyme patterns need be repeated from strophe to strophe.

Onomatopoeia

The formation or use of words which carry in their pronunciation a suggestion of their meaning. Such words (*hum, moan, murmur, bang, hiss, chugged, buzz*) are called *onomatopoeic words*.

Open Couplet

See Couplet, p. 324.

Paradox

A figure of speech in which an apparently self-contradictory statement turns out, upon closer examination, to express a truth. John Donne was fond of the figure, and in the last three lines of his "Holy Sonnet XIV" he employed *paradox* twice:

> Take me to You, imprison me, for I
> Except You enthrall me, never shall be free;
> Nor ever chaste, except You ravish me.

The ideas that Donne will be free when imprisoned, or chaste when ravished, seem to be false because they are self-contradictory. But they reveal a truth when read in their spiritual contexts: a man's soul is free only when subordinated to God's will; it is chaste and pure only when it has submitted to God's power.

Parody

A literary form of burlesque in which a particular author's language, style, or subject matter are imitated for the purpose of comedy or derision. Poems are often the subjects of *parody* when the original was marked by either an excessively simple or an excessively pompous style. This anthology contains no specific parodies of other lyric poets, though Christopher Marlowe's "The

Passionate Shepherd to His Love" has been parodied by other poets, most effectively by Donne's "The Bait." In a more general sense E. E. Cummings' "next to of course god" can be called a parody of much unthinking and chauvinistic patriotism.

Pastoral

A poem dealing with the idyllic life of shepherds. From the time of its inception with Theocritus in the third century B.C., *pastoral* poetry has been highly conventional and artificial. It has never sought to present a realistic description of rustic life. In English literature the pastoral has been importantly used for elegies, in which a surviving shepherd (the poet) laments the death of another shepherd (the deceased friend). The genre is represented in this anthology with Milton's "Lycidas," Shelley's "Adonais," and Arnold's "Thyrsis."

Pathetic Fallacy

A term coined by the English critic John Ruskin and used in literary criticism to describe a poetic passage in which nature is so strongly personified that it responds in a human way to some human action. The following lines from Allen Tate's "Ode to the Confederate Dead" illustrate the *pathetic fallacy*:

> You hear the shout—the crazy hemlocks point
> With troubled fingers to the silence which
> Smothers you.

Pentameter

A line of poetry consisting of five metrical feet (see METRICAL FOOT, p. 328).

Personification

A figure of speech in which inanimate objects or abstract notions are embodied with human qualities. The thing so personified, if it is an abstract quality, is called a *personified abstraction* and is often capitalized as a proper noun. Grey uses *personification* in the following stanza from "Elegy Written in a Country Churchyard":

> Let not Ambition mock their useful toil,
>   Their homely joys, and destiny obscure;
> Nor Grandeur hear with a disdainful smile
>   The short and simple annals of the poor.

Prosody

The theory underlying the principles of meter, rhyme, stanzaic pattern, and other components of poetic composition.

Pun

A play upon words having the same or similar sounds and more than one meaning. The real estate salesman who tells you to "get a lot while you're young" is punning on the multiple meaning of "lot."

Quatrain

The term refers either to a complete poem consisting of four lines or to a four-line stanza in a longer poem. The *quatrain* has been a popular stanza in lyric as well as narrative poetry, and it has accommodated various line lengths and rhyme patterns. The most frequently used quatrains in lyric poetry have been iambic tetrameter or pentameter quatrains rhyming *aabb*, *aaba*, or *abab*.

Run-on Line

Another name for enjambment (see p. 326).

Sestet

The term refers either to a complete poem consisting of six lines or to a six-line stanza or division within a longer poem. The last six lines of an Italian sonnet are referred to as the *sestet* when they form a complete syntactical and substantive unit.

Simile

A figure of speech which calls attention to the similarity between two persons or objects. Unlike a metaphor (see p. 328), the *simile* expresses the comparison with the use of the words *like* or *as*. Shelley employs a simile in the following lines from "Stanzas Written in Dejection, Near Naples":

I could lie down like a tired child
And weep away the life of care.

Occasionally, the simile makes use of more than one comparison, as in the following lines from T. S. Eliot's "The Hollow Men":

Our dried voices, when
We whisper together
Are quiet and meaningless
As wind in dry grass
Or rats' feet over broken glass
In our dry cellar.

Sonnet

Originally introduced into England from Italy in the sixteenth century, the *sonnet* has become a popular lyric form in English verse. Basically, the sonnet consists of fourteen iambic pentameter lines, though at least two distinct types can be identified according to rhyme scheme and internal division. The *Italian* (or

Petrarchan, after the Italian sonneteer Petrarch) sonnet is divided into an octave (rhyming *abbaabba*) and a sestet (rhyming *cdecde, cdcdcd, cdedce,*) or other combinations without a couplet ending. This anthology contains several Italian sonnets, and Keats' "On First Looking into Chapman's Homer" (p. 264) provides a suitable example for analysis. The second major sonnet type is called the *English* (or Shakespearean) sonnet. It is divided into three quatrains and a final couplet (rhyming *ababcdcdefefgg*). Since this anthology contains no examples of this type, a complete sonnet from Shakespeare is presented here for illustrative purposes:

> That time of year thou mayst in me behold
> When yellow leaves, or none, or few, do hang
> Upon those boughs which shake against the cold,
> Bare ruined choirs, where late the sweet birds sang.
> In me thou see'st the twilight of such day
> As after sunset fadeth in the west;
> Which by and by black night doth take away,
> Death's second self, that seals up all in rest.
> In me thou see'st the glowing of such fire,
> That on the ashes of his youth doth lie,
> As the death-bed whereon it must expire,
> Consumed with that which it was nourished by.
> This thou perceivest, which makes thy love more strong,
> To love that well which thou must leave ere long.

Spondee

A metrical foot consisting of two accented syllables (see METRICAL FOOT, p. 328).

Symbol

Literally speaking, a *symbol* is something which stands for or suggests something else. That basic meaning carries over to the meaning of a symbol in literature; it is a word or group of words which communicate beyond the literal or denotative level. A symbol participates in a poem in two ways. First, it is part of the literal meaning. The shepherd's pipe in Arnold's "Thyrsis" is first of all a shepherd's pipe, with which the shepherd makes his rude music. Second, however, the same pipe symbolizes the making of poetry. Hence, when Arnold says of Thyrsis (actually his friend and fellow poet Arthur Hugh Clough) that "his piping took a troubled sound," he is using the symbol of the pipe to refer to the fact that Clough had turned his poetical attention to contemporary problems. Similarly, the image of the lone tree which recurs in the same poem symbolizes a kind of stability and hope amidst despair.

Synecdoche

A figure of speech in which the name of a part is used to signify its whole. When Charles Lamb laments the passing of "the old familiar faces," he is using synecdoche.

Synesthesia

A figure of speech in which an image appealing to one sense is described in terms of another sense. *Synesthesia* appears often in such common expressions as "cool music" and "loud color." Similarly, Alan Seeger uses this figure in "I Have a Rendezvous with Death" when he speaks of spring coming back "with rustling shade."

Tetrameter

A poetic line consisting of four metrical feet (see METRICAL FOOT, p. 328).

Theme

Used with regard to literature, the word *theme* refers to the abstract concept which is treated in a particular work. In highly didactic works like Shelley's "Song to the Men of England" or Morris' "The Day Is Coming" the theme is directly stated as a course of action to be followed. Most lyric poems, however, do not contain a direct statement of theme. The reader must determine from the total impact of the poem what it was that the author intended to say. The theme of a lyric poem, or the statement the author wishes to make about the human condition, may indeed be very simple, as it is in Burns' "To a Mouse." On the other hand, it might be profound and complex, as in Eliot's "The Hollow Men."

Tone

The *tone* of a literary work refers to the general attitudes of the author toward both his subject and his audience as those attitudes can be inferred from the work itself. We may, for example, say that the tone of a passage or entire work is serious or playful, impersonal or intimate, ironic or serious, exhortative or suggestive. In longer works like Milton's *Paradise Lost* or Byron's *Don Juan* the tone may shift from one book or canto to another. In most lyric poems, however, the pervading tone remains—or should remain—consistent throughout.

Trimeter

A poetic line consisting of three metrical feet (see METRICAL FOOT, p. 328).

Trochee

A metrical foot consisting of an accented syllable followed by an unaccented syllable (see METRICAL FOOT, p. 328).

INDEX

Authors, Titles, and First Lines of Poems

Authors' names are in bold types;
titles are in roman;
and first lines are in italic.